PUBLIC LANDS MANAGEMENT IN THE WEST

PUBLIC LANDS MANAGEMENT IN THE WEST

Citizens, Interest Groups, and Values

Edited by
BRENT S. STEEL

PRAEGER

Westport, Connecticut
London

Library of Congress Cataloging-in-Publication Data

Public lands management in the West : citizens, interest groups, and
    values / edited by Brent S. Steel.
        p. cm.
    Includes bibliographical references and index.
    ISBN 0–275–95695–4 (alk. paper)
        1. Public land—West (U.S.)—Management. 2. Public land—
    Management—Public opinion. 3. Public opinion—West (U.S.)
    I. Steel, Brent.
    HD243.W38P83 1997
    333.1'0978—dc20   96–26878

British Library Cataloguing in Publication Data is available.

Library of Congress Catalog Card Number: 96–26878
ISBN: 0–275–95695–4

First published in 1997

Praeger Publishers, 88 Post Road West, Westport, CT 06881
An imprint of Greenwood Publishing Group, Inc.

Printed in the United States of America

The paper used in this book complies with the
Permanent Paper Standard issued by the National
Information Standards Organization (Z39.48–1984).

10 9 8 7 6 5 4 3 2 1

Copyright Acknowledgments

The editor and publisher gratefully acknowledge permission to use the following material:

Chapter 2 is a revised version of "Conflicting Values about Federal Forests: A Comparison of National and Oregon Publics," by Brent S. Steel, Peter List, and Bruce Shindler from *Society and Natural Resources*, vol. 7 (1994): 137–153. Published by Taylor & Francis, Inc., Washington, D.C. Reproduced with permission. All rights reserved.

Chapter 3 is a revised version of "Sources of Variation in Attitudes and Beliefs about Federal Rangeland Management," by Mark Brunson and Brent S. Steel from *Journal of Range Management*, vol.
49 (1996): 69–75. Reproduced with permission.

*This book is dedicated to the memory of my student
and friend Vicki Jansen-Kingen*

Contents

Tables and Figure

TABLES

FIGURE

Preface

In recent years, the use of public lands in the Western United States has become the subject of national as well as regional debate. Public concern for wildlife, fish species, wilderness preservation, recreational access, and other values associated with these lands has increased substantially since the 1960s. These concerns have clashed with the traditional extraction orientated policies that have dominated the use of these lands for over a century, resulting in often acrimonious public controversy and frequent litigation. At the heart of this debate are differing philosophical and normative views about the natural environment and appropriate human relationships to that environment. These views in turn are connected to different conceptions of how the proper management of natural resources ought to be organized and carried out.

To a substantial degree, philosophical orientations and public values concerning the environment set parameters for public policy, both for policies protecting ecosystems and for programs aimed at maintaining the economic and cultural vitality of natural resource-dependent communities. In many areas sustained public support is essential to the successful implementation of public policies seeking to balance out environmental and socioeconomic objectives. Despite the importance of public attitudes and beliefs in this area, relatively little is known about the interaction between public values and public policies affecting the physical environment. Not only do public values about natural environmental systems affect the overall public policy process and the character of management of natural resource systems employed by government, but public values also strongly affect the psychological, sociological, and economic systems of the many traditionally resource dependent communities throughout the American West.

The analysis of public values pertaining to the environment, consequently, is integral to finding acceptable solutions for fundamental (often contentious) resource management problems. It is the intent of this book to provide an *interdisciplinary* perspective on assessing public values regarding the environment, and to discuss their relationship to natural resource problems in the West.

Contributors to the volume represent the academic disciplines of anthropology, forest and rangeland resources, environmental policy, philosophy, and political science. Most of the authors have extensive experience working with federal natural resource agencies, and most have published scholarly articles and books concerning issues of public lands management in the West.

This book is organized into three parts. The first section provides an introduction and general overview of values associated with public forest and rangeland management. The introductory chapter by Steel and Lovrich reviews the various economic, social, and political factors leading to changing natural resource management paradigms in contemporary America. In Chapters 2 and 3 data from national and regional surveys concerning public forest and rangeland management issues are examined. In each case, survey findings indicate that while there is more support for the natural resource extraction lifestyle and industry in the West when compared to the rest of the nation, both national and western publics are increasingly *biocentric* in their orientations toward public lands management. All three chapters in this section suggest that natural resource agencies may well encounter more resistance to traditional management practices in the future if their practices do not incorporate the wider public's views featuring the protection of environmental systems on public forests and rangelands.

The second section of the book focuses on the various interests and publics engaged in natural resource issues in the West. Chapters in this section examine the role of interest groups, industry, government officials, and rural and urban publics involved in public lands management issues. Chapter 4 by Steel and Pierce and Chapter 5 by Salazar suggest that environmental groups and industry are well positioned to continue conflict over public lands management in the future. While it is difficult to categorize industry and environmental groups into specific issue agendas or policy positions, both types of groups have different kinds of resources available for successfully contesting public land management plans on the local, state, regional, and national levels well into the future.

The remaining chapters in this section compare rural and urban constituencies concerning their orientations toward public lands management issues and the resources available to influence public lands policy. Chapter 6 by Brunson, Shindler, and Steel argues that while there are indeed strong rural-urban differences in preferences concerning public lands management among citizens, there also is some ground for policy compromise. The authors found significant numbers of rural and urban residents favorable to balancing both environmental and economic values on public lands. However, Chapter 7 by Witt and Alm and Chapter 8 by Simon examine a recent political trend that increasingly makes such compromise unlikely-the development of the county supremacy movement in many rural western counties. The authors argue that rural resource-based communities are at a disadvantage compared to urban or core communities when it comes to influencing natural resource policy. Urban cores--which include both industry and environmental interests--have economic, political, and social advantages that lead to their domination of public lands issues. As a consequence, the people and local leaders of many rural resource-based counties express frustration and powerlessness which is manifested in the "county supremacy" and "wise use" movements. These developments also are discussed in Chapter 9 by DeVine and Soden.   In their chapter on public lands management in Nevada, the authors argue that while "states rights" and "county rights" movements will continue to be popular in states such as Nevada, their long-term political success is unlikely.

The final section of the book concludes with several case studies of public lands management issues in Washington, Oregon, and Alaska. These chapters illustrate the complexities and possibilities of public lands management at the local level. Richard Hansis's Chapter 10 suggests that for some specific sites on public lands, particularly those where both rural and urban publics have developed considerable emotional attachments, there is a strong consensus concerning preferred management strategies. Hansis argues that natural resource agencies should heed public preferences in these situations or risk further alienation of an already cynical public. Chapter 11 by Shindler reports on local perspectives of alternate harvest practices in Alaska's Tongass National Forest. His findings indicate that dealing with complex problems with a single management practice may be problematic; citizens tend to view ecosystem management actions as commonly involving a range of issues and a complexity of choices. If we expect informed public judgments about these management systems, we will need to learn how to more properly frame the questions involved. Finally, in Chapter 12 Jennifer Gilden demonstrates the special way change in timber-dependent communities affects women. In response to the rapidly changing economy in natural resource dependent communities, women are attempting to diversify within their traditional caretaker roles.

Part I: Public Values, the Environment, and Public Lands

Chapter 1

An Introduction to Natural Resource Policy and the Environment: Changing Paradigms and Values

Brent S. Steel and Nicholas P. Lovrich

Public lands in the western United States have become the subject of both a national and regional debate concerning the proper use and long-term well-being of forests and rangelands. Timber extraction and grazing historically have been the primary economic products derived from public lands in the region, with mineral extraction and fossil fuel collection taking a position of secondary importance in most (though not all) areas. However, public concern for wildlife habitat, protection of fish species, wilderness preservation, recreational access, and other nonextractive use values associated with these lands has increased substantially since the 1960s, and the primacy of management for timber and grazing has become the subject of increasing controversy and litigation, particularly with regard to federal forest and rangelands (Wondolleck, 1988). At the heart of this debate are differing values and interests concerning the natural environment and the proper relationship of humans to their ecological surroundings. These views in turn are connected to different conceptions about how the management of common pool natural resources ought to be provided for in the contemporary setting.

The purpose of this chapter is to provide a brief introduction to these differing value orientations toward the environment, and toward the management of natural resources in the national context. We will begin with a brief literature review concerning changing values toward the environment in the United States, and then identify some of the socioeconomic factors that are believed to be responsible for the development of conflicting natural resource management paradigms concerning public lands. Next, we discuss these competing management paradigms and then present some national level public opinion data concerning general orientations toward the environment and toward the management of natural resources. Subsequent chapters will compare national and regional perspectives concerning the management of western public lands, and identify the various conflicting interests and publics that continue to be involved in the overall policy debate. In the concluding part of the book, several case studies of public lands management issues in the West are presented to provide a local context perspective on these complex issues. After all, it is the local resource extraction-dependent communities in the West that will ultimately be most profoundly affected by this overarching conflict.

VALUE CHANGE CONCERNING THE ENVIRONMENT AND NATURAL RESOURCES: A BRIEF LITERATURE REVIEW

In the decades following World War II a number of fundamental changes transpired in the industrial nations, especially those usually identified as the "Western Democracies" (Dalton, 1988). In contrast to the prewar period, economic growth in the 1950s and 1960s was so rapid that fundamental structures of society were altered, and social commentators began to note a new stage of development. This new stage or phase of socioeconomic development in advanced industrial society has been assigned the label "postindustrial" in the social science literature on modernity and postmodern intellectual thought (Rosenau, 1992).

A substantial number of studies are available for review which examine in considerable depth the social, economic, and political implications of postindustrialism (Touraine, 1971; Bell, 1973; Heisler, 1974; Huntington, 1974). While some definitional disagreement is present among scholars, a few commonly agreed upon central features of this new type of society can be identified. Postindustrial societies are characterized by the following traits: economic dominance of the service sector over those of manufacturing and agriculture; complex nationwide communication networks; a high degree of economic activity based upon an educated workforce employing scientific knowledge and technology in their work; a high level of public mobilization in society (including the rise of new social causes such as the civil rights movement, the antiwar movement, the antinuclear movement, the environmental movement); increasing population growth and employment in urban areas (and subsequent decline in rural areas); and historically unprecedented societal affluence (Bell, 1973; Galston, 1992; Inglehart, 1977; Tsurutani, 1977). It is argued that the advent of postindustrial society has altered individual value structures among citizens (particularly younger persons) such that "higher order" needs (self-actualization) have supplanted more fundamental subsistence needs (basic needs, material acquisition) as motivation for much societal behavior (Abramson and Inglehart, 1995; Inglehart, 1991; Flanagan 1982; Yankelovich, 1981). Value changes entailing greater attention to "postmaterialist" needs are thought to have brought about changes in many types of personal attitudes--including those related to natural resources and the environment (Steger, Pierce, Steel, and Lovrich, 1989).

What this means for natural resource policy is that structural change in the economy featuring growth of urban service economies (or "the core") with concomitant decline in natural resource rural economies (or "the periphery") has lead to urban service areas exerting ever more influence over life in rural areas. This influence derives from their greater economic and political power, their superior technical expertise, and their substantial knowledge and information base (i.e., scientific knowledge, policy process knowledge, timely access to information, etc.) and control of mass communications channels, which tend to be increasingly effective measures for the propagation of their values and belief systems (Pierce, Steger, Steel and Lovrich, 1992). Finally, with the advent of postmaterialist value orientations in these core urban service areas, urban mass publics and elites have come to have belief systems concerning natural resource issues and land use policy in the periphery that are quite different from the economic growth oriented views that used to predominate in the past. Increasingly, then, natural resource-based communities at the periphery become subject to the environment protective rules devised in urban cores (Dietrich, 1992). This state of affairs eventually leads to sharp conflict with the periphery, and ultimately to the urban service core, mandating severe changes in land use practices and policies in the periphery, which come to be seen as challenging the customary and much preferred "way of life" of rural citizens (Carroll, 1995).

FACTORS ASSOCIATED WITH CHANGING NATURAL RESOURCE MANAGEMENT PARADIGMS

Most scholars investigating the topic of postindustrial society tend to agree that a relatively small number of key socioeconomic factors have led to the development of conflicting core versus periphery natural resource management paradigms, resulting in frequent policy conflict and occasional complete stalemate in advanced industrial societies. The thirty-year-long standoff between the national authorities and local farmers backed by environmental activists at Tokyo's Narita airport, the two-decade-long Sagebrush Rebellion in the American West, and the continuing battle over farmland preservation in California are examples of such impasse situations (Dalton and Kuechler, 1990). Among the most salient factors generally thought to be involved are the following:

Population Change: Postindustrial societies experience a shift in population from periphery to urban core areas. For example, during the 1980s and 1990s more than one-half of all rural counties in the United States lost population while urban core counties (includes both urban and suburban communities) grew at a rapid rate. This rural outmigration in most instances led to the most highly educated and/or skilled younger cohorts leaving rural areas to take up residence in the urban core (Deavers, 1989). Such persistent population migration dynamics have led to the acquisition of increased economic and political power by urban core elites and exacerbated the decline in influence enjoyed by elites based in the periphery (Beale and Fuguitt, 1990; Freemouth, 1993).

Economic Change: With the development and growth of the urban tertiary sector (and subsequent decline in the manufacturing, natural resource, and agricultural sectors) in the United States, urban core employment grew by 18 percent in the 1980s while rural employment grew by only 8 percent (Galston, 1992). In addition, unemployment and poverty rates were significantly higher and wages were significantly lower in the periphery when compared to the urban core (Gorham and Harrison, 1990; Shapiro and Greenstein, 1990). Substantial economic decline in the rural periphery often leads to a felt imperative to increase natural resource extraction among its residents in order to sustain community viability, while growth in the urban service industry creates a contrary imperative toward nonmaterial uses of natural environments (Nicholson, 1987; Stern, Young, and Druckman, 1992; Yankelovich, 1994).

Technological Change: The role of technological innovation and change is central to the relationship between core and periphery. Technological innovations have led to increased efficiency and productivity in manufacturing industries, in agriculture, and in natural resource extraction/processing industries. Once labor-intensive work on public lands is now primarily technology intensive, feeding further the process of outmigration to urban areas. In addition, these technological advances have led to a more central role in the (core) economy for theoretical and mathematical knowledge and for research and development investments as opposed to physical capital. This in turn has led enhancement of the importance of universities, think tanks, and the diverse media devoted to the creation and transmission of specialized information. As a result of these changes we now have far more information being generated concerning the condition and consequences of land use patterns (i.e., satellite photography, geographic information system [GIS] maps), and this information has been proliferated among individuals, interest groups, political elites, and to the investigative reporter using the high tech media channels produced in postindustrial society (Iyenger and Kinder, 1987; Kellner, 1990; Rothman, 1979).

Value Change: It has been argued by many that the advent of postindustrial society has altered individual value structures among citizens (particularly younger cohorts) such that "higher order" needs (e.g., quality of life) have begun to supplant more fundamental subsistence needs (e.g., material acquisition) as the motivation for much societal behavior (Aaron, Mann, and Taylor, 1994; Inglehart, 1991; Flanagan, 1982; Yankelovich, 1981). Value changes entailing greater attention to "postmaterialist" needs are thought to have brought about changes in many types of personal attitudes, including those related to natural resources and the environment (Catton and Dunlap, 1980; Lovrich and Pierce, 1986).

In fact, some observers have suggested that the development of the environmental movement was, in great measure, a product of the vast socioeconomic changes evident in postwar advanced industrial societies (Caldwell, 1992; Milbrath, 1984; Van Liere and Dunlap, 1980). The development of environmental consciousness and the advent of the environmental movement in the urban core has resulted in the open questioning of many of the traditional political and economic institutions of modern society (Habermas, 1981; Offe, 1985). These changing value orientations among individuals, groups, and elites in the urban core pose serious consequences for land use in the periphery, and have led in time to the articulation of two conflicting natural resource management paradigms concerning the use of public lands. These conflicting paradigms have been well articulated by Brown and Harris (1992).

The two competing natural resource management paradigms identified by Brown and Harris--derived from the ideas of Gifford Pinchot and Aldo Leopold, respectively--have been labeled the "Dominant Resource Management Paradigm" and the "New Resource Management Paradigm" (see Table 1.1). The former world view advocates the anthropocentric belief that the management of federal forests and rangelands ought to be directed toward the production of goods and services beneficial to humans. The latter paradigm has emerged more recently and grown rapidly in popularity in postindustrial society. It has a biocentric view toward forest management that emphasizes maintaining intact all the elements of forest and rangeland ecosystems, and is best summarized in the words of Leopold (1949: 262): "A thing is right when it tends to preserve the integrity, stability, and beauty of the biotic community. It is wrong when it tends otherwise."

A passage from William Kittredge's *Who Owns the West?* (1996: 5) is quite descriptive of these conflicting paradigms, and characterizes well the situation in which many western communities now find themselves:

Again our culture in the West is remixing and reinventing itself. It's a process many locals, descendants of people who came west only a few generations back, have come to hate; some think they own the West because their people suffered for it, and in that way they earned it. They feel that it's being taken away from them, and they're often right; they think they are being crowded out, and they are. They feel that nobody in greater America much cares about their well-being or dreams, and they are right.

The following section provides a national perspective concerning these issues, and generally supports Kittredge's assessment of the national public's sentiments concerning these broad matters of public affairs.

NATIONAL ORIENTATIONS TOWARD THE ENVIRONMENT AND NATURAL RESOURCES

In the most thorough and comprehensive review of recent trends in American public opinion toward the environment, the widely cited Environmental Sociologist Riley Dunlap (1992) concludes the following:

- Public environmental concern developed dramatically in the late 1960s coinciding with other new social movements

- After a decline in environmental concern in the 1970s there has been a significant and steady increase in both public awareness of environmental problems and support for environmental protection efforts

- By Earth Day in 1990, public concern for the environment reached unprecedented levels in the United States

Table 1.1
Conflicting Natural Resource Management Paradigms

New Resource Management Paradigm	*Dominant Resource Management Paradigm*
[Biocentric]	[Anthropocentric]
Nature for its own sake	Nature to produce goods and services primarily for human use
Emphasize environmental protection over commodity outputs	Emphasize commodity outputs over environmental protection
General compassion for future generations (long-term perspective)	General compassion for this generation (short-term perspective)
Less intensive rangeland management; stream protection, less grazing, etc.	Intensive rangeland management; maintain traditional grazing practices, etc.
Less intensive forest management; selective cutting, prescribed fire, watershed protection, etc.	Intensive forest management; clearcuts, herbicides, slash burning, road-building, fire suppression, etc.
Limits to resource use and growth; earth has a limited carrying capacity	No resource shortages; science and technology will solve production shortages
New politics, consultative and participative	Old politics, determination by experts
Decentralized and devolved decision making	Centralized and hierarchical decision making

Source: Revised from Brown and Harris, 1992.

An indication of the strong public support expressed for environmental protection and the environmental movement are results from a 1989 Gallup survey where 41 percent of respondents considered themselves "strong environmentalists" and 35 percent called themselves (not strong) "environmentalists" (*Gallup Report*, 1989). Only one in five of the survey respondents stated that they were "not an environmentalist." In addition, 85 percent of those surveyed indicated that they worry about the loss of natural habitat a "fair amount" to a "great deal" (58% said they worry a "great deal"). Perhaps one of the most important findings of the survey was that around half (49 percent) of the survey respondents reported that they had "contributed money to an environmental, conservation or wildlife preservation group." Given these findings, it is not surprising to see that declining populations of certain birds and animals have generated much public concern and considerable activism (Daly and Cobb, 1990).

In a recent (1993) national survey conducted by a multi-disciplinary team of researchers at Washington State University and Utah State University (in conjunction with the Sustainable Forestry Program, Oregon State University), individuals from randomly selected households were asked to indicate their level of agreement or disagreement with a variety of statements concerning natural resource management and public policies pertaining to the environment (Steel and Brunson, 1993). The survey results (see Table 1.2) derived from over 1,300 national interviews unequivocally indicate strong support for protecting plant and animal species.

A majority of citizens in the national cross-section survey disagreed with the statement that "plants and animals exist primarily for human use." In addition, a majority of respondents (47.5%) disagreed with the anthropocentric statement "humankind was created to rule over the rest of nature." Most striking is the strong support registered for the biocentric statements that "humans have an ethical obligation to protect plant and animal species" and "wildlife, plants and humans have equal rights to live and develop on the earth." While one may take issue with the leading wording of these statements (Brechin and Kempton, 1994) or question the commitment to supportive behavior on the part of responding individuals (Dunlap, Grieneeks, and Rokeach, 1983), they do indicate very strong support for protection of nature in the national public policy context. The same high level of support for environmental protection has been documented in a number of studies of the "New Environmental Paradigm" (NEP) conducted by Riley Dunlap and his associates in recent years (Dunlap, 1992).

It was suggested earlier that a number of scholars have suggested that there are growing generational differences in value orientations toward the environment and natural resources in postindustrial society (Inglehart, 1995; Pierce, Lovrich, Tsurutani, and Abe, 1986). These differing orientations were argued to be the product of postmaterialist values among younger, post-World War II generational cohorts. The survey findings presented in Table 1.3 provide some empirical evidence for this hypothesis among the American national survey respondents. For most of the indicators presented in Table 1.3, younger cohorts register greater concern for protecting nature than do older cohorts; the most striking finding is for the first indicator, where 79.5 percent of the 18 to 29 age group disagreed with the statement "plants and animals exist primarily for human use." This finding compares to 36.6 percent of the 61-plus age group disagreeing with the statement. What this means for natural resource management on public lands, if the trend continues, is increasing generational conflict. It seems clear from this survey evidence that Roderick Nash's theme of an emerging "rights of nature" ethic is deeply imbedded in the cognitive maps (the "hearts and minds") of contemporary

Table 1.2
National Attitudes Toward Natural Resources and the Environment

A.   Plants and animals exist primarily for human use.
            strongly disagree   31.8%
            disagree   23.2%
            neutral   13.4%
            agree   13.8%
            strongly agree   17.8%

B.   Humankind was created to rule over the rest of nature.
            strongly disagree   31.4%
            disagree   19.4%
            neutral   12.4%
            agree   10.1%
            strongly agree   26.6%

C.   Humans have an ethical obligation to protect plant and animal
      species.
            strongly disagree   5.6%
            disagree   1.6%
            neutral   4.2%
            agree   23.1%
            strongly agree   65.5%

D.   Wildlife, plants & humans have equal rights to live and develop
      on the earth.
            strongly disagree   10.2%
            disagree   11.7%
            neutral   7.5%
            agree   23.2%
            strongly agree   47.4%

American youth (Nash, 1989). Similarly, findings from recent studies of
generational patterns of belief and opinion on environmental issues in Canada
suggest a similar pattern of pro-environmental orientations among the younger age
cohorts (Pierce, Lovrich, Steger, and Steel, 1993).

     To assess the strength of the American public's commitment to environmental
protection vis-à-vis the economy, a 1992 national survey of citizens conducted at
Oregon State University asked respondents to self-select their position on a scale

Table 1.3
Generational Differences in Environmental Values

	DISAGREE (%)	NEUTRAL (%)	AGREE (%)
A.	Plants and animals exist primarily for human use.		
18 to 29 years	80.6	12.1	7.3
30 to 45 years	62.7	10.0	27.3
46 to 60 years	52.2	8.4	39.4
61-plus years	32.9	19.2	47.9
B.	Humankind was created to rule over the rest of nature.		
18 to 29 years	64.8	15.2	20.0
30 to 45 years	60.3	9.5	30.2
46 to 60 years	42.8	10.4	46.8
61-plus years	36.5	14.7	48.8
C.	Humans have an ethical obligation to protect plant and animal species.		
18 to 29 years	11.5	3.6	84.8
30 to 45 years	2.6	4.1	93.3
46 to 60 years	11.9	2.0	86.1
61-plus years	8.1	4.6	87.3
D.	Wildlife, plants & humans have equal rights to live and develop on the earth.		
18 to 29 years	8.8	1.9	89.3
30 to 45 years	23.3	8.0	68.7
46 to 60 years	24.6	9.8	65.6
61-plus years	21.4	7.1	71.5

regarding the importance of managing natural resources for both environmental preservation and economic development considerations (Steel et al., 1993). Table 1.4 summarizes the survey results gathered on this economics versus environment trade-off question concerning the specific natural resource of public forest lands.

Table 1.4
Economic Versus Environmental Trade-Offs in Natural Resources Policy–1992

Many federal forest management issues involve difficult trade-offs between natural environmental conditions (wildlife, old growth forests) and economic considerations (employment, tax revenues). Where would you locate yourself on the following scale concerning these issues?

The highest priority should be given to maintaining natural environmental conditions even if there are negative economic consequences.	42.0%
Both environmental and economic factors should be given equal priority in forest management policy.	46.6%
The highest priority should be given to economic considerations even if there are negative environmental consequences.	11.4%

The largest single response for the sample is found at the midpoint--a near majority favored an equal balance between environmental and economic components in natural resource management. It should be noted, of course, that 42 percent of the national sample expressed a higher regard for environmental concerns than for economic considerations.

Additional questions asked of American households by the Gallup Organization during its 1992 "Health of the Planet Survey" (Gallup International, 1992) reveal the strength and broad geographic and socioeconomic sweep of public support for environmental protection in the United States. The survey results displayed in Table 1.5 indicate quite clearly that the level of concern for environmental conditions is both strongly felt and of widespread currency, both with respect to general pro-environmental attitudes and more locale-specific "not in my backyard" sentiments (Bullard, 1994; Rabe, 1994).

While Americans tend to think of their own local communities as being fairly safe and well preserved, they are inclined to believe that the nation as a whole is in

Table 1.5
National Public Opinion Concerning the Environmental Health of the Planet

A. *Overall, how would you rate the quality of the environment in our nation: very good, fairly good, fairly bad, or very bad? In your local community? In the world as a whole?*

	Percent Rating Very/Fairly Bad
In my community	28%
In the nation	46%
In the world	66%

B. *Now let's talk about the world as a whole. Here is a list of environmental issues that may be affecting the world as a whole. As I read each one, please tell me how serious a problem you personally believe it to be in the world: very serious, somewhat serious, not very serious, or not serious at all or you don't know enough about it to judge?*

	Percent Saying "Very Serious"
Loss of species	50%
Loss of rain forest	63%

C. *With which one of these statements about the environment and the economy do you most agree? "Protecting the environment should be given priority, even at the risk of slowing down economic growth? Or, "Economic growth should be given priority, even if the environment suffers to some extent."*

Percentage that chose protecting the environment over economic growth.	59%

D. *Increased efforts by business and industry to improve environmental quality might lead to higher prices for things you buy. Would you be willing to pay higher prices so that industry could better protect the environment, or not?*

Percent saying they are willing to pay higher prices to protect the environment.	65%

rather bad environmental shape. With respect to worldwide conditions, Americans are inclined to express the view that things are in rather bad shape with two out of three Americans feeling that the quality of the environment in the world is in very bad or fairly bad shape. In situations where trade-offs between the environment and economic considerations occasion conflict, nearly six in ten Americans favor giving preference to the environmental values at stake. Would these same citizens be willing to pay the costs of greater effort to protect and preserve the environment? Very nearly two in three survey respondents answered in the affirmative to the query "Would you be willing to pay higher prices so that industry could better protect the environment, or not?"

CONCLUSION: FINDING A MIDDLE GROUND THAT CAN PROVIDE FOR CORE VERSUS PERIPHERY FAIRNESS AND INTERGENERATIONAL JUSTICE

The foregoing discussion of societal value changes taking place in the setting of postindustrial America involving conflicting views of what public policy ought to be on public lands in the West with respect to urban core and rural periphery populations and with respect to older generations and the younger cohorts provides an appropriate backdrop to the chapters to follow. As economic growth and the increasing application of technology to societal needs have transformed our politics and called into question our previously boundless faith in progress, we have found ourselves questioning our conventional values, discovering ever broader stakeholders in decisions about our natural resources, and needing to work out some difficult trade-offs between deeply felt needs and values. As we become increasingly likely to be the denizens of cities and metropolitan areas, we are inclined to develop sympathy for the Spotted Owl and the Pacific Salmon and other endangered species, and we become desirous of preserving the old growth forests and other national treasures for our children and their offspring to marvel at and derive inspiration from as they come to learn of the spiritual and/or aesthetic value of natural preserves. Too often, however, we forget about the families and communities of the periphery, about the value they attach to the rangeland and forests and fish habitats that have provided for their livelihood. For their part, the residents of the periphery too often refuse to believe that the inexorable forces of societal change will require a fundamental change in how they will have to relate to the public lands and waters around them. Both sides in the core and periphery spheres have much to learn and think through. Similarly, the generations have interests that are not entirely compatible with respect to natural resources and our posterity; there is ample room for better understanding in this relationship as well.

It is the hope of the several authors contributing to this volume that their research and considered observations will promote an informed and productive dialogue on difficult value trade-off issues across the urban/rural and younger/older dividing lines of society. Change has come to the West rapidly, showing little mercy for those caught in its grip. When we think of the state of Nevada (the Silver State) just forty years ago being the most rural state in the United States and now being the most highly urbanized, we begin to get a good sense of the scale and scope of change affecting our lives as citizens of the American West. Under the pressure of this type of change we need studies of the type reported here, we need case studies of attempts to come to grips with change of the sort included here, and we need to encourage and support efforts to promote public deliberation and dialogue. As Jane Mansbridge (1983) has argued, we need to move "beyond advocacy democracy" to achieve some sort of policy learning (Jenkins-Smith and Sabatier, 1993). While there is no assurance that collaborative processes will lead to consensus (Kelman, 1992), it is also clear that some noteworthy successes at collaborative environmental policy negotiations have occurred (Crowfoot and Wondolleck, 1990; Fiske, 1991). Knowing this, should this approach not be given increased opportunity to succeed? It is also clear that "civic journalism" (Dahlgren and Sparks, 1991; Fouhy, 1994) can do much to promote the type of public discussion and deliberation which occasions a "coming to public judgment" (Yankelovich, 1991; Gundersen, 1995). It is the hope of the contributors to this volume that our work will contribute both to future research and to the sorely needed deliberative processes facing our states. The pending devolution of governmental responsibilities to states and local governments means that the form and content of countless policy deliberations will be critical to an effective balancing of values and interests in conflict. Federal government agencies retaining control of public lands in the West will continue to face challenges to their policies (and even their very authority), and they too will need to promote the goals of collaborative problem solving and support the efforts of responsible journalists seeking to promote public education on environmental issues. It is our dearest hope that we daughters and sons of the West prove equal to the momentous challenges facing us all, and that our efforts here improve the prospects for ultimate success.

Chapter 2

Managing Federal Forests: National and Regional Public Orientations

Brent S. Steel, Peter List, and Bruce Shindler

The Pacific Northwest has become the focus of a regional and national debate concerning the use and well-being of public forest lands. Timber has been historically the primary economic product from forested areas in the region. However, public concern for wildlife, fish, wilderness, recreation, and other values associated with these lands has increased substantially since the 1960s, and the primacy of management for timber has become the subject of increasing controversy and litigation, particularly with regard to federal forest lands (Wondolleck, 1988: 9). At the heart of this debate are differing philosophical and normative views about forests and human relationships to forests.

One school of thought, derived from such important early foresters as Bernhard Fernow and Gifford Pinchot, approaches natural resource management with a utilitarian or resource conservation focus. This view advocates the wise use of forests for the betterment of humankind and is based mostly on anthropocentric assumptions. The other, contrasting view of forestry is related to the ideas of John Muir and Aldo Leopold. This approach to forest management is more biocentric in orientation and favors the extension of ethical consideration to all parts of forests, including birds, mammals, plants, insects, and such elements as forest streams and soils. The purpose of this study is to investigate the degree to which the public embraces these differing value orientations toward federal forests in the national context and in Oregon where the current debate has serious consequences for both timber production and the forest environment.

This study has four specific goals. First, it identifies and reviews these value orientations toward forests. Second, it compares the orientations of national and Oregon publics toward federal forest lands. Third, it investigates several factors correlated with changing value orientations toward forests. In conclusion, it examines the relationship between these orientations and federal forest management preferences in the national and regional context. Data utilized in this study are drawn from national and regional surveys of citizens conducted in the fall of 1991.

CHANGING VALUES CONCERNING PUBLIC FORESTRY

Since the days of W. J. McGee and Gifford Pinchot, public forestry has endorsed a resource conservation philosophy about forests and other natural resources. This conservation policy has many dimensions and has evolved over time, but was grounded originally on several ethical and political principles concerning natural resources: the wise human use and development of resources; the preservation and protection of those resources for future generations; and the democratic allocation of those resources for the greater public good, as opposed to monopolistic economic interests in society (Clary, 1986; Hays, 1959; Nash, 1973; Pinchot, 1910).

The Pinchotian ideology is based on anthropocentric thinking about human relationships to forests. An anthropocentric orientation is a "human centered orientation toward the non-human world" (Eckersley, 1992) and thus gives a central position in these relationships to humans, human needs and human satisfactions. Moreover, it assumes that the nonhuman part of the environment is "material to be used by humans as they see fit" (Scherer and Attig, 1983), which means that it is defined in terms of the resources it provides to humans rather than to other species (Scherer and Attig, 1983). The nonhuman world is "reduced to a storehouse of resources and is considered to have instrumental value only" (Eckersley, 1992). There is no notion that the nonhuman parts of nature are valuable in their own right or for their own sake. The value that nonhuman objects, species and processes in nature have is not "intrinsic" or "inherent"; it is value for humans (Naess, 1989). In addition, this orientation presumes that while humans have direct ethical duties or responsibilities to each other, they have only indirect duties to nonhumans or to the nonhuman parts of the environment. Humans form an ethical community with each other, but non-human organisms and natural objects are neither members nor primary constituents of this community. Thus, providing for human uses and benefits is the primary aim of natural resource allocation and management, whether those uses are for commodity benefits (e.g., timber and forage) or for aesthetic, spiritual or physical benefits (e.g., wilderness and outdoor recreation). In short, it emphasizes the instrumental value of forests for human society rather than their inherent worth.

This conservation ethic has been advocated for years by many officials and employees in federal resource agencies such as the U.S. Forest Service (see Wondolleck, 1988). Clearly the view has been modified since Pinchot's day to include such concepts as sustained yield and recreation. Yet its basic principles have remained fairly stable over time, and these added components are still valued for their instrumental contribution to human society. Many foresters believe that it has served forestry and other natural resource professions well (e.g., Barton, 1992).

In recent years, however, a new orientation about nature has emerged in our society which is more "biocentered" or "ecocentered" in its philosophical character (List, 1993; Nash, 1989, 1973; Worster, 1977). Moreover, this new approach has been applied to forestry (Coufal 1989; McQuillan, 1990; Rolston and Coufal, 1991). It is an orientation that can be traced back to Charles Darwin's ecological ideas, and in the United States owes a good deal to such figures as John Muir, Liberty Hyde Bailey, and especially Aldo Leopold (Worster, 1977).

A biocentric orientation to nature does not give primacy to human wants and desires. Instead it is a nature-centered or ecocentered approach. That is, it elevates the requirements and values of all natural organisms, species, and ecosystems to center stage and, in some versions, makes the earth or nature as a whole the focus of "moral considerability." This orientation does not deny that human desires and human values are important, but it places them in a larger, natural or ecological context. In addition, it assumes that environmental objects have inherent as well as instrumental worth. This orientation thus values the nonhuman world for its own sake rather than only for the sake of its utility to humans (Eckersley, 1992; Scherer and Attig, 1983).

In contrast with the resource management philosophy, this biocentered orientation tells us that human economic uses and benefits are not necessarily the most important uses of forests. There are noneconomic values and inherent values in forests that are just as distinctive as, and in some cases more significant than, economic ones. Human economic rationales and social benefits should not dominate our thinking about forests or our behavior in them. In matters of human management, these values are to be equally respected and preserved even if they conflict with human-centered values.

Both John Muir and Aldo Leopold advocated the importance of some of these noneconomic and inherent values in nature. Muir was particularly taken with aesthetic and spiritual values in the wilder parts of our continent, but rejected the idea that nature was created for humans to use. Leopold too referred to noneconomic values as "aesthetic" and "ecological" but sometimes called this kind of value "philosophical" (Leopold, 1949). To him wild creatures and objects have value because of their natural beauty and because of their ecological roles and functions in the land community. He formulated this general idea in a now famous land ethic principle that "a thing is right when it tends to preserve the integrity, beauty and stability of the biotic community" (Leopold, 1949).

Leopold's land ethic is often called biocentered or ecocentered because he deflated the role of humans in nature, making them more like coequals with other species. His way of phrasing this was to talk about humans as "plain members" and "citizens" in the land community (Leopold, 1949). In addition, he argued that ecological scientists need to make land health the focus of their practical relationships and promote the long-term ecological capacity of the land to renew itself.

In the 1970s, a more vigorous version of this biocentered view emerged with the development of "deep ecology," a philosophy that went beyond the land ethic to emphasize the biocentric equality of all natural species (Devall and Sessions, 1985; Naess, 1989, 1973). Deep ecologists argue that humans need to change their ecological consciousness about nature and thus reaffirm their basic connections to all life forms. Once humans come to experience nature and natural creatures for what they are, their narrow human concerns will be submerged into a larger natural whole and their behavior toward wild beings and objects will change as well (Devall and Sessions, 1985). The practioners of this philosophy do not always claim that they are advocating an "ethic," but it is clear that implementing their philosophical ideas would fit well into a biocentered orientation toward the environment (Devall and Sessions, 1985; Wuerthner, 1991).

Moreover, while these value orientations are not mutually exclusive (except perhaps in their most extreme forms) and are multidimensional, we believe that they can be arrayed on a continuum with the most anthropocentric orientation on one end and the most biocentric orientation on the other. Somewhere in between the two ends one gets a mixture of the orientations, something like a Leopoldian land ethic position.

In addition, we believe that there is a connection between the value orientations that people hold toward forests and their attitudes about what is desirable in forest management. In fact we hypothesize that a person's views about the techniques of forest management (e.g., clear-cutting) and the policy directions of forestry (e.g., participation by citizens in forest planning) are directly related to these values about forests. If they adopt an anthropocentric, utilitarian, or Pinchotian orientation, they will be more inclined to favor certain traditional approaches to forest management. On the other hand if they accept a more biocentered, Leopoldian orientation, they will be more inclined to reject those traditional approaches and favor a more ecocentered style of forest management.

SOURCES OF VARIATION IN VALUE ORIENTATIONS TOWARD FORESTS

A number of authors have addressed various aspects of the relationship between social values, values toward forests, and attitudes toward forest management (e.g., Brown and Harris, 1992). These discussions imply that the current debate about the disposition of public forests in the United States is, at heart, not only a professional and technological debate, but a debate about how forest ecosystems should be defined, philosophically. The differences between the more traditional, anthropocentric view of forests and the emerging biocentric view thus cannot be settled by appeal to facts alone (see Greber and Johnson, 1991). Factual information does not speak for itself; it exists in a cultural context, within a set of assumptions about its relevance, and these assumptions include important value orientations (Dake and Wildavsky, 1991, 1990). It is our underlying values, to a large degree, that determine what facts will count as important. For these reasons, it is important to understand what those values are and to determine their connections with other relevant social, political, and cultural factors.

In our judgment, value orientations concerning forests are influenced by a variety of factors. Primary influences include sociodemographic characteristics, self or group interest, sociopolitical value orientations, and geographical location.

Sociodemographic Factors: Group-based social attributes have long been a salient feature of research concerning environmental values (Dunlap et al., 1983; Milbrath, 1984; Siegelman and Yanarella, 1986; Van Liere and Dunlap, 1980, 1981;). Among the most commonly employed measures are gender, age, and education. Age (or for some researchers "political generation") is a widely used variable in evaluating environmental orientation. Citizens in Western democracies born after World War II are considered to be more likely than older persons to focus on environmental concerns (Dalton, 1988; Inglehart, 1990; Inglehart and Flanagan, 1987; Pierce et al., 1992); consequently, age (as an indicator of cohort) is an important background factor in any environmental study.

In addition, there may be a link between value orientations toward forests and gender. There is some evidence to suggest that women are socialized to perceive moral dilemmas in terms of interpersonal relationships, and to seek to resolve them by an ethic of care. Men, in contrast, may tend to perceive moral dilemmas in terms of more impersonal features of situations and to resolve them by appeal to rules of justice and rights (Gilligan, 1982). This differential socialization experience might lead women to take a more (personally) protective and biocentered view toward nature (see Mohai, 1992; Steger and Witt, 1989). We hypothesize that women would tend to have more biocentric values toward forests while men would tend to have more anthropocentric forest values.

Level of formal educational attainment is included in this analysis because it is broadly associated with having a strong impact on environmental values (*Gallup Report*, 1989; Inglehart, 1990; Milbrath, 1984; Steel, Soden, and Warner, 1990). Those individuals with higher levels of educational attainment are significantly more likely to have value orientations sympathetic to environmental concerns when compared to individuals with less formal education. According to Howell and Laska (1992), this relationship is not surprising because "the evidence on both sides of an environmental issue frequently addresses a very complex etiology of causes comprehended more easily by the better educated" (p. 141). We hypothesize this relationship to hold true for value orientations toward forests, with higher levels of formal education associated with more biocentric ethical values.

The last sociodemographic variable included in this study is place of residence-rural versus urban. Some studies have suggested that urban populations are much more likely to have proenvironmental values due to their better access to information and educational opportunities, and because they "are more likely to experience environmental problems firsthand due to industrial activities and high concentrations of people" (Howell and Laska, 1992: 141). If this relationship holds true for value orientations toward forests, then we hypothesize more biocentric orientations in the relatively treeless urban areas than in the countryside. This is consistent with the idea of wilderness as a desirable place, and the interest in wilderness preservation has grown out of our urban culture (Nash, 1973).

Interest Factors: Two important factors that would obviously affect value orientations toward forests are attachment to the timber industry and membership in an environmental organization. An individual's value orientation toward the environment may very well be influenced by where her or she stands in relation to the productive arrangements of society (see Douglas and Wildavsky, 1982). Persons who rely on the timber industry for their economic well-being, for example, are more likely to look at commodity interests as most beneficial. Environmentalists, on the other hand, may tend to view forests in terms of broader public goals and to promote the preservation of natural resources (Dennis and Zube, 1988; Hendee, Gale, and Harry, 1969). Some observers have identified environmentalists and other contemporary social movements as engaging in "elite challenging" or "outside lobbying" strategies due to the grassroots nature of most movements and the use of unconventional forms of political participation to achieve their policy objectives (e.g., demonstrations, boycotts, etc; Inglehart, 1990; Sussman and Steel, 1991).

Sociopolitical Orientations: value orientations toward forests are also conceivably influenced by, or are a component of, general political and social values. For example, the liberal-left perspective has been identified with support for natural resource preservation (Steel, Steger, Lovrich and Pierce, 1990) and higher levels of environmental risk perceptions (Steel, Soden and Warner, 1990). Other research suggests that citizens on the left-liberal end of the political spectrum support "policy proposals emanating from the environmental movement," while those on the right-conservative side of the spectrum have been found to be "less supportive or even hostile to environmental concerns" (Calvert, 1987: 2). We hypothesize that those on the left would be more likely to have biocentric orientations toward forests while those on the right would have more anthropocentric orientations. In part, this is due to conservative attachment to the status quo and use of the marketplace to allocate values. Liberals are more likely to critique the existing economic and political system and to support noneconomic uses of forest lands.

Although the value of the unidimensional left-right spectrum remains substantial, it has become evident that a number of new sociopolitical issues cut across traditional ideological cleavages. Ingelhart's (1990) and Dalton's (1988) research into value orientations identifies postmaterialism as a new, central feature of postwar generations. Postmaterialism, in contrast to a materialist value priority, is less concerned with economic growth and security issues than it is with Maslowian higher order values such as love for the aesthetic qualities of the environment. We expect that citizens with postmaterialist value orientations will have more biocentric views of forests while those with materialist values will give greater emphasis to human management of nature.

Geographical Location: One major goal of this study is to compare the value orientations of citizens in the national and regional context. When compared to the national public, citizens of the Pacific Northwest may have a somewhat different value orientation toward forests due to identification with the natural resource extraction culture and industry. One widely held view suggests that much of the concern over preserving old growth forests in the Pacific Northwest originated with policy makers and public opinion from the Midwest and East Coast. As Timothy Egan has commented: "Environmentalists have learned that taking their case to a larger audience may be the best strategy for preserving forests" (1991: 26, 27).

METHODOLOGY AND MEASUREMENTS

Samples: In order to investigate national and regional views of forest values among citizens, four waves of mail surveys (and a telephone call reminder) were sent to random samples of the Oregon and national publics. Names, addresses, and telephone numbers were provided by a national survey research company that has comprehensive lists of public telephone directories.[1] Survey design and implementation followed Dillman's (1978) "Total Design Method" and potential respondents were offered a copy of the aggregate results upon completion of the project to encourage responses. For the national sample, 1,603 surveys were mailed out and 1,094 were returned, for a response rate of 68.4 percent; the response rate for the Oregon sample was 75.7 percent, with 872 of 1,152 surveys returned.

Dependent Variable: The indicator we used to assess value orientations concerning forests, what we call our "Forest Values Scale" or FVS, asked respondents to identify their level of disagreement or agreement with the eight statements listed in Table 2.1. The statements were selected to cover various dimensions of anthropocentric and biocentric views concerning forests, and were drawn from a review of environmental attitude research and the literature of environmental ethics.[2] Some of the statements were chosen because they seemed to represent key tenets of anthropocentric thinking about the environment and, by extension, about forests as components of the environment. For example, the statement "plants and animals exist primarily for human use" has long been identified as a component of Western anthropocentric thinking about nature, and is derived in part from the Christian religion (White, 1967). On the other hand, the statement "humans should have more love, respect, and admiration for forests" is an adaption of a Leopoldian statement about the land community (Leopold, 1949), and it is likely a value statement that a wide variety of individuals would agree with, whether they are more anthropocentrically or more biocentrically inclined. Finally, the judgments that "forests have a right to exist for their own sake, regardless of human concerns and uses" and "wildlife, plants and humans have equal rights to live and develop" are clearly more biocentric in character (Devall and Sessions, 1985; Naess, 1989, 1973).   The five response categories for the FVS ranged from "strongly disagree" to "strongly agree." After recoding items so that higher numbers reflected a biocentric position and lower numbers reflected an anthropocentric position, the responses were summed to form an indicator of forest values ranging from 8 to 40.[3]

Independent Variables: The independent variables used to assess the impact of demographics, interest factors, and value orientations are presented in Table 2.2. The demographic factors examined as predictors of value orientations concerning forests include age in years, gender, level of formal educational attainment,[4] and an indicator that assesses the city size where each respondent resides (URBAN).[5] To assess an individual's perspective or interest concerning forests, two indicators were used. Respondents whose families depend on the timber industry for their economic livelihood were categorized as TIMBER[6] while those belonging to an environmental organization were classified as GREEN. The indicators used to assess the political and social value orientations of respondents include Inglehart's (1990) postmaterialist value indicator (POSTMATERIAL)[7] and a self-assessment measure of general political orientation (IDEOLOGY).[8]

FINDINGS

Univariate Findings: Table 2.1 reports the distribution of responses for eight indicators of values concerning forests. The mean scores for seven of the eight items suggests that both the Oregon and national samples tend to be more biocentric in orientation than anthropocentric.[9] The only indicator where both samples responded in an anthropocentric manner was the second item, which stated that "forest resources can be improved through human management." Most of the national and Oregon publics agreed with this statement (mean scores of 4.17 and 4.23 respectively).

When mean scores between respondents of both samples are compared, the national public is significantly more likely to have stronger biocentric views than the Oregon public for six of the eight items listed. At the bottom of Table 2.1 an additive scale mean and reliability coefficient are reported for the national and Oregon samples. The mean scores for the additive scale (Forest Values Scale) and the reported *t-test* statistic suggest that the national sample is significantly more likely to have stronger biocentric views toward forests than the Oregon sample. While this is consistent with the beliefs of those who suggest that the national public is more biocentric toward national forests than are Western residents, the mean scores for individual items and the additive scale suggest that Oregon respondents are more biocentric in overall orientation than they are anthropocentric. The differences between the two samples lie in the intensity of value orientations and not in their direction.

Summary measures for the various independent variables used in the forthcoming multivariate analyses are presented in Table 2.2. In regard to the four sociodemographic variables, the average age for national respondents is 48.8 years and for Oregon respondents it is 50.3 years. Women constitute half of the national sample and 52 percent of the Oregon sample. For the variable EDUCATION, we find that the average level of formal educational attainment for each sample is "some college" (mean scores of 5.04 and 5.27). For the final variable URBAN, the average national respondent is slightly more likely to live in a large urban area (mean = 4.15) than Oregon respondents (mean = 3.70).

With regard to the interest indicators, Oregon respondents are much more likely than national respondents to be dependent on the timber industry for their economic livelihood (21% and 11% respectively). National respondents are slightly more likely to identify themselves as members of an environmentalist organization than Oregon respondents (16% and 10% respectively).

Table 2.1
Forest Values Scale: Comparing National and Oregon Publics

	NATIONAL mean (s.d.)	OREGON mean (s.d.)	t-ratio
The primary use of forests should be for products that are useful to humans.	2.31 (1.24) n=1069	2.53 (1.27) n=856	-3.94**
Forest resources can be improved through human management.	4.17 (1.07) n=1076	4.23 (.95) n=857	-1.09
Forests should be used primarily for timber and wood products.	1.99 (1.10) n=1073	2.23 (1.17) n=858	-4.72**
We should actively harvest more trees to meet the needs of a much larger human population.	2.21 (1.21) n=1069	2.14 (1.25) n=852	1.23
Plants and animals exist primarily for human use.	2.58 (1.47) n=1074	3.36 (1.42) n=858	-5.31**
Humans should have more love, respect, and admiration for forests.	4.37 (.98) n=1077	4.04 (.90) n=860	3.02*
Forests have a right to exist for their own sake, regardless of human concerns and uses.	3.57 (1.32) n=1069	3.32 (1.40) n=848	4.04*
Wildlife, plants, and humans have equal rights to live and develop	3.88 (1.37) n=1069	3.68 (1.23) n=854	3.10*
Additive scale mean:	28.78	25.20	5.18**
Cronbach's Alpha:	.82	.81	

Note: The scale used for the individual items was 1 = strongly disagree to 5 = strongly agree. For the additive scale, items were recoded so that higher numbers reflect a biocentric position and lower numbers reflect an anthropocentric position.

* Significant at $p < .05$; ** Significant at $p < .01$.

Table 2.2
Distributional Characteristics for Hypothesized Determinants of Forest Values Orientation

Variable Name	Variable Description	NATIONAL mean (s.d.)	OREGON mean (s.d.)
AGE	Respondent age in years	48.8 (17.2) n=1,075	50.3 (16.1) n=863
GENDER	Dummy variable for gender 1 = Female 0 = Male	.50 n=1,064	.52 n=870
EDUCATION	Level of formal education 1 = Some grade school to 8 = An advanced degree	5.04 (1.41) n=1,078	5.27 (1.53) n=871
URBAN	Respondent residence 1 = Rural area to 7 = City of 250,001 plus	4.15 (2.22) n=1,060	3.70 (2.15) n=865
TIMBER	Economic livelihood dependent upon industry 1 = Timber dependent 0 = Else	.11 n=1,068	.21 n=839
GREEN	Member of environmentalist organization 1 = Member 0 = Else	.16 n=1,066	.10 n=838
IDEOLOGY	Subjective political orientation 1 = Very liberal/left to 7 = Very conservative/right	4.25 (1.43) n=1,069	4.23 (1.45) n=850
POSTMATERIAL	Postmaterial values dummy variable 1 = postmaterialist values 0 = mixed and materialist values	.21 n=1,067	.17 n=868

There is a similar distribution of responses among the national and Oregon samples for the subjective political orientation indicator (IDEOLOGY). The average respondent for both samples is slightly to the right of center. For the postmaterialist values indicator, we find that 21 percent of the national sample and 17 percent of the Oregon sample demonstrate postmaterialist values.

Multivariate Analyses: Ordinary least squares estimates for the Forest Values Scale are presented in Table 2.3. The *F*-test results indicate that both models are statistically significant, however the adjusted R^2s suggest that the scale works better for the national sample ($R^2 = .31$) than the Oregon sample ($R^2 = .21$). This finding may be because ethical views toward national forests in Oregon are more complicated, given the immediate conflicting environmental and economic risks facing the region and the greater familiarity with the issues involved.

For the national sample model, we find that when controlling for the independent effects of all variables, all but the variable EDUCATION have statistically significant impacts. In the Oregon model, only URBAN does not have a statistically significant impact. For the demographic variables in each model, both the younger and the female respondents are significantly more likely to have biocentric orientations than their counterparts. Education has a significant impact only in the Oregon model, with the more highly educated having more biocentric values than their less formally educated counterparts. For the variable URBAN, national respondents living in large urban areas are significantly more likely to have strong biocentric values than those from smaller cities or rural areas. When controlling for the independent effects of all variables, there is little difference in value orientations between Oregon respondents living in urban and rural locations.

As expected, those national and Oregon respondents who depend on the timber industry for their economic livelihood are significantly less likely to have biocentric ethical orientations than their non-timber dependent counterparts. National and Oregon environmental organization members are more likely to have biocentric orientations than those who are not members of such organizations.

The final two variables concern dimensions of political orientation and are statistically significant in each model. When controlling for the independent effects of other variables, those national and Oregon respondents who identified themselves as liberal are more likely to have biocentric value orientations toward forests than self-identified conservatives. IDEOLOGY had the largest standardized regression coefficients in both models, suggesting that political orientation is the most important predictor of value orientations toward forests. The second political value indicator shows that national and Oregon postmaterialists are more biocentric in orientation than those with mixed and materialist values. This relationship was expected since it was hypothesized that higher order values (self-actualization) are consistent with a biocentric view of the world.

FOREST VALUES AND POLICY PREFERENCES

The data presented in Table 2.4 illustrate the relationship between forest value

Table 2. 3
OLS Estimates for the Forest Values Scale

	NATIONAL		OREGON	
	b	ß	b	ß
AGE	-.04***	-.12	-.08***	-.17
GENDER	1.35***	.11	2.30***	.18
EDUCATION	.15	.03	.54***	.13
URBAN	.11**	.08	.01	.01
TIMBER	-1.67***	-.10	-1.00***	-.08
GREEN	2.78***	.17	3.03***	.14
IDEOLOGY	-1.50***	-.36	-1.20***	-.27
POSTMAT	1.17**	.09	.97**	.07

$R^2 = .31$		$R^2 = .21$
Adjusted $R^2 = .31$		Adjusted $R^2 = .21$
$F = 55.44***$		$F = 26.79***$

* Significant at $p < .05$; ** Significant at $p < .01$; *** Significant at $p < .001$.

orientations and agreement/disagreement with nine federal forest policy statements.[10] The Forest Values Scale was divided into three categories of orientation for presentation purposes--anthropocentric, intermediate, and biocentric. Each figure in the table represents the percentage of respondents within each category which agrees with the specific policy statement.

Two general patterns are reflected in the data. First, those respondents with biocentric orientations are more likely to support policies less intrusive and damaging of federal forest lands than are those with anthropocentric orientations. For example, both national and Oregon respondents with biocentric orientations are more likely to support a ban on clear-cutting, establishment of more wilderness areas, greater protection for fish and wildlife habitats, and protection of the remaining "old growth" forests. Anthropocentric respondents are more likely to support opening wilderness areas to logging, giving economic concerns a higher priority in federal forest decisions, setting aside endangered species laws to preserve

Table 2.4
Value Orientations Toward Forests and Federal Forest Policy Preferences

| | | *Forest Values Scale Support* | | |
		Anthro-pocentric	Inter-mediate	Biocentric
		percentage agree		
Clear-cutting should be banned on federal forest land.	National	39.7	65.3	82.7
	Oregon	29.1	54.5	89.9
More wilderness areas should be established.	National	49.4	79.5	88.5
	Oregon	21.7	50.0	76.3
Greater protection should be given to fish and wildlife habitats on federal forest lands.	National	65.4	80.9	86.3
	Oregon	23.7	50.3	87.7
Greater efforts should be made to protect the remaining "old growth" forests.	National	49.5	87.0	92.3
	Oregon	8.5	47.3	92.2
Endangered species laws should be set aside to preserve timber jobs.	National	31.5	9.7	8.6
	Oregon	80.1	31.7	5.7
Federal forest management should emphasize timber and lumber products.	National	42.4	25.3	14.2
	Oregon	80.1	22.7	5.8
Some existing wilderness areas should be opened to logging.	National	46.4	20.8	16.1
	Oregon	66.3	30.2	5.8
The economic vitality of local communities should be given the highest priority when making federal forest decisions.	National	50.6	34.0	23.8
	Oregon	84.3	48.1	10.3
Survival of timber workers and their families is more important than preservation of old growth forests.	National	40.1	9.7	6.1
	Oregon	66.9	4.9	2.1

Note: The FVS scale was collapsed to produce three categories of orientaion: anthropocentric, moderate, and biocentric. All group comparisons in this table are statistically significant at .05 (Chi Square).

jobs, emphasizing timber products in federal forest management, and choosing timber jobs and families over preservation of old growth.

The second pattern suggests that value orientations toward forests manifest different levels of agreement between the national and Oregon samples for the nine policy statements listed. This is most visible for respondents with anthropocentric orientations. Oregon anthropocentric respondents are much more likely to support human uses of forests than their national counterparts. For example, while over 49 percent of national anthropocentric respondents agreed that greater efforts should be made to protect old growth forests, only 8.5 percent of anthropocentric Oregonians agreed with this statement. One of the most pronounced contrasts concerns the setting aside of endangered species laws to preserve timber jobs. Over 80 percent of anthropocentric Oregonians agreed with this statement compared to 31.5 percent of similar respondents in the national sample.

For those individuals with intermediate orientations, we find that national respondents are much more likely to oppose many traditional forestry practices than Oregon respondents. National respondents with intermediate orientations, for example, were more likely than Oregon respondents to support greater protection of fish and wildlife habitats (80.9% and 50.3% respectively) and greater efforts to protect the remaining old growth forests (87% and 47.3% respectively). Those national and Oregon respondents with biocentric orientations on the FVS scale were more similar than different.

What these findings suggest is that anthropocentric national respondents are more sympathetic to preservationist management policies than are their Oregon counterparts. Anthropocentric Oregon respondents are much more likely than their national counterparts to accept traditional forest practices (such as clear-cutting) and to prefer policies that support the economic interests of timber communities. This orientation was found to be related to their favorable attitudes toward the natural resource extraction culture and industry.

CONCLUSION

Several important findings emerge from this analysis. Overall, both national and Oregon publics tend to be more biocentric in orientation than anthropocentric. These results are consistent with other analyses that show greater public support for the environment in recent years (Dunlap, 1992). When the national and Oregon samples are compared, however, the national public was found to have even stronger biocentric values than the Oregon public. It was suggested that these more strongly anthropocentric individuals in Oregon may be related to economic reliance on the timber industry and/or identification with the natural resource extraction culture evident in the western United States.

When the correlates of value orientations toward forests were examined, we found that younger cohorts, women, members of environmental organizations, liberals, and postmaterialists in both samples were significantly more likely to have biocentric orientations toward forests than older cohorts, men, those who are economically dependent on the timber industry, conservatives, and materialists. Given the decline in timber industry employment and the stronger biocentric views of younger cohorts (and possibly future generations given current trends), we would expect the national and Oregon publics to become even more biocentric in their attitudes toward federal forests in the future.

The last section of this study examined the relationship between these forest value orientations and federal forest management preferences. Findings suggest that those national and Oregon respondents with biocentric orientations were much more likely to oppose traditional management practices than those with anthropocentric orientations. This pattern was most pronounced in the Oregon sample, where anthropocentric respondents preferred policies that preserve timber jobs and local communities over the protection of endangered species and old growth forests. It should be noted, however, that large numbers of anthropocentric national respondents preferred policy preferences more sympathetic to the preservation of natural environmental systems.

This cross-sectional study suggests that natural resource agencies with significant responsibilities for managing federal forests, such as the U.S. Forest Service and the Bureau of Land Management, may encounter even more resistance from the public in the future if they continue traditional management practices (e.g., clear-cutting) and fail to protect environmental systems such as old growth forest stands and endangered species. We believe that there is strong support among the Oregon and especially the national public for a less commodity-based, more environmentally and ecologically sensitive, holistic and multiple-valued approach to federal forest management. Even residents of a major timber producing state are largely in favor of forest policies that emphasize a more ecosystemic approach to managing federal forest lands. But to more fully validate these conclusions a longitudinal study of forest values and federal forest management policies will be needed.

NOTES

1. Previous research (Leuthold and Scheele, 1971) has suggested that samples drawn from municipal telephone directories will tend to underrepresent some racial minorities (e.g., African Americans), those individuals with highly mobile occupations, and lower income, less educated people.

2. We modified the statements to apply them more specifically to forests (see Devall and Sessions, 1985; Dunlap and Van Liere, 1978; and Leopold, 1949).

3. A previous reviewer of this chapter suggests that the Forest Values Scale measures a utilitarian versus preservation value continuum rather than an utilitarian versus biocentric one. The authors agree that some of the statements in the scale are utilitarian in content; this is appropriate since anthropocentric forest values are associated with a utilitarian perspective. However, the authors also believe that the scale is multidimensional and while a biocentric orientation may tend to be more preservationist in its content, this is not what is measured directly by the biocentric statements in the scale (e.g., "forests have a right to

exist for their own sake, regardless of human concerns and uses").

4. The question used was, "What is your highest level of education?" The following response categories were provided: (1) never attended school, (2) some grade school, (3) completed grade school, (4) some high school, (5) completed high school, (6) some college, (7) completed college, (8) some graduate work, and (9) an advanced degree.

5. Respondents were asked "Which of the following best describes your place of residence?" The response categories provided were: (1) rural area, (2) city of 2,500 or less, (3) city of 2,501 to 25,000, (4) city of 25,001 to 50,000, (5) city of 50,001 to 100,000, (6) city of 100,001 to 250,000, and (7) city of 250,001 plus.

6. The question used was: "Do you or any of your immediate family depend upon the timber industry for your economic livelihood?"

7. The question used to construct Inglehart's (1990) postmaterial scale is: "There is a lot of talk these days about what your country's goals should be for the next ten to fifteen years. Listed below are some of the goals that different people say should be given top priority. Would you please mark the one goal you consider the most important in the long run. What would be your second choice? Please mark that second choice as well." The response categories provided were: (1) Maintaining order in the nation, (2) Giving people more say in important governmental decisions, (3) Fighting rising prices, (4) Protecting freedom of speech. Respondents are considered to have postmaterialist value orientations (i.e., Maslow's "higher order" values) if they selected both (2) and (4) responses. If the respondent selected items (1) and (3), they were considered to have "materialist" value orientations (i.e., lower order values). Any other combination was considered a "mixed" orientation.

8. The question and scale used to ascertain subjective political ideology was, "On domestic policy issues, would you consider yourself to be:"

Very	1----2----3----4----5----6----7	Very
Liberal	Moderate	Conservative

9. Disagreement with the first five items and agreement with the last three items were considered to be biocentric responses.

10. Most of the forest policy statements were drawn from a 1990 University of California, Davis, questionnaire on national forest policy practices (Sabatier, Loomis, and McCarthy, 1990), and suitably reworded for our study. The remainder were constructed by the authors from other discussions of forest policy (see DeBonis, 1989).

Chapter 3

Sources of Variation in Attitudes and Beliefs About Federal Rangeland Management

Mark Brunson and Brent S. Steel

Public concern about the natural environment and its management has increased in the past quarter-century (Dunlap, 1992). Rangeland policy and practices increasingly come under public scrutiny, especially on federal lands. Yet little social-scientific research has examined the American public's attitudes toward range practices and policies, demands for rangeland uses, or beliefs about the quality of range environments. For citizens to make informed choices about the future of federal lands, they need help from range professionals who understand the nature and origins of the public's beliefs and attitudes--not simply among traditional grazing or hunting publics but across a much wider spectrum of society. A successful manager of public rangelands in the coming decades must be able to translate public attitudes into supportable policies that address both forage and nonforage values.

Because traditional range uses occur mostly in the rural West, we might expect rural and western populations to be more supportive of current range policy than urban and eastern populations. However, previous research on environmental attitudes suggests that the picture may be more complicated than that. Attitudes toward natural resources gradually are shifting to an amenity-oriented view (Brown and Harris, 1992), and this trend is more pronounced in cities and suburbs than in rural areas (Buttel, 1987). Moreover, persons who hold generally environmentalist views may oppose environmentally motivated management actions that restrict their own personal choices (Noe and Hammitt, 1992), and Western economic interests are more closely tied to range commodities. Environmental attitudes also are related to knowledge about the quality of those environments (Pierce, Lovrich, Tsurutani, and Abe, 1989), and such knowledge is likely to be greatest in the Intermountain West and Great Plains.

However, Gallup polls (e.g., Graham 1991) usually find little regional variation in environmental attitudes. Similarly, a forestry survey by Shindler, List and Steel (1993) found relatively few differences in responses from Oregon and the nation as a whole. One reason may be that while natural resources are economically important in the West, the region is also highly urbanized (Brunson and Kennedy, 1994). Traditional concepts of "rural" or "urban" are confounded as urbanites move to the rural West, usually because of the region's amenities (Rudzitis and Johansen, 1991; Rasker, 1993). As a result, a rural environmentalist voice is emerging in debates over natural resource issues (Fortmann and Kusel, 1990).

This chapter examines how these various influences are linked to differences in attitudes and beliefs about federal rangelands and their management. It describes results of a 1993 study focusing on (a) differences in attitudes and beliefs about federal range management associated with the local or regional importance of rangelands, and (b) associations between overall environmental attitudes, attitudes toward federal range management, and beliefs about environmental conditions on federal rangelands.

METHODS

Sampling: Data come from three parallel surveys: two telephone surveys of randomly selected households, one conducted nationally and the other in Oregon; and a mail survey of residents of 17 Oregon counties where rangeland environments predominate and livestock grazing contributes significantly to local economies. Sample frames were provided by a national survey research firm that draws households at random from a database of current telephone directories. There was no geographic stratification within samples. Dillman's (1978) total design method guided survey design and implementation. For the national survey, we contacted 2,000 households and completed 1,360 interviews, a 68 percent response rate. In the Oregon survey, we contacted 1,500 households and completed 1,003 interviews (67%). Both telephone surveys were conducted between March and June 1993, using identical questionnaires. A mail survey, containing all questions from the telephone survey plus several others, was sent to 500 residents of eastern Oregon counties in September 1993. We received 280 usable responses and 64 other surveys were undeliverable, a 64 percent response rate.

Response rates are consistent with our previous mail and telephone surveys on environmental issues (e.g., Shindler et al., 1993), and were within Dillman's (1978) guidelines. Many persons who declined to respond said they had no opinion about rangelands or their management. Therefore results may tend to emphasize the views of those most likely to be concerned about rangeland policy.

Survey Instrument: Survey questions covered: (1) attitudes toward management of federal rangelands, (2) knowledge about the environmental condition of federal rangelands, (3) confidence in organizations and institutions involved in range management, (4) relative influence that different rangeland constituencies should have on policy development and implementation, and (5) attributes of respondents that could influence beliefs, including their overall attitudes toward the relationship between society and the natural environment as well as demographic characteristics. Many questions were adapted from a recent study of public attitudes about federal forest management in Oregon and in the United States (Shindler et al., 1993). The national survey and its implications are discussed further in Brunson and Steel (1994).

The primary attitude/belief measure was a series of questions asking people for their level of agreement with statements about rangelands and range management. For each question, respondents were asked to choose a response of 1 (strongly disagree), 2 (disagree), 3 (neutral), 4 (agree) or 5 (strongly agree). For statements about the environmental condition of rangelands, respondents could also choose a "don't know" response. No more than 4 percent answered "don't know" to any single question. Data from "don't know" responses are excluded from analyses reported here.

Respondents were asked to give their views about "federal lands such as those managed by the Bureau of Land Management and the U.S. Forest Service," with particular attention to rangelands. To further clarify the attitude object, a definition of "rangeland" was given. Choosing a definition was problematic, as there are many such definitions and none is universally accepted (Holechek, Pieper, and Herbel, 1989). To ensure a valid telephone survey, the definition could be no more complex than a single phrase. The phrase we chose was "places that have arid climates, where grassland or desert environments are *more common* than heavily forested ones (although forested areas may be present)." In the Oregon surveys, eastern Oregon was identified as an example of a range environment.

Table 3.1 lists the attitude and belief items specific to rangelands and their management. Six items were used to evaluate beliefs about the environmental condition of federal rangelands. Ten items were used to evaluate attitudes toward management of those lands. Shortened versions of these statements will be used in subsequent tables to describe the relationships between survey samples or attitude/belief items. An additional item provided further insight into range management attitudes. Respondents were asked which of three choices is "the proper model of management to follow on federal rangelands." Choices were: "*agricultural*, emphasizing the efficient production of forage to provide meat products for society"; "*multiple benefits*, emphasizing a long-term sustainable balance between human and ecological concerns"; and "*preservation*, emphasizing minimal alteration and interference in rangelands by humans."

ANALYTICAL METHODS

Two comparative approaches were used: a simple East-West comparison looked for regional differences in attitudes and beliefs and a comparison across differing scales of analysis examined differences associated with a population's proximity (and presumed familiarity) with federal rangelands. For the first comparison,

Table 3.1
Statements Used as Attitude and Belief Items

Attitude Statements
The economic vitality of local communities should be given the highest priority
    when making decisions about federal rangelands.
Livestock grazing should be banned on federal rangelands.
More wilderness areas should be established on federal rangelands.
Livestock grazing should be permitted in rangeland wilderness areas.
Greater protection should be given to fish such as salmon in rangelands.
Greater efforts should be made to protect rare plant communities on federal
    rangelands.
Endangered species laws should be set aside to preserve ranching jobs.
Federal rangeland management should emphasize livestock grazing.
Greater efforts should be given to protect wildlife on federal rangelands.
Ranchers should pay more than they do now to graze livestock on federal land.

Belief Statements
Most federal rangelands are overgrazed by cattle and/or sheep.
Soil erosion is only a minor problem on federal rangelands.
Populations of most wildlife species on federal rangelands have remained
    constant or are increasing.
The quality of water from federal rangelands has decreased markedly in the
    past 50 years.
The extent of overgrazing on federal lands has decreased markedly in the
    past 50 years.
The loss of streamside vegetation is a serious problem on federal rangelands.

---

respondents from the *national sample only* were divided into two groups based on
whether their region contains rangelands or large amounts of federal land. The
rangeland group included the 11 Western states plus Alaska, Hawaii, Kansas,
Nebraska, and North and South Dakota. *T*-tests were used to compare mean
responses to attitude and belief items, and chi-square tests were performed on the
categorical question. An alpha of .05 was used to measure significant differences.
    The second comparison was made between each of the three samples, using one-
way analysis of variance (ANOVA) to compare for differences in mean responses
to attitude and belief items. This approach was chosen because it allowed us to
compare attitudes in a Western state that has significant amounts of federal
rangelands with those of the nation as a whole, while simultaneously comparing
attitudes in grazing-dependent portions of a typically urbanized Western state with
those of the state as a whole. In so doing, we also addressed a theoretical issue of
how the scale at which political opinions are measured may reflect differences in

beliefs about the attitudes within a political constituency. The eastern Oregon sample provided an analysis at the U.S. House of Representatives level, while the Oregon sample offered an analysis at the U.S. Senate level, and the national sample an analysis at the Executive Branch level.

Pearson product-moment correlations were used to test for associations between beliefs about environmental conditions, attitudes toward specific range management issues, and general environmental attitudes. All three samples could be combined (N = 2,643) for this analysis, since we were looking only for associations within the individual response patterns of each study participant. Because Pearson correlations are a powerful test and significance is dependent upon sample size, values for R as low as .067 may be judged significant at the .05 level when a sample surpasses 2,500 cases-even though such an association would explain less than one-half of 1 percent of the total variance in responses. Accordingly, we chose a standard based on politically practical significance rather than statistical significance: correlations are judged as significant only when more than 10 percent of the total variance is explained (R = .316; $\alpha < .001$).

Three variables are used to describe overall environmental attitudes. These were obtained by multivariate analysis of a nine-item Likert-type scale partially based on the New Environmental Paradigm scale of Dunlap and Van Liere (1978) and used in recent research on public attitudes toward federal forest management (Shindler et al. 1993). The nine statements described attitudes toward the relationship between society and natural resources, natural resource scientists, or nature itself. Factor analysis (varimax rotation) of the combined samples revealed a three-dimensional attitude construct (Table 3.2). These dimensions can be characterized as describing, (1) attitudes concerning human domination of nature (hereafter referred to as DOMINION), (2) attitudes concerning the ethical relationship between society and nature (ETHICS), (3) and attitudes concerning the extent to which science and technology have exceeded natural limits (SCIENCE).

RESULTS AND DISCUSSION

Regional Comparisons: In general, attitudes in the national and Oregon samples reflected public preferences for a more preservationist, less livestock-oriented approach to federal rangeland management. The eastern Oregon sample was more favorable toward traditional uses such as livestock grazing and hunting. Comparisons between the rangeland (western) and nonrangeland regions (Table 3.3) found significant differences for seven of the 10 attitude items. Residents of the rangeland region were more likely to agree that grazing should be allowed in wilderness and that endangered species laws should be set aside to protect ranching jobs. They were less likely to believe more wilderness is needed, grazing should be banned, ranchers should pay higher grazing fees, or greater efforts are needed to protect fish and rare plants. However, even where statistically significant differences were found, there was no case in which one region supported a statement while the other opposed it. A significant difference was found in

Table 3.2
Factor Analysis of General Environmental Attitude Statements

	Factor 1	Factor 2	Factor 3
Attitude Statement	DOMINION	ETHICS	SCIENCE
Plants and animals exist primarily for human use.	.8970	-.0671	.0154
Humankind was created to rule over the rest of nature.	.8796	-.0626	-.0403
Humans have an ethical obligation to protect plant and animal species.	-.1365	.7705	.1048
Humans and nature can live together in productive harmony.	.2435	.7470	-.0732
The earth should have far fewer people on it.	-.1663	.1174	.4810
Wildlife, plants, and humans have equal rights to live and develop on the earth.	-.3948	.6676	.1874
Technology will find a way of solving the problem of shortages of natural resources.	-.3446	.2310	-.4440
People would be better off if they lived without so much technology.	-.0096	.2122	.7521
Technical and scientific experts are usually biased.	.2769	-.0962	.7250

Note: Varimax rotation. Eigenvalues: 2.2787; 1.6194; 1.4386. Percent of variance explained: 59.3.

responses to the question about a proper range management model (Table 3.4): Westerners were *more* likely to support a preservation model of range management than were easterners.

Regional differences were found for two of the six belief statements (Table 3.3) about environmental condition of rangelands. Residents of the nonrangeland region were more likely to believe that riparian vegetation loss is a serious problem, and that the extent of overgrazing on federal rangelands has decreased.

Generally the results of the regional attitude comparison are in predictable directions, with the Western states showing greater preference for management that stresses traditional or utilitarian uses and less preference for protective management. However, differences in support were slight, and never did one region support a policy that the other rejected. Similarly, results of the belief comparison suggest that the public in Western states is no more or less aware of the environmental condition of rangelands than easterners. Responses reflect a generalized belief that federal rangelands have suffered environmental damage, and this pessimism is no less in the West than in the East.

Two results were in directions that were *not* predicted. Westerners were *more* likely to support a preservationist approach to range management, and they were *less* likely to know that the extent of overgrazing in their region has decreased over the past half-century. A potential explanation for this, and for the relative lack of regional variation overall, is that most residents of the West live within 100 miles of the Pacific Ocean, where amenity uses of public lands are important but grazing uses are not.

COMPARISONS ACROSS POLITICALLY RELEVANT SCALES OF GRAZING DEPENDENCY

The eastern Oregon sample differed from the Oregon statewide and national samples on all 18 attitude and belief items (Table 3.3). *F*-tests for differences in means were significant at the .0001 level for all 18 comparisons. Responses from the Oregon sample were generally between those of the national and eastern Oregon samples, suggesting that support for the more environmentalist positions of the national group was moderated somewhat by closer proximity to rangelands and grazing-dependent communities. However, Oregonians generally responded more like the national public than like a grazing-dependent public: the average difference in means between Oregon and the nation was 0.37, while the average difference in means between Oregon as a whole and its eastern counties was 0.51.

In all cases, residents of the grazing-dependent region of eastern Oregon were more supportive than the national or statewide samples of statements advocating traditional or utilitarian uses, and less supportive of statements urging greater protection of nonforage resources. For four items (ban livestock grazing, more wilderness areas, protect rare plants, higher grazing fees) the eastern Oregon sample was the only one whose mean response was at or below the neutral midpoint, showing that policies supported in national or statewide polls may not be favored

Table 3.3

Differences in Attitudes and Beliefs About Federal Rangelands and Their Management Between Regions and Politically Relevant Scales of Range Dependency

	REGION		SCALE OF DEPENDENCY		
Attitude Items	East[1]	West	U.S.	Ore.	E. Ore.
Priority to local economy	3.05	3.01	3.04[a]	3.10[a]	3.63[b]
Ban livestock grazing	3.24	3.06**	3.17[b]	3.16[b]	1.87[a]
More wilderness areas	4.17	3.53***	3.93[c]	3.13[b]	2.20[a]
Allow wilderness grazing	2.53	2.78**	2.62[a]	2.62[a]	3.23[b]
More protection for fish	4.18	3.81***	4.04[c]	3.51[b]	3.04[a]
More protection for rare plants	4.13	3.91**	4.05[c]	3.37[b]	2.87[a]
Repeal endangered species laws	2.06	2.33**	2.16[a]	2.75[b]	2.99[c]
Emphasize livestock grazing	2.78	2.74	2.77[a]	3.00[b]	3.22[c]
More protection for wildlife	4.40	4.40	4.40[c]	4.22[b]	3.24[a]
Ranchers should pay more	3.93	3.69**	3.84[c]	3.25[b]	3.00[a]
Beliefs					
Most rangelands are overgrazed	3.46	3.58	3.51[c]	3.27[b]	2.75[a]
Soil erosion is minor problem	2.43	2.32	2.39[a]	2.59[b]	3.05[c]
Wildlife populations increasing	1.98	2.00	1.98[a]	2.31[b]	3.12[c]
Water quality markedly worse	4.40	4.41	4.40[a]	4.22[b]	3.13[c]
Overgrazing is down markedly	2.32	2.18*	2.27[a]	2.24[a]	3.15[b]
Serious riparian vegetation loss	4.30	4.07***	4.22[b]	4.18[b]	3.27[a]

Note: *T*-tests for differences in mean Likert scale responses; significance shown by *<.05, **<.01, *** <.001; scale values range from 1 = strongly disagree to 5 = strongly agree. a, b, c = Different superscript letters indicate statistical differences in means (F-test, p<.0001).

in grazing-dependent communities. For two other items (allow wilderness grazing, emphasize livestock) the eastern Oregon sample was the only one with a mean response *above* neutral, showing that locally favored actions lacked national support.

The Oregon and national samples differed on seven of the 10 attitude items. The gap was largest on issues of wilderness designation, rare plant protection, endangered species laws, and grazing fees. Partly this may be a side effect of statewide concern about economic effects of species-protection laws on the state's timber industry. There was no difference in attitudes toward giving priority to local communities, banning grazing on federal lands, or wilderness grazing. In only one case did the national public support or oppose a statement when the Oregon public did not: Oregonians were neutral on the subject of emphasizing livestock grazing on federal rangelands, while the national public opposed such an approach.

The three samples also differed significantly in their preferences for a range management model (Table 3.4). The most prominent source of variation in responses was that residents of eastern Oregon were less than half as likely as the other two groups to support a preservationist model. The eastern Oregon population was the most supportive of a multiple benefits approach like that of the U.S. Forest Service and Bureau of Land Management.

Responses to the belief items (Table 3.3) show that eastern Oregon residents differed from the other two samples on all six beliefs, while the Oregon and national samples differed on four of the six. Eastern Oregon responses tended to be noncommittal, never straying far from the neutral point. For four of the six items, the eastern Oregon sample gave slightly positive responses while the other two groups held negative beliefs about rangeland environments. Differences between the Oregon and national samples were much smaller ($\bar{x} = .17$) than those between the Oregon statewide and eastern Oregon samples ($\bar{x} = .78$).

Table 3.4
Differences in Preferences for Range Management Model

	--- Percent ---				
	REGION[1]		**SCALE OF DEPENDENCY**[2]		
Management Model	**East**	**West**	**U.S.**	**Ore.**	**E. Ore.**
Agricultural	11.1	12.6	11.6	15.5	14.3
Multiple benefits	69.4	58.4	65.2	58.7	75.3
Preservation	19.6	29.0	23.1	21.8	10.4

1. $\chi^2 = 17.8$, $p < .001$
2. $\chi^2 = 37.0$, $p < .001$

ATTITUDE/BELIEF CORRELATIONS

Correlations between general environmental attitudes and specific attitudes or beliefs are shown in Table 3.5. Seven of the 10 specific attitudes are correlated with the DOMINION attitude scale, and five are correlated with the ETHICS scale. None of the specific attitudes is correlated with the SCIENCE scale. Only one specific attitude item (ban livestock grazing) is not strongly correlated with *any* of the three general attitude scales. The DOMINION scale is strongly correlated with four of the six belief items, the ETHICS scale with two items, and the SCIENCE scale with none of the items. Belief in the seriousness of riparian vegetation loss is the only one not strongly correlated with at least one general scale.

Attitudes and beliefs about rangelands both appear to be strongly associated with general attitudes toward human dominion over nature. People who believe that the world and its resources were created for human use are more likely to support traditional uses of range *and* more likely to believe that those uses have not had a deleterious effect on public rangelands (or that such effects are being ameliorated without abandoning traditional uses). Specific attitudes and beliefs are also related, although less definitively, to beliefs about the ethically proper relationship between humans and nature. People who value a harmonious relationship between nature and society are more likely to favor protective actions and an increase in grazing fees, and more likely to believe most rangelands are overgrazed and most streams polluted. However, there is not as strong a relationship between protective attitudes or pessimistic beliefs and the general attitude that human technologies have overstepped their bounds. This may be because the public blames range environmental problems on livestock grazing, a "low-tech" use, rather than on a technology such as chaining or herbicide sprays.

Correlations between specific attitudes and beliefs are shown in Table 3.6. Two items, beliefs that riparian vegetation loss is a serious problem and attitudes toward a total ban on livestock grazing, had no significant correlations. Eighty percent of the remaining 45 pairs had attitude/belief correlations above R = .316. All 36 significant correlations were in the expected direction; that is, negative beliefs about range environments were associated with support for protective actions, and positive beliefs about rangeland conditions correlated with support for traditional actions. Strong associations were found even where no causal connection between belief and attitude was readily discernible (e.g., "soil erosion is only a minor problem on federal rangelands" X "endangered species laws should be set aside to preserve ranching jobs," R = .499).

Social-psychological theory suggests that attitudes toward a specific object (e.g., management of federal rangelands) are products of individuals' values and their beliefs about that object (Ajzen and Fishbein, 1980). Values, defined as beliefs about desirable end-states and modes of conduct, tend to be more stable and enduring that beliefs or attitudes about specific objects (Rokeach, 1979). In this study, values are reflected in the general attitude scales: the DOMINION scale reflects religious or materialist modes of conduct, the ETHICS scale reflects biocentrism and an end state of natural harmony that Rokeach (1979) called "world

Table 3.5
Correlations Between General Environmental Attitudes and Attitudes Toward Range Management Practices or Beliefs About Range Environmental Condition

| | ---------------- General attitudes ---------------- | | |
Attitude Items	DOMINION[1]	ETHICS	SCIENCE
Priority to local economy	.352*[2]	-.088	-.087
Ban livestock grazing	-.166	.199	.040
More wilderness areas	-.365*	.381*	.135
Allow wilderness grazing	.372*	-.195	-.096
More protection for fish	-.349*	.442*	.132
More protection for rare plants	-.362*	.413*	.092
Repeal endangered species laws	.428*	-.246	-.066
Emphasize livestock grazing	.408*	-.124	-.067
More protection for wildlife	-.248	.450*	.172
Ranchers should pay more	-.270	.358*	.134
Belief Items			
Most rangelands are overgrazed	-.416*	.401*	.152
Soil erosion is minor problem	.532*	-.173	-.043
Wildlife populations increasing	.454*	-.224	-.070
Water quality markedly worse	-.247	.434*	.171
Overgrazing is down markedly	.323*	-.133	-.047
Serious riparian vegetation loss	.157	.121	-.163

1. Dimensions derived from factor analysis of a general attitude scale (Table 3.2)
2. Asterisk indicates correlations explaining >10% of variance in responses (R > .316).

of beauty," and the SCIENCE scale reflects rationalist-technical modes of conduct.

Humans are motivated to maintain consistency in environmental attitudes (Heberlein 1981). However, as they learn more about an attitude object they are more likely to encounter conflicts between values. Then they must develop what Tetlock (1986) called integrative complexity or "trade-off reasoning," which can lead to seemingly inconsistent attitudes. Tetlock (1986) offers the example of someone who values a "world of beauty" and a "comfortable life," and who experiences value conflict in forming an attitude toward the question: "Should public park lands be opened to mining and exploration in order to promote economic growth and prosperity?" That person may favor mining in parks for economic reasons while still holding environmentalist attitudes in a general sense.

Table 3.6
**Correlations Between Specific Attitudes Toward Range Management
and Beliefs About Range Environments**

	Range Environment Beliefs					
	A	B	C	D	E	F
Attitudes						
Priority to local economy	-.300	.400*	.461*	-.241	.411*	-.229
Ban livestock grazing	.221	-.197	-.221	.207	-.143	-.015
More wilderness areas	.439*	-.398*	-.443*	.419*	-.325*	.032
Allow wilderness grazing	-.371*	.423*	.467*	-.395*	.405*	.101
More protection for fish	.424*	-.386*	-.395*	.415*	-.306	.015
More protection for rare plants	.517*	-.413*	-.470*	.423*	-.368*	-.040
Repeal endan-gered species	-.393*	.499*	.486*	-.313	.424*	.138
Emphasize live-stock grazing	-.342*	.430*	.471*	-.142	.381*	-.208
More protection for wildlife	.422*	-.292	-.378*	.632*	-.282	.190
Ranchers should pay more	.433*	-.301	-.364*	.347*	-.237	.040

Note: Asterisk indicates correlations explaining >10% of variance in responses
(R > .316).   A = Most rangelands are overgrazed, B = Soil loss is a minor problem, C = Wildlife is increasing, D = Water quality is worsening, E = Overgrazing is reduced, F = Riparian vegetation loss.

Because integrative complexity is a product of increasingly complex chains of reasoning about an attitude object, we can expect correlations between general and specific attitudes to be larger when respondents have *not* thought much about the attitude object and so have not encountered value conflicts. Strong correlations between values and beliefs about rangelands would suggest that those beliefs are a product of general environmental values rather than of complex or sustained reasoning about rangelands-especially if the beliefs are not factually supported. Because attitudes are the products of an exceedingly complex information-processing system (the human brain), attitude/belief correlations above our alpha of .316 are relatively rare. The large number of highly significant correlations found here may be considered evidence that those attitudes and beliefs are products of a relatively simple cognitive structure with respect to rangelands. In other words, public attitudes toward specific range practices or policies are more likely to derive from people's general sense of the state of the environment and its proper stewardship than from any deeply rooted, highly reasoned beliefs or attitudes about rangelands.

Further evidence of this can be found in the rather monolithic structure of specific attitude/belief correlations. Respondents tended to believe either that rangeland conditions are uniformly bad or worsening and that protective actions are needed, or that rangeland conditions are uniformly good or improving and that traditional management is best. Nationally and in Oregon, there were more people in the former camp than the latter.

One belief and one attitude existed independently of other values, attitudes, or beliefs measured here. Belief that riparian vegetation loss is a serious problem on rangelands was not strongly associated with any general or specific attitude. That may be because this was the only belief that was both demonstrably true and environmentally pessimistic, so that agreement with the item could result from either environmental ideology or knowledge about rangelands. Attitudes toward a total ban on livestock grazing likewise were not associated with any general environmental value or belief. Environmentalism alone apparently cannot explain support of the "Cattle-Free" movement, but must be considered along with other factors warranting further study, such as vegetarianism or inconvenience to recreation users.

CONCLUSIONS AND IMPLICATIONS

This study examined variation in public attitudes and beliefs about federal rangelands and their management as a function of region, local importance of range uses, and environmental value/belief/attitude associations. We found relatively weak support for an East-West dichotomy on range issues, but much better support for a dichotomy between urbanized areas throughout the United States and those rural regions where rangelands are important to local economies. This could eventually translate to a loss of political power for range constituencies in the United States Senate if Western urban interests assert their environmental views more strongly, but it is less likely to affect votes in the House of Representatives. We also found evidence that attitudes and beliefs about rangelands are typically part of a poorly developed cognitive structure rooted in simplistic, value-based ideas about the goodness or badness of range practices and conditions.

A fundamental presumption of survey research is that responses reflect preexisting ideas that guide behavior. However, recent research suggests that when faced with questions about issues about which they have given little prior thought, respondents may construct answers on the spot (Tourangeau and Rasinski 1988). Measurement thus can *create* public opinion instead of *capturing* it (Simmons, Bickart, and Lynch, 1993). This phenomenon might tempt range managers to simply disregard the results of surveys like this. However, Simmons et al. (1993) also found that respondents may be motivated to act consistently with their spuriously formed opinions. Given that possibility, the American political process makes it entirely possible for "created" public opinion to become public policy. For example, members of Congress whose districts do not contain rangelands may base votes on results of published opinion polls or informal surveys mailed to constituents. If our political system allows rangeland policy to be based on uninformed opinion, it becomes the responsibility of the range profession to create a better-informed public than now exists.

An information campaign about range management should be just that: a systematic program to let the public know what rangelands are, how they function ecologically and socially, what problems they face and the values they support. Our results show that such efforts are as badly needed in the urban areas of the West as anywhere else. The temptation may be strong to try to induce change in attitudes through a slick, Madison Avenue style approach, but the likelihood of quick success is not great because rangeland attitudes are strongly tied to values, and value-based attitudes can be highly resistant to change (Heberlein, 1981). A more promising long-term strategy is to take advantage of the growing notoriety of rangelands-keeping range issues in the public eye whenever possible, so that a gradually better-informed public begins to make the kind of "trade-off reasoning" that comes as greater understanding creates in people a need to resolve value conflicts.

Part II: Interests and Publics

Chapter 4

Political Communication Strategies of Interest Groups and Industry in Federal Forest Policy

Brent S. Steel and John C. Pierce

Public policy disputes in the natural resource and environmental policy area increasingly turn on scientific and technical issues, the presence of which challenges the public's capacity for understanding and influencing the courses of government action (Nelkin, 1979). In their lobbying efforts, interest groups and industry often serve as important mechanisms for pressing their various constituents demands in those scientifically and technically complex policy areas such as federal forest policy (Berry, 1989). The advocacy role taken by interest groups frequently is framed in the context of the information sharing function they increasingly perform in modern, postindustrial democracies. As Jeffrey Berry has argued, "Interest groups *educate* the American public about political issues. With their advocacy efforts, publications, and publicity campaigns, interest groups can make people better aware of both policy problems and proposed solutions" (1989: 7; emphasis in original).

This chapter focuses on the communication of information to citizens, natural resource agencies, and legislators by interest groups and industry involved in the federal forest policy debate in the State of Oregon. In looking at the communication activities of these organizations, the analysis will focus on: (1) the types of information used; (2) the character of communication strategies; (3) the frequency of communication by groups designed to influence citizens, agencies, and legislators; and (4) the correlates of perceived success of this political communication. Data utilized in this study are from an interest group and industry survey conducted in 1992. Industry and interest groups involved in the federal forest planning process in at least one of Oregon's 13 national forests were included in the study.

THE POLICY CONTEXT

Timber and grazing have been the primary products from public range and forest lands in the western United States. However, management for timber and grazing primacy over other noncommodity values has become the subject of increasing controversy and litigation as the effects of logging and grazing primacy on wildlife, fish, and long-term sustainability of ecosystems and their associated human communities have become evident (Dietrich, 1992; Wilkinson, 1992). Local, regional and national interests and policy advocates from the research/academic realm urge a varied and often contradictory set of policy recommendations on federal and state governments and natural resource agencies. The offered solutions range from proposals to continue near historic levels of timber cutting and increased grazing to those that would drastically reduce human management of public lands.

A wide array of interest groups and industry organizations have become involved in the federal forest policy debates, and their methods of influencing forest policy are quite diverse (Salazar, Gonzales, and Steinberg, 1990). Not only do these groups tend to frame ecological and social problems differently, but they also tend to use information, organizational personnel, financial resources, and time in different ways to achieve their policy objectives.

Historically, a tight community of natural resource agencies and commodity interests largely determined the direction of federal natural resource policy (see Mather, 1990; Reisner, 1986). This policy process has been described as an "iron triangle" or a "subgovernment" (Berry, 1989: 172, 184). In recent years, however, new groups and interests have entered the process, often challenging the status quo and sometimes leading to considerable policy unpredictability (Force and Williams, 1989; Shindler et al., 1993). An outcome of this development in the Pacific Northwest frequently has been virtual paralysis in the implementation of traditional harvest-oriented forest policy, and the introduction of considerable inconsistency in forest management practices.

All of this political change suggests a policy area featuring continuing flux and unpredictability. Because of this disequilibrium, it is important to understand the information strategies used by interest groups and industry in the forest policy process in the coming years of change. It has been noted that disequilibrium in society or in a specific policy arena is often a stimulant to interest group formation and heightened group activity (Salisbury, 1975; Petracca, 1992).

Some observers have suggested that under disequilibrium conditions public interest groups, such as those organizations composing the environmental movement, often serve as important mechanisms for pressing the public's concerns in scientifically and technically complex policy areas such as natural resource issues (Freudenberg and Skinsapir, 1992; Milbrath, 1984). The advocacy role taken by public interest groups is frequently framed in the context of the information sharing function interest groups perform in modern, postindustrial democracies (Pierce et al., 1992). Industry organizations, on the other hand, often command substantial financial resources at their disposal to influence the policy process. According to some observers (Lindbloom, 1977), this often gives business a privileged position in the American policy process: "both legislators and the administration in power are especially eager to please those in the business community because they don't want to suffer the electorate's wrath after an economic turndown" (Berry, 1989: 205).

To be sure, industry also influences the public by providing information and communicating its policy preferences. This is especially true in the policy area of public lands such as federal forests. With approximately three-fourths of the public now identifying themselves as "environmentalists" and 44 percent opposing harvesting of timber on federal lands (*Gallup Poll Monthly*, 1991; *American Forests*, 1994; also see Dunlap, 1992), the natural resource industry has a vested short and long-term interest in taking its case to the public.

In the context of policy area flux and the high level of environmental awareness among the American public, public interest groups have substantial influence on public natural resource decisions despite fewer financial resources because of their grassroots support organizations and because of greater "value congruence" with the general public (see chapters 1, 2, and 3). Environmental groups tend to succeed in the policy process because of their "elite challenging" orientation and their ability to gain passage of laws that maintain avenues for citizen involvement and legal challenge to how forest resources are being managed on public lands.

GROUPS AND POLITICAL COMMUNICATION

While much has been written about interest groups both as organizations and as political actors with policy agendas and strategies for implementing these agendas, relatively little work has been done to document the growing ability of groups to generate and disseminate a wide variety of types of information. Rather than operating exclusively in the realm of conventional lobbying and membership electoral mobilization, interest groups increasingly are concerned with the gathering and distribution of complex scientific and technical information. In recent decades, environmental groups have directed their efforts toward "influencing specific legislative and administrative actions," and "groups had to know how the political system worked, how to identify decision makers and how their minds worked" (Ingram and Mann, 1989: 144).

While interest groups differ in their capacity to generate information, they are likely to vary in the effort expended in communicating this information and in the scope or range of types of information communicated. The following passage is relevant to the communication efforts of the interest groups studied here, since interaction between group representatives and government officials goes both ways:

Messages are communicated through an interaction process. There is constant mutual feedback between sender and receiver so that both parties are communicators, or givers and receivers, at the same time. The environment within which communication occurs is a significant part of the communication picture, because of its role in shaping both process and contents of communication. (Vasu, Stewart, and Garson, 1990: 147)

Providing information to members is not always an important function identified by scholars of interest groups. Following the reasoning of Mancur Olson, specialized information (publishing newsletters, magazines, or journals; providing information or data services; sponsoring research activities; running seminars, conferences or workshops) is considered a private good and a separate incentive to group membership (Ingram and Mann, 1989). However, other scholars reverse the logic of Olson's reasoning on its head by arguing that "Provision of private goods is a by-product of the lobbying function. Magazines and outings serve to reinforce or increase members' utility for environmental goods the group seeks to obtain and to impress members with groups' accomplishments" (Mitchell, 1979: 109).

When group communications with government are considered, the interactional nature of information sharing is evident. Interest groups use their specialized information to insure access to government officials. Information pertaining to highly complex economic, technical, or scientific problems provided by interest groups is especially important to legislative staff and to both high-ranking and middle-level civil servants (Schlozman and Tierney, 1986).

In regard to public communication in the federal forestry policy debate, Mather (1990) has argued that the debate has become increasingly salient to the public. As a result of active group advocacy in this issue arena by environmental and conservation groups, a far larger proportion of the general public has become involved in the public policy process than ever before. This has led industry to adopt a similar strategy to counteract environmental criticism of forest harvesting practices on public lands. As Berry argues, "Interest groups have strong reasons to convince people at the grass roots of the righteousness of their arguments, believing that changed public opinion will eventually lead to changed elite opinion" (1989: 99).

The following analyses will focus on industry and interest group communication strategies, frequency of communication, the types of information communicated, and self-assessed success in communication with the public, legislators, and natural resource agencies (all of which are important actors in the forest policy process). Multivariate analyses also are provided to assess how different strategies, types of information, and frequency of communication relate to self-perceived success. The results will provide insight into the political success potential of the different interests in the federal forest policy arena.

DATA AND MEASUREMENTS

The data employed in the following analyses are derived from mail surveys of officers of public interest groups and industry representatives who have been involved in federal forest policy in at least one of Oregon's 13 national forests.[1] During the spring of 1992 each national forest provided its public participation list, which contains the names and addresses of individuals, interest groups, and industry representatives who have participated in the forest planning process. After the elimination of duplicate listings, questionnaires were sent to industry representatives and public interest groups with individual memberships. Survey development and implementation followed Dillman's *Mail and Telephone Surveys* (1978). For the industry survey, 176 surveys were delivered and 133 were returned, for a response rate of 75 percent. For the interest group survey, 415 groups were sent surveys with 326 returned, producing a response rate of 78 percent.

In order to determine group communication strategies with the public, interest group and industry officers were asked to indicate if their organization has a regular means of communicating with the public, and if they do *regularly communicate* what forms of communication are used.[2]   Groups and industry also were asked the *frequency of communication* with elected and appointed national government officials concerning federal forest policy.[3] In addition, each group was asked what *types of information* they communicate to legislators, agencies, and the public.[4] Groups then were asked what *communication strategies*[5] they use to communicate information to members of Congress and natural resource agencies, and then how *successful*[6] they perceive their communication attempts to have been.

Organizations are categorized into five groups according to their interest in the management of federal forest lands.[7] Often these different types of groups are at odds over the management of public forest lands-for example, timber production versus wildlife habitat, hunting versus wildlife watching. Steel, Steger, Lovrich, and Pierce (1990) found strong policy differences toward the management of public lands between hunting and fishing, snowmobile/mechanized vehicle, and wildlife watching groups in Ontario and Michigan. Passive recreation (e.g., bird watchers) and environmental groups preferred a preservationist management approach to public lands while hunting groups and mechanized vehicle groups preferred a multiple-use approach.

Data for the first four categories are from the Oregon federal forest interest groups survey, while data for the fifth category are from the Oregon forest industry survey. Group categories and examples are as follows:

1. *Environmental Protection/Conservation*: Membership groups interested in the preservation or conservation of federal forest lands

2. *Intensive Recreation*: Membership groups representing, for example, fishing, hunting, snowmobiling, or power boating, interests. These groups a interested in intensive use of federal forest lands

3. *Passive Recreation*: Membership groups representing, for example, hiking, crosscountry skiing, mountain climbing, and wildlife watching interests. These groups are interested in more passive and potentially less environmentally damaging activities

4. *Industry-Related Groups:* Membership groups representing natural resource extraction interests on federal forest lands. Examples of these groups include mining groups, logging groups, woods products unions, and wise-use groups

5. *Industry*: Nonmembership commercial organizations interested in natural resource extraction from federal forest lands. Industries in this category,

include sawmills, logging companies, millworks, mining companies, timber trucking companies, and helicopter logging concerns

RESULTS

Public Communication: The findings displayed in Table 4.1 report group communication strategies to inform the public. As one could expect in a politicized issue area such as federal forest policy, a majority of groups listed have some regular means of communicating with the public. For the four types of membership organizations, over 82 percent regularly communicate their preferences to the public. Industry organizations, on the other hand, are less likely (59 percent) to communicate directly with the public.

The preferred forms of public communication for membership groups appear to be the print media approach of newsletters (98 percent and over) and magazines (75 percent and over). Two other written forms of communication are also popular with many groups and include special reports and newspapers. A majority of environmental groups reported using these two additional forms of communication. In fact, environmental groups were the most likely to use all of the forms of communication listed. As suggested previously, environmental groups depend on public support more than most organizations to promote their policy agenda.

Frequency of Communication: The data displayed in Table 4.2 provide some insight into the frequency of group communication with national government officials involved in the federal forest policy debate. For all of the national government officials listed-including both elected and appointed officials-environmental groups indicated more frequent contact with all the officials when compared to all other organized interests. This was generally followed by the frequency of industry communication with the listed officials. As Wondolleck has suggested concerning public lands policy, "given their [industry and environmentalist] dissatisfaction with the formal administrative decision-making process, industry and environmental groups are both encouraging Congress and the Secretaries of Agriculture and Interior to take action to end the impasse" (1988: 12). The officials most frequently targeted by environmental groups include elected officials and their staff, followed by mid-level personnel in agencies and heads of agencies. Industry organizations indicated the second highest level of communication with mid-level personnel and agency heads.

An interesting pattern evident in the table is the frequency of contact with mid-level personnel in agencies (e.g., USDA Forest Service and USDI Bureau of Land Management). These officials often have significant discretionary powers in the implementation of public lands management policy and are therefore important targets for communication of group preferences. Another interesting finding is the high level of contact with government scientific experts by environmental groups. Environmental groups often do their own scientific research because they "question not only the substance of Forest Service decisions, but also the process by which these decisions are being made" (Wondolleck, 1988: 11, 12).

Table 4.1
Group Communication Strategies

Does your Organization have a regular means of communicating with the public? (Percentage)

	Envir.	Passive Rec.	Intense Rec.	Indus. Group	Indus.
YES	82	86	84	93	59
NO	17	14	16	7	41

If "yes," what forms of communication are used? (Percentage)

	Envir.	Passive Rec.	Intense Rec.	Indus. Group	Indus.
Newsletter	100	100	98	100	36
Magazine	100	100	75	100	14
Promotional memberships	19	14	3	12	NA
Special reports	52	28	44	56	31
Workshops	48	36	25	50	13
Videotapes	33	21	17	25	21
Newspapers	54	50	37	37	41
Radio	30	29	15	25	27
Television	37	29	4	6	29
	n=126	n=28	n=142	n=32	n=133

Types of Communicated Information: The findings presented in Table 4.3 reflect the types of information that interest groups and industry communicate to legislators, natural resource agencies, and the public in order to influence federal forest policy. Five different types of information were identified by organizations as useful in policy debates: scientific, political, value positions, legal, and economic information.

Table 4.2
Frequency of Group Communication with National Government Officials
Concerning Federal Forest Policy

	Envir.	Passive Rec.	Intense Rec.	Indus. Group	Indus.
	mean	mean	mean	mean	mean
Elected officials or their staff F-test = 4.89 p = .003	3.84	2.73	2.98	2.80	3.36
Heads of agencies, departments or commissions. F-test = 3.33 p = .003	3.65	3.00	3.11	3.07	3.32
Mid-level personnel in agencies, depts. or commissions F-test = 2.74 p = .053	3.69	2.04	3.62	3.73	3.54
Legal experts in government F-test = 0.53 p = 0.65	2.31	2.10	2.11	2.20	2.22
Scientific experts in government F-test = 11.95 p = .000	3.78	1.05	2.33	1.79	2.37
	n=126	n=28	n=142	n=32	n=133

Note: A Likert response format was used with 1 = never and 5 = often.

Not surprisingly, most businesses communicate economic information to legislators (79 percent), natural resource agencies (81 percent), and the public (88 percent). Most industry-related groups, environmental groups, and intensive recreation groups also use economic information to influence federal forest policy.

Environmental groups, however, were most likely to use value positions in the policy debate. What is most striking about the results is the number of environmental groups who say they communicate *scientific* information to legislators, natural resource agencies, and the public. This finding supports the growing body of literature that suggests that the primary role of interest groups is changing from classic lobbying activities to one of making strategic use of information to structure the nature of the policy debate in government and the public mind (Pierce et al., 1992). In fact, environmental groups were the most likely to communicate a variety of information types to legislators, natural resource agencies, and the public.

Communication Strategies: The data presented in Tables 4.4 and 4.5 provide some insight into the communication strategies of groups involved in the federal forestry process. The first table reports strategies to communicate with members of Congress. For environmental, passive recreation, intensive recreation, and industry-related groups the most used strategy is "building public support for proposals" in order to influence Congress. Given earlier discussion concerning the increasing "publicness" of federal forest policy this strategy is not surprising. While it could be argued that environmental groups are already "preaching to the converted," given the strength of public support for environmental causes (see chapters 1, 2, and 3) they still must inform the public of impending changes concerning management. Groups that engage in activities potentially damaging to federal forests-such as natural resource extraction and intensive recreation interests-also have a need to present their side of the issues to the public.

Testifying at public congressional hearings and providing information directly to Congress members were both popular strategies among most of the groups questioned in Oregon. Congress's role in the federal forest debate has been pivotal in recent years. The recent timber salvage legislation passed in 1995 is an excellent example of why groups must take their case to Congress. The "salvage rider" allows harvesting of dead and dying timber on western public lands and resurrects many old growth timber sales which that stopped by the endangered listing of the western spotted owl. Other recent actions by Congress include a moratorium on endangered species listings under the endangered species act and budget cuts to agencies that play a key role in species protection such as the U.S. Fish and Wildlife Service, the Department of Interior, and the National Marine Fisheries Service.

The data presented in Table 4.5 suggest strategic differences among groups in their efforts to inform natural resource agencies such as the USDA Forest Service and the Bureau of Land Management. Environmental groups are the only organizations which tend focus on the public for helping to inform and influence natural resource agencies. Over 60 percent of the environmental groups studied here use "testifying at public hearings" as a strategy and 76 percent say they build "public support for proposals." Industry and industry-related groups are most likely to work behind the scenes and provide "information on pending policies" (62% and 74% respectively).

Table 4.3
Types of Information Communicated to Legislators, Agencies, and the Public

	Envir.	Passive Rec.	Intense Rec.	Indus. Group	Indus.
Percentage Communicating Information:					
LEGISLATORS					
Scientific	51	14	18	50	35
Political	37	14	14	31	35
Value positions	69	21	24	25	61
Legal	44	14	28	37	24
Economic	59	36	56	50	79
NATURAL RESOURCE AGENCIES					
Scientific	52	14	24	62	35
Political	32	14	14	37	35
Value positions	68	29	24	37	58
Legal	41	14	27	37	26
Economic	61	43	66	56	81
PUBLIC					
Scientific	63	14	24	37	37
Political	51	21	20	31	41
Value positions	69	29	25	6	56
Legal	54	14	27	31	26
Economic	51	36	56	56	88
	n=126	n=28	n=142	n=32	n=133

Note: The description of each category of information provided to groups is as follows: *scientific information* (e.g., reports on scientific studies, etc.); *political information* (e.g., news on sources of policy support or opposition); *value positions* (e.g., ethical arguments concerning resource uses, etc.); *legal information* (e.g., news cases or administrative rulings); *economic information* (e.g., findings on cost-benefit studies, etc.).

* $p < .05$; ** $p < .01$; *** $p < .001$

Table 4.4
Communication Strategies for Influencing Members of Congress Concerning Federal Forest Policy

	Envir.	Passive Rec.	Intense Rec.	Indus. Group	Indus.
	Percentage Using Communication Strategy:				
Testifying at public hearings	60	50	34	44	50
Providing information on pending legislation	63	43	39	56	67
Building public support for proposals	70	57	42	62	56
Identifying experts on natural resource/ environmental issues	48	21	24	50	33
	n=126	n=28	n=142	n=32	n=133

Perceived Communication Success: Perceptual data cannot tell us who actually is "successful" in communicating information, but it does allow for self-evaluation of influence in the federal forestry policy process.. The results displayed in Table 4.6 provide some insight into each group's perception of its own success in transmitting information to various parties.

With regard to legislators, 50 percent of the industry-related groups considered themselves successful, followed by environmental groups (42 percent), industry (35 percent), intensive recreation (33 percent), and passive recreation (12 percent). Almost 70 percent of environmental groups considered themselves successful at informing natural resource agencies, followed by 57 percent of industry-related groups and 43 percent of intensive recreation organizations. Only 31 percent of industry and 37 percent of passive recreation groups rated themselves as being successful in their advocacy.

Table 4.5
Communication Strategies for Group Influence of Natural Resource Agencies
Concerning Federal Forest Policy

	Envir.	Passive Rec.	Intense Rec.	Indus. Group	Indus.
	Percentage using communication strategy:				
Testifying at public hearings	62	50	38	37	59
Providing information on pending policies	54	36	42	62	74
Building public support for proposals	76	36	42	37	39
Identifying experts on natural resource/ environmental issues	36	21	18	31	25
	n=126	n=28	n=142	n=32	n=133

As for informing the general public, fewer organizations considered themselves successful. Industry-related groups (46 percent) and environmental groups (45 percent) were most likely to consider themselves successful as compared to only a third of businesses and 25 percent or less of recreation groups. Certainly these latter organizations are aware of their standing among the public (see chapters 1, 2, and 3).

Multivariate Analyses: In order to determine the impact of communication frequency, types of information, communication strategies, and group type on perceived success in the federal forestry debate, ordinary least squares estimates for influencing legislators, natural resource agencies, and the public are presented in Table 4.7. The independent variables for these models were presented in Tables 4.2 through 4.5. For the information type and communication strategy independent variables, indicators were recoded as dummy variables (1 = information type or strategy used; 0 = other). The frequency of communication variables are included as coded in Table 4.2. The organizational type variable is controlled in each model

Table 4.6
Self-Assessed Success of Interest Group and Industry Attempts to Influence the Federal Forest Policy Process

Question: On matters affecting federal forest policy, how successful would you say your organization is in its attempts to inform legislators, natural resource agencies, and the general public?

	Envir.	Passive Rec.	Intense Rec.	Indus. Group	Indus.
LEGISLATORS					
%successful	42	12	33	50	35
%uncertain	34	50	33	21	29
%unsuccessful	25	38	34	29	36
NATURAL RESOURCE AGENCIES					
%successful	69	37	43	57	31
%uncertain	24	37	36	21	32
%unsuccessful	7	25	21	21	37
GENERAL PUBLIC					
%successful	45	25	22	46	31
%uncertain	34	37	40	38	36
%unsuccessful	21	37	38	15	33
	n=126	n=28	n=142	n=32	n=133

Note: A Likert format response category was provided with 1 = not successful and 5 = very successful. Categories were collapsed for presentation purposes.

through the use of dummy variables (1 = environmental or industry group; 0 = other). Because it is necessary to omit one dummy category for each model to be estimated, the category representing recreation groups (both intensive and passive) is omitted. The dependent variables included for each model are the same as those presented in Table 4.6. The F-test results indicate that all three models are statistically significant, and adjusted R^2s range from .32 to .36.

For the frequency of communication variables included in the models, we find that frequent contact with elected officials, agency heads, and mid-level personnel is associated with perceived success with legislators, natural resource agencies, and the public in federal forest policy. An additional variable--frequency of contact with scientific experts -- is also significantly correlated with perceived success in

Table 4.7
Ordinary Least Squares Estimates of Self-Perceived Success Influencing Legislators, Agencies, and the Public Concerning Federal Forest Policy

	Legislators		Natural Resource Agencies		Public	
	b	**Beta**	*b*	**Beta**	*b*	**Beta**
Communication Frequency						
Elected officials	.23**	.25	.26**	.17	.06	.03
Agency heads	.28***	.29	.23***	.27	.05	.02
Mid-level personnel	.11*	.11	.15*	.17	.02	.03
Legal experts	.02	.03	.05	.06	.07	.05
Scientific experts	.05	.05	.12*	.15	.04	.05
Information Type						
Scientific	.15*	.10	.17**	.26	.25*	.13
Political	.24**	.15	.45**	.18	.03	.02
Values	.18*	.13	.32*	.13	.21*	.12
Legal	.40**	.16	.06	.03	.12	.05
Economic	.08	.03	.08	.04	.37***	.18
Strategies						
Testifying	.18	.07	.02	.01	.06	.03
Info. on legislation	.03	.02	.35*	.14	.19*	.11
Public support	.16*	.11	.17*	.11	.28*	.12
Identify experts	-.02	-.01	.18	.08	.05	.02
Groups						
Environmental	.08	.05	.20*	.10	.19*	.11
Industry	.06	.04	.16*	.09	.07	.06
R^2 =	.36		.37		.32	
Adj. R^2 =	.31		.33		.30	
F =	8.81***		9.09***		7.23***	

$* p < .05; ** p < .01; *** p < .001$

communicating with natural resource agencies. Not surprisingly, none of these variables was found to be significantly related to perceived success in communicating with the public.

For the variables assessing the type of information used to communicate with legislators, natural resource agencies, and the public in the federal forest debate, both scientific information and value information were significantly related to perceived success in all three models. This is an important finding given both the highly technical nature of these management issues and the strong value-based emotions surrounding forests. Not surprisingly, the use of political information was significantly related to perceived communication success with legislators and natural resource agencies. Use of poll data or promises of support/opposition are commonly made by groups involved in such a volatile policy arena. Legal information was only related to perceived success with legislators and economic information was only significantly related to perceived success with the public. These management issues often are framed in economic terms by industry when communicating with the public, and, in turn, environmental/conservation groups have returned the charge, claiming subsidies of public timber harvests by the federal government due to below-market timber sales and government road building.

As for the communication strategy variables included in each model, only building public support is significantly related to perceived communication success with legislators, natural resource agencies, and the public. Certainly this is supportive of previous discussion suggesting the public nature of federal forestry issues in the West. Providing information on impending legislation is significantly related to perceived success in communicating with agencies and the public. For example, recent attempts by Congress to rewrite or even gut the Endangered Species Act have generated much comment by all groups involved in federal forest policy.

For the dummy variables controlling for group type, we find no significant differences between environmental groups and industry in perceived communication success with legislators. However, for natural resource agencies both environmental groups and industry are significantly more likely than recreation groups to perceive communication success. Finally, for perceived communication success on federal forestry issues with the public, environmental groups are significantly more likely to perceive success when compared to industry and recreation groups. Given the widespread support of environmental groups among much of the public this finding is to be expected.

CONCLUSIONS

This chapter has presented evidence from a study of the advocacy groups active in the management of Oregon's 13 national forests. It has investigated the resources and strategies of public interest groups and industry representatives involved in forest management decisions in the early 1990s. On the basis of survey data collected among 133 business representatives and 326 public interest groups involved in federal forest policy, it is clear that the interest communication of various kinds of information is central to the practical dynamics of a contentious, value-laden, and scientifically/technologically complex policy area. The character of the policy process clearly reflects an intersection between an interest group's perception of its own strengths, resources, and positions, and the nature of the criteria that characterize decision-making loci in the policy process. To be sure, some interests may well be disadvantaged in the new information age of interest group politics. At the same time, it is clear that these interests recognize the importance of the strategic calculus that guides their information and communication behavior in attempting to achieve their goals.

NOTES

1. The 13 national forests included in the study are: Deschutes, Fremont, Malheur, Mt. Hood, Ochoco, Rogue River, Siskiyou, Siuslaw, Umatilla, Umpqua, Wallowa-Whitman, Willamette, and Winema.

2. The question used was: "Does your organization have a regular means of communicating with the public? If yes, what forms of communication are used?" The response categories provided were: newsletter, magazine, promotional memberships, special reports, workshops, videotapes, newspapers, radio, and television.

3. The question used was: "When communicating information on federal forest land policy with national government officials, how frequently do representatives of your organization interact with the types of officials listed below?" The types of officials provided were: elected officials or their staff, heads of agencies, mid-level personnel in agencies, departments, or commissions, legals experts in government, and scientific experts in government. (Response categories were: 1 = never to 5 = often).

4. Organizations were asked: "What kinds of information concerning federal forest issues does your organization communicate (if any) to legislators, natural resource agency personnel, and the public?" The types of information provided were: scientific, political, value positions, legal, and economic.

5. Groups were asked: "Which of the following information strategies does your organization typically use to inform members of Congress/natural resource agencies?" The response categories provided were: testifying at public hearings, providing information on pending legislation, building public support for proposals, identifying experts on natural resource/environmental issues.

6. The question used was: "On matters affecting federal forest policy, how successful would you say your organization is in attempts to inform legislators, natural resource agencies, and the general public?" (Response categories were: 1 = not successful to 5 = very successful. Categories were collapsed for presentation purposes in Table 4.6)

7. Group categories were formulated using the *Directory of Oregon Forest Interest Groups* published by Oregon State University Extension (Corvallis,OR: April, 1993). For purposes of this chapter, Berry's (1989: 4) definition of interest groups was used to identify organizations involved in federal forest policy: "an interest group is an organized body of individuals who share some goals and who try to influence public policy." Berry argues that industrial organizations, such as specific timber companies, fall outside this definition and should be examined separately from interest groups (1989: Ch. 1). Consequently, we have made a distinction between groups that represent industry (i.e., have membership) and industry itself.

Chapter 5

Political Resources and Activities of Environmental Groups in Washington State

Debra Salazar

During the last three decades, environmental concerns have become institutionalized in American public policy making. This institutionalization is evident in the passage of numerous statutes related to the environment, the creation of environmental regulatory agencies at both national and state levels of government, and the organization of thousands of environmental interest groups across the country. These groups have become key players in environmental politics at all levels of government.

But as the environmental movement has secured access to policy-making processes, observers have noted divisions within the movement.[1] While there is disagreement regarding the nature and sources of these divisions, typically analysts distinguish between mainstream organizations headquartered in Washington D.C. and grassroots groups throughout the country. Grassroots groups are distinguished by class diversity among members, local focus, unconventional political style, the prominence of volunteers, and efforts to democratize environmental science and politics (Gottlieb, 1993). These characteristics are in contrast to mainstream environmental organizations, which dominated by middle- and upper-class staff and leaders, have a national and increasingly global focus, rely on conventional political tactics such as lobbying and litigation, and are staffed by professionally trained experts (Dowie, 1992; Gottlieb, 1993).

This division within the movement is claimed as a source of both strength and weakness (Dunlap and Mertig, 1992). Diversity of organizational styles and practices is seen as an asset with particular elements of the movement positioned to take advantage of particular opportunities. In contrast, environmental activists on each side often criticize those on the other side of the cleavage as ineffective or lacking a fundamental understanding of environmental problems. While there is likely some truth in both claims, clearly the differences among environmental groups have implications for the nature of environmental politics. Professional and bureaucratic organizations with access to financial resources and technical expertise will conduct themselves differently from organizations run by lay volunteers who must educate themselves about the technical aspects of environmental problems. These groups will approach politics with different values and different orientations to authority and compromise. Thus, the existence of a central cleavage among environmental groups may explain much about contemporary environmental politics.

The purpose of this chapter is to explore this variation among environmental groups at the state level. The geographic focus is the state of Washington. Because political resources circumscribe the political activities in which interest groups engage, these resources will be the analytical focus of the chapter. Political resources are the assets groups use to influence public policy. Reliance on particular resources is important both because of its effect on the quality of political interactions and the magnitude of political influence that groups exercise.

This chapter addresses four questions. First, do environmental groups in Washington State differ with respect to key organizational and political attributes? That is, can we discern systematic variation among these groups similar to that observed between national and grassroots groups? Second, what kinds of political resources do environmental groups find important to their efforts to influence public policy? Third, can we discern patterns in the use of political resources? What is the underlying structure of these resources? Finally, how are political resources related to political activities? These questions are examined within the context of a sample of environmental groups in Washington State.

THE NATURE OF POLITICAL RESOURCES

Political resources are the tools organizations use to influence public policy. They are assets that groups can expend on particular endeavors. A group's success depends, in part, on both the quality and quantity of political resources at its disposal. Aldrich (1979) identified four types of resources: money, personnel, information, and products and services. Benson (1975) argued that the most important resources are money and authority. Ingram and Mann (1989) identified ideological appeals, having effective leadership, and forming coalitions, as the bases for the success of environmental groups in influencing policy making. The literature is rich in discussions of how groups have used particular resources in support of particular policy ends. Very few studies, however, have developed systematic analyses of the different kinds of political resources that organizations use to influence the making of public policy.

Schattschneider's (1960) analysis of conflict expansion offers an important insight regarding political resources. He suggested that the pressure group system, a small and closed network, responded to particular kinds of political resources. If an actor is not endowed with these resources, she or he has an incentive to attempt to expand an issue or conflict beyond the pressure group system to the broader electorate, where, presumably, different kinds of resources hold value.

Salazar (1989) drew on Schattschneider to define two types of political resources, *instrumental resources* and *direct electoral support*. The latter is tied to the direction and strength of public opinion on particular issues and becomes important only when a conflict has been expanded. The scope of expansion must include what Cobb and Elder (1983) have called the attentive public and perhaps the general public. Instrumental resources include money, mailing lists, and volunteer campaign workers, assets that can be transferred among issues. Salazar argued that resources could be distinguished by whether they were tied to a particular issue. This typology was designed to generate insights regarding the necessary conditions for and consequences of conflict expansion. Resources, in this model, are those that groups can offer politicians and the issue is the unit of analysis. When the group is the unit of analysis and resources are defined more broadly, finer distinctions among kinds of resources are useful.

Schlozman and Tierney (1986) constructed a list of eight political resources and asked organizational representatives to identify the two most important and the two least important. They interviewed individuals from 175 organizations that were represented in Washington, D.C. Schlozman and Tierney's list includes: a reputation for being credible and trustworthy, a wide circle of contacts, well-known and respected leaders, control over technical information, an appealing cause, strategically placed allies, a large membership, and a large budget. By far, respondents believed a reputation for credibility to be among the most important resources and a large budget to be among the least so. This was true for all four types of organizations (corporations, trade associations, unions, and citizens' groups) that Schlozman and Tierney studied.

Laumann and Knoke (1987) compiled a list of eight political resources for their study of the health and energy national policy domains: technical expertise, funds to mobilize support for a policy proposal, staff or facilities useful for mobilizing support, formal authority, connections to influential organizations, reputation as an impartial mediator, ability to mobilize public opinion, and ability to mobilize members or employees. They asked organizational informants to name other groups with which they were familiar and to identify the resources these groups use to influence policy making.

Laumann and Knoke went beyond ascertaining which resources were most valued by attempting to discover the underlying structure of political resources. They used a typology developed by Laumann and Pappi (1976) to construct their list of resources and then factor analyzed their data to discover empirical groupings. The typology has two dimensions: locus of influence base and scope of convertibility. The second dimension distinguishes among resources by the range of contexts (general or specific) in which a resource will be effective. The first dimension distinguishes between resources that reflect or inhere in an organization's standing in the policy community and those that are more idiosyncratic and reflect characteristics of an organization's leaders or staff. Laumann and Knoke refer to the poles of this dimension as institutional (or positional) and personal.

Their factor analysis generated three factors and did not indicate groupings consistent with the typology. The first factor included one resource: formal authority. The second, reputation as an impartial mediator, was also a single-variable factor. The third factor, which Laumann and Knoke termed mobilizable resources, accounted for 74 percent of the common variance in the health domain. This factor includes variables of all four types defined by the Laumann and Pappi (1976) typology. In fact, the results of the factor analysis are unrelated to the typology, and the mobilizable resource factor seems best interpreted as a residual category.

Pross (1992) used organizational resources as one element of his typology of pressure groups. Pross focused on resources, such as membership (size and quality), budget, staff, volunteers, and reputation. He argued that the possession of such resources as well as of policy capacity distinguished between institutionalized and nascent groups.

Pierce et al. (1992) drew on Pross's work in their study of environmental groups in Ontario and Michigan. Their principal component factor analysis revealed three factors underlying a set of eleven resources. The first factor, financial resources, included the size of an organization's annual budget, the extent of external financial support, whether or not an organization employs paid staff, and whether or not it enjoys tax exempt status. The second factor, human resources, comprised: a chapter-based organizational structure, the number of volunteers available to the organization, the number of individual members, and the percentage of revenue raised from dues. Finally, three resources-presence of organizational members, affiliations with provincial or state organizations, and affiliations with national organizations-loaded highly on the third factor, networking resources. Pierce and his coauthors contended that the differential access of groups in their sample to financial, human, and networking resources would be reflected in the nature of their interactions with public officials.

My review of previous research indicates that three considerations ought to guide the study of political resources. First, results will be most meaningful if resources are defined strictly, as things (tangible or intangible) that are available for use. There is ambiguity in the literature with respect to the difference between a resource and an action. The list of political resources used for this study does not include the uses to which things are put. For example, mobilization of members is not a resource but a process. Resources such as a charismatic leader, a mailing list, and the occurrence of a disaster can be used to mobilize members. But mobilization is not a resource. Second is Schattschneider's insight about the importance of the issue in defining politics. Much of politics is about defining issues in terms favorable to various political actors. Thus, an appealing cause may be a key political resource for an interest group. Finally, the list of political resources used for this study was constructed with an eye to clarifying relations among resources. In particular, resources are defined such that the analysis should determine if resources are allocated among groups according to whether they reflect institutionalized or personalized attributes of organizations.

To construct a list of resources, I drew heavily on Schlozman and Tierney's indicators, Laumann and Knoke's mobilizable resource factor, and interviews conducted with staff of environmental groups in other states. A total of 10 indicators was used: a large budget, a large membership, computer equipment and databases, professional lobbyists, staff expertise on environmental politics, staff expertise on the technical elements of environmental problems, a wide circle of contacts, a reputation for being credible and trustworthy, an appealing cause, and volunteer staff. In the following section, I describe the sample used to analyze relations among these resources.

THE SAMPLE

Data used in this paper are part of a larger dataset regarding environmental policy making in the state of Washington. The study focuses on the period 1987, 1988, which corresponds to the most recent complete session of the Washington state legislature at the time data were collected. The data for this chapter focus on the structural attributes of environmental groups.

The sampling frame for environmental groups was constructed from three sources: (1) a list of Washington environmental groups compiled by Draffan (1987); (2) the directory of the Washington Environmental Council (an umbrella organization of environmental groups in the state); and (3) rosters from legislative committee hearings regarding environmental bills and issues during 1987 and 1988. The complete list consisted of over 300 environmental groups. The population was stratified into two categories. One category consisted of the 24 groups most active in the state legislature during that session (i.e., groups that testified five or more times during the 1987, 1988 session). The second category consisted of the remaining groups in the population. I refer to the first set of groups as the L(legislature) groups and the second set as the non-L groups. A random sample of one hundred of the non-L groups was selected for the study, as well as all of the L groups.

Representatives of each organization were contacted by phone and asked to participate in the study. Representatives of 22 of the 24 L groups were interviewed personally (92% response rate). Obtaining a sample of non-L groups was more difficult. The sampling frame included groups with duplicate names, groups formed after the period defined for study, groups that no longer existed (and for which I was unable to track down former leaders), and groups that were not citizen-based environmental groups. Some of these were professional associations or resource development associations. After eliminating these groups from the sample list, 73 groups remained. Completed, usable questionnaires were received from 51 non-L groups (response rate of 70%) for a total sample of 73 organizations.[2]

STRUCTURAL ATTRIBUTES OF ENVIRONMENTAL GROUPS

The first question posed in this study is: Are there structural differences between environmental groups that appear regularly at the state legislature and those that do not? The literature indicates that differences should exist with respect to four characteristics: size, the level of bureaucratization and professionalization of groups, the degree of internal democracy, and sources of funding.[3] Eight variables were used to capture these dimensions (Table 5.1). The groups do differ significantly in size, as measured by number of members, with the L groups having nearly 10 times as many members , on average, as the non-L groups. The number of full-time employees is an indicator of both size and professionalization, and the two sets of groups also differ significantly with respect to this variable. A chi-square test indicated a p value equal to 0.001 for the distributions of values for the ordinal variable, number of full-time employees.[4] Of course, number of employees is also an indicator of financial resources and, as expected, the L groups clearly have more access to these.

The bureaucratization variable is an additive index that ranges from zero to five. Informants were asked to indicate whether their organizations had: written rules, a system of files, a board of directors, division of labor among individuals, and division of labor among departments. Scores for this variable are the sum of yes responses. Comparison of means indicates the L groups score significantly higher on this variable.

An index of member participation in organizational decision making was created to measure the extent of internal democracy for the groups. Informants were asked to assess the extent of member participation through a series of channels (member polls, elections, task forces, meetings). Each item was coded from 0 to 4 (no members participate to 76, 100% participation). The index was created by summing scores and dividing by the number of items. Participation is generally low by this measure and there is no significant difference between the two types of groups. Thus, for our samples, members of less institutionalized groups do not appear to participate in organizational decision making any more than their counterparts in more established groups. The generally low levels of participation in decision making are consistent with other studies of citizens' groups.[5]

Finally, sources of organizational funding were elicited. Environmental groups in Washington draw nearly three-fourths of their revenue from members and approximately 10 percent through grants from other organizations (e.g., foundations). The L groups draw nearly twice as much of their revenue from the latter source than do the non-L groups. This could serve to constrain the former groups' choice of political activities.[6]

THE DISTRIBUTION OF POLITICAL RESOURCES

Each of the respondents was asked to select two issues on which the organization had concentrated most during 1987 and 1988. For each issue, respondents were presented with the list of ten resources and asked to indicate how important (scale of 1 to 5) each resource was for their organization's efforts to influence policy. Examination of the responses to this question (Table 5.2)

Table 5.1
Structural Characteristics of Two Types of Environmental Groups

	All Groups	Groups Prominent at State Legislature	Groups Not Prominent at State Legislature	T-test
Age (years)	21.6	25.1	20.4	0.85
Number of members	3,147	8,308	921	2.40*
Bureaucratization[a]	3.62	4.00	3.45	2.02*
Member participation[b]	1.04	1.19	0.98	1.30
Percent budget from members	72.4	70.6	73.2	-.036
Percent budget from other organizations.	9.6	15.2	7.1	1.91
Number of full-time employees[c]		1 to 5	0	
Number of volunteers[d]		30 plus	21-30	
	n=73	n=22	n=51	

* Significant at $p < .05$; ** Significant at $p < .01$; *** Significant at $p < .001$.
a. Entries are sample means.
b. Variable is scaled from 0 to 5.
c. Variable is scaled from 0 to 4.
d. Entries are median categories.

indicates variation among environmental groups with respect to the importance of each resource as well as consistency in the most and least valued resources. Money-driven resources such as budget, computer equipment,[7] and lobbyists are of no more than moderate importance for three-fourths of the groups. On the other hand, 88 percent of the groups consider a reputation for being credible to be of much or very much importance (a result that supports Schlozman and Tierney's findings). Also, resources such as contacts, an appealing cause, volunteers, and technical expertise are considered relatively important for most of the groups.

However, there is considerable variation in the importance environmental groups attribute to a large membership and political expertise.

These results are consistent with Schlozman and Tierney's findings regarding citizens' groups. They found reputation most frequently mentioned as a key resource, followed by an appealing cause, a large membership, and technical expertise (volunteers were not included in their study). The one resource where these findings diverge from theirs is a wide circle of contacts, generally regarded by my respondents as important but not so regarded by respondents in Schlozman's and Tierney's study. This difference may be an artifact of the way the questions were posed. Schlozman and Tierney asked respondents to choose the two most important resources. I asked that respondents assess the importance of each resource.

Comparison of the importance attributed to political resources by the two samples of groups reveals patterns of difference and similarity. Difference of means tests indicate significant differences with respect to the importance of a large membership, computer resources, professional lobbyists, political expertise, and a wide circle of contacts (Table 5.3). The L groups found these resources to be of more importance than did the non-L groups, The only resource that the non-L groups rated more highly was volunteers, but this difference was not statistically significant. In general, both sets of groups tend to find the same resources of value. The primary difference between the two sets is that the non-L groups concentrate on a smaller number of resources and the L groups use a greater variety of political resources. The sample as a whole is homogenous and consistent with Schlozman and Tierney's findings.

Principal components factor analysis was used to discern underlying relationships among the ten political resources. Principal components analysis is a data reduction technique used to construct linear combinations of variables that explain the total variation in a set of variables (Dillon and Goldstein 1984).[8] Each principal component is a linear combination of the larger set of variables. The goal is to get the smallest number of components that will explain the largest amount of total variance. The first step in the analysis presented here is to discover if political resources are interrelated in a manner that is consistent with the Laumann and Pappi (1976) typology. In a subsequent section the results of the principal components analysis will be used to assess relations among political resources and political activities.

Because of concern about differences between the two types of groups, I analyzed just the non-L groups and the total sample of both types of groups separately. Analyses of the 10x10 correlation matrices produced the same three-factor model for both datasets. The results were sufficiently similar that I report only the results of the full sample.

Recall that I expected to find two factors, one corresponding to positional resources and the other to idiosyncratic or personal resources. But a three-factor model best accounts for variation among the observed variables in this sample.

Table 5.2
Political Resources of Environmental Groups in Washington State

	Percentage of Organizations Finding Each Resource of Importance [n=73]:				
Political Resource	**No**	**Slight**	**Moderate**	**Much**	**Very Much**
Budget	42.5	26.0	19.2	5.5	6.8
Membership	20.5	13.7	15.1	28.8	21.9
Computers & databases	48.0	16.4	23.3	8.2	4.1
Professional lobbyists	53.4	15.1	13.7	13.7	4.1
Political expertise	21.9	13.7	16.4	31.5	16.4
Technical expertise	12.3	11.0	13.7	38.4	24.7
Contacts	6.8	5.5	19.2	46.6	21.9
Reputation for credibility	1.4	2.7	8.2	32.9	54.8
Appealing cause	6.8	15.1	5.5	34.2	38.4
Volunteers	8.2	9.6	11.0	17.8	53.4

Kim and Mueller (1978) suggest that factors with eigenvalues of at least one be included in the model.[9] The third factor generated by these data had an eigenvalue of 1.25 (versus 1.60 for the second factor and 0.72 for the fourth factor). Further, a plot of eigenvalues against the number of factors indicated a marked discontinuity at three factors.

Varimax rotation was used to obtain the orthogonal set of factors displayed in Table 5.4. Component loadings reflect the relations among the original variables and the components or factors. Eight of the variables load unambiguously on only one factor. For two of the variables, interpretation of loadings is more problematic.

Table 5.3
Importance of Political Resources for Two Types of Environmental Groups

	Groups Prominent at State Legislature	Groups Not Prominent at State Legislature	T-test
Budget	2.45	1.92	1.75
Membership	3.86	2.88	2.76**
Computers & databases	2.46	1.86	1.98
Professional lobbyists	2.82	1.65	3.97***
Political expertise	3.68	2.80	2.52*
Technical expertise	3.86	3.37	1.48
Contacts	4.23	3.49	2.78**
Reputation for credibility	4.54	4.29	1.15
Appealing cause	3.96	3.76	0.58
Volunteers	<u>3.82</u> n=22	<u>4.06</u> n=51	-0.70

* Significant at $p < .05$; ** Significant at $p < .01$; *** Significant at $p < .001$.

Though the loadings do not perfectly reflect expectations, there is a good deal of correspondence, indicating that resources are allocated among groups in a manner that is consistent with the typology.

Factor one reflects idiosyncratic attributes of groups, those useful in mobilizing other resources. An appealing cause, volunteers, a reputation for credibility, and a wide circle of contacts load most highly on this factor. The inclusion of the issue variable in this factor indicates that the manner in which groups use issues as political resources is related to personalized rather than institutionalized attributes of groups. Thus, if one were interested in predicting the circumstances under which

Table 5.4
Principal Components Analysis of Environmental Groups' Political Resources (Varimax Rotation; n=73)

Political Resources	Component Loadings		
Appealing Cause	.814	.129	.086
Volunteers	.767	.113	.031
Reputation for Credibility	.686	.061	.418
Contacts	.601	.329	.327
Budget	.210	.870	-.030
Membership	.247	.814	.008
Computers & Databases	.104	.682	.347
Professional Lobbyists	-.123	.628	.533
Technical Expertise	.289	-.049	.882
Political Expertise	.201	.287	.812
Eigenvalue	4.132	1.595	1.250
% of total variance explained	23.4	25.1	21.3
Cumulative percent = 69.8			

conflicts would be expanded, examination of the types of people who lead and staff the relevant organizations should prove more useful than focusing on organizational variables.

Factor two comprises organizational assets, including budget, membership, computer resources and professional lobbyists. These are the resources for which there were the greatest differences between the L and non-L groups. Thus, the institutional/idiosyncratic dimension discriminates between the two sets of environmental groups sampled. Organizational resources are much more important for the L groups.

Factor three includes both technical and political expertise. Professional lobbyists, which loads most highly on the organizational factor (two), also loads moderately on factor three. This loading may reflect the role of lobbyists in state and local environmental groups. These groups cannot afford to pay high-powered lobbying firms, and thus their lobbyists are generally semiprofessionals who work for the group part-time and/or for a small salary. For many groups, their value may reflect the attributes of the person who happens to hold the position rather than institutional attributes of the organization. Because of the nature of many of the groups (low budgets, low levels of specialization and division of labor), expertise inheres in individuals rather than in organizational positions. A reputation for credibility also loads moderately high on factor three, giving weight to an interpretation of this factor as having a base in both expertise and personal attributes. Thus, the idiosyncratic or personal attributes of an organization contribute to its expertise or knowledge base.

In sum, the principal components analysis indicates that political resources are allocated according to institutional and personal attributes of groups. Further, expertise emerges as a separate locus of influence, closely linked to the personal attributes of staff and leaders.

POLITICAL RESOURCES AND POLITICAL ACTIVITIES

Political resources are important because of their effects on what groups do and on their effectiveness. There are numerous kinds of activities in which interest groups engage. Walker (1991) factor analyzed interest group involvement in eight kinds of activities. He derived two factors including four activities each. Inside strategies include legislative lobbying, administrative lobbying, litigation, and electioneering. Outside strategies comprise use of the mass media, protests, providing speakers at public forums, and sponsoring conferences. Walker tested the effects of four independent variables on the importance of each strategy for groups. For citizens' groups, the existence of local chapters was positively related to the use of outside strategies. Chapter organization was used as an indicator of decentralization (Walker 1991).The size of paid staff was positively related to inside strategies, while the extent of external financial support was negatively related to use of inside tactics. Walker argued that heavy reliance on patronage moderates citizens' groups political activities while a large staff encouraged the use of inside strategies.

Respondents for this study were given a list of various political activities and asked which they engaged in during 1987, 1988. The activities were grouped into categories and coded 1 if an organization engaged in any activity in the category and 0 if it did not. The seven categories of activities were: conservation (e.g., build or maintain trails in natural areas), litigation, demonstrations or protests, public outreach (e.g., manage an environmental information center), work with the business community, involvement in election campaigns, and testifying in legislative hearings.

The likelihood of engaging in each kind of activity was compared for the two types of groups in the sample. The L groups are more likely than non-L groups to engage in every activity except conservation (see Table 5.5). The differences are statistically significant with respect to working with business, elections, and testimony at legislative hearings (Table 5.5). For each of these activities the L groups are at least one and one-half times as likely to engage in it than are the non-L groups. This pattern is consistent with the advantages the L groups have in access to political resources (Table 5.3).

Table 5.5
Political Activities of Two Types of Environmental Groups

Political Activity	*Percentage of Groups Engaging in Each Activity*				
	L Groups	Non-L Groups	Chi-square	*p*	Yule's Q
Testify	100.0	66.7	9.560	.002	1.00
Elections	50.0	23.5	4.991	.025	.53
Litigation	31.8	21.6	.869	.351	.26
Public Outreach	72.7	54.9	2.040	.153	.37
Conservation	50.0	66.7	1.806	.179	.33
Demonstrations	50.0	37.2	1.031	.310	.26
Work with Business	77.3	51.0	4.389	.036	.53
	n= 22	n= 51			

To assess more directly the effect of resources on political activities, a series of logit regressions was estimated. For each type of political activity, the effects of the three types of political resources, two sources of funding, and the levels of bureaucratization and member participation in organizational decision making were assessed (Table 5.6).[10]

Litigation, testifying, and electoral activity are part of Walker's (1991) inside strategy category. Expertise is positively related to the first two activities and organizational assets is positively related to all three (though the relation to testify is not significant). Mobilization resources are not significantly related to any of the inside tactics. These results suggest that access to resources influences decisions about engagement in political activities. That the coefficient for mobilization resources was not significant for any of three models may indicate that these resources are more important for effectiveness than for choice of strategies.

Grants, which is an indicator of patronage, has a negative effect on testify. In contrast, member contributions appear to encourage the use of litigation as a tactic. These results are consistent with Walker's (1991) finding that patronage discourages political activities of citizens' groups. While bureaucratization does not appear to have much effect on use of any of the inside tactics, participation is strongly related to electoral activity. Perhaps groups that actively engage their members are best able to use that activism in election campaigns. Alternatively, activist members may find electoral politics important.

Public outreach and conservation are outside strategies. While conservation is not a conventional political activity, it is an important one for environmental groups. Organizational assets do not have a statistically significant effect on either activity but the coefficient for outreach is much larger than that for conservation. Similarly, expertise and bureaucratization have significant effects on outreach. Clearly, organizational capacity is important for groups engaged in this type of activity. Member participation and mobilization resources also promote outreach activities. Thus, both institutionalized and personalized resources contribute to the initiation and maintenance of public outreach programs.

Consistent with the fact that conservation is not an overtly political activity, political resources appear to have no effect on it. Dependence on grants for revenue is negatively related to conservation, member participation positively so. Intriguingly, in all three models where the grants variable is significant, its effect is negative. Thus, financial reliance on patronage appears to discourage electoral and legislative as well as conservation actions. These results give no clues about the kinds of activities that patronage may support. In contrast, member participation may promote outreach, conservation, and electoral activity, tactics for which an active membership may provide the human resources that are essential to success.

CONCLUSIONS

In this chapter, I have attempted to discern whether the division within the environmental movement between national and grassroots groups can be observed between institutionalized and grassroots groups in Washington State. These groups

Table 5.6
Effects of Political Resources on Activities of Environmental Groups

	Testify	Electoral Activity	Litigate	Public Outreach	Conservation
Constant	2.593*	-2.146*	-3.750**	-3.050**	2.005*
	(1.669)	(1.498)	(2.247)	(1.593)	(1.485)
Organi-zational Assets	.200	.543**	.523*	.315	-.118
	(.340)	(.297)	(.347)	(.308)	(.281)
Expertise	.931***	.060	.953***	.378*	-.142
	(.348)	(.293)	(.407)	(.301)	(.290)
Mobili-zation Resources	.297	.059	.077	.767**	-.242
	(.301)	(.287)	(.405)	(.349)	(.308)
Grants	-.050**	-.033*	.017	.019	-.040**
	(.025)	(.025)	(.026)	(.020)	(.021)
Member Contrib.	-.015	.004	.033*	-.001	-.013
	(.015)	(.011)	(.021)	(.012)	(.012)
Bureau-cracy	-.053	.102	-.103	.549**	-.268
	(.275)	(.294)	(.295)	(.311)	(.265)
Parti-cipation	.401	.928**	-.088	1.470***	.752**
	(.490)	(.457)	(.478)	(.600)	(.435)
LR Statistic	13.090*	9.836	13.321*	22.830**	11.853
Pseudo R^2	.165	.112	.184	.245	.128

N = 69, df = 7

Note: Dependent variable is coded 1 if organization engaged in an activity, 0 if not. Top entry in each cell is logit coefficient. Entries in parentheses are standard errors. Probabilities for *T*-tests are based on one-tail values: *p < 0.10, **p < 0.05, ***p < 0.01.

do indeed differ with respect to key organizational attributes, political resources, and political activities. The grassroots (or non-L) groups have fewer members and smaller staffs, are less bureaucratized, and derive less of their revenue from external sources than the institutionalized (or L) groups. The grassroots groups also use a smaller array of political resources and tend to engage in a smaller set of political activities than the institutionalized groups. While this chapter has not examined environmental groups' issue agendas or positions, it is reasonable to infer the two types of groups will also differ in these regards. We should expect to find differences within the state and local environmental communities regarding willingness to compromise and orientation to authority. Environmental politics generally, and public lands politics more specifically, will reflect these differences within the environmental movement. If the patterns I have observed in Washington exist in other states, then public lands contests, whether fought on the regional, state, or national levels, will exhibit similar patterns of conflict, though not necessarily influence.

A second goal of this chapter was to examine patterns in the use of political resources. Resources fall into three groupings: organizational assets, mobilization resources, and expertise. Environmental groups in Washington State tend to rely more on expertise and mobilization resources than on organizational assets. Grassroots groups are especially reliant on mobilization resources and appear to have very little access to organizational assets relative to the institutionalized groups. Thus for state and local environmental groups in Washington State, politics is about defining issues and mobilizing volunteers through networks of contacts more than about raising large sums of money and hiring professional lobbyists. While these generalizations hold for both types of groups in the sample, they are especially true of grassroots groups.

Technical expertise is a key resource for all groups because environmental problems have important technical elements. But the manner of building such expertise probably differs between the two types of groups. Institutionalized groups, with larger paid staffs and more bureaucratized structures, are more likely to hire their experts. Further, institutionalized groups find political expertise more important for their efforts than do grassroots groups. This is consistent with the former groups' greater involvement in electoral and legislative politics and in working directly with business interests.

Environmental groups political resources are related to their political activities. Expertise and organizational assets tend to be positively related to the use of inside political tactics. Mobilization resources appear to support public outreach activities.

Recently, the federal role in public land management has reemerged as a focus of political conflict. The 1994 elections brought many wise-use advocates to Congress. They have used their positions to promote denationalization of the public lands. State and/or local control of public lands would certainly shift the balance of power in public lands politics in many locales. Jurisdictional change would work to the advantage of some interest sectors and the disadvantage of others. But, if the findings reported here hold true across the West, the internal politics of the environmental movement are likely to be similar in a new land management regime. To the extent that divisions within the environmental movement promote conflict about goals and strategies, we will see such conflict over local and regional as much as national decisions about land use allocations and management practices. To the extent that diversity is an advantage, this advantage can be exercised regardless of jurisdiction.

NOTES

1. See, for example, Dunlap and Mertig (1992), Dowie (1992), Gottlieb and Ingram (1989).

2. An additional problem I encountered was refusal to participate. Informants from several groups who declined to complete questionnaires were interviewed. In all cases, these were groups from the less conventional segment of the environmental movement; their philosophies ranged from deep ecology to bioregionalism (see Borrelli 1988 or Gottlieb 1993 for discussions of these positions). These informants believed that structured questionnaires were inappropriate for eliciting information about their groups. Though some representatives of radical environmental groups did participate in the study, the findings probably do not adequately reflect characteristics of this segment of the environmental movement.

3. See, for example, Gottlieb (1993), Dowie (1992; 1994), and Dunlap and Mertig (1992).

4. This variable was scaled from 1-5 as follows: zero employees, 1-5, 6-10, 11-15, greater than 15.

5. See, for example, Rothenberg's (1992) study of Common Cause.

6. See Gottlieb (1993) for a discussion of the role of foundations in shaping the agendas of national environmental groups.

7. The distribution of responses on this variable indicates that the computers and databases item was presented to respondents slightly ahead of its time. It is likely that had the question been asked several years later, many more groups would have found this resource important.

8. Principal components differs from common factor analysis in that the latter is used to discover unobserved factors that explain the *common* variance or *correlation* among a set of observed variables while the former is used to explain total variation (Kim and Mueller, 1978).

9. This criterion suggests that if a factor is to be included, it ought to account for more variance than a single variable (Dillon and Goldstein, 1984).

10. Results for five of the seven activities are presented here. The other two models did not generate significant coefficients.

Chapter 6

Consensus and Dissension Among Rural and Urban Publics Concerning Forest Management in the Pacific Northwest

Mark Brunson, Bruce Shindler, and Brent S. Steel

Media depictions of the debate over forestry in the Pacific Northwest offer images of conflict between polarized, monolithic interests: jobs versus owls; environmentalists versus loggers; small mill towns versus. large metropolitan areas (Doherty, 1993). Efforts to preserve old growth forests are often described as the imposition of urban values on rural people at the expense of resource-based livelihoods and cultures. This image is fostered by anti-environmentalist "wise-use" organizations seeking to restore a resource extraction emphasis in Western public lands policy and management (Krakauer, 1991). Some academic analysts also have suggested the existence of a rural-urban dichotomy in attitudes toward environmental preservation (Tichenor et al., 1971; Tremblay and Dunlap, 1978), although more recent studies have indicated that this view is too simplistic (Freudenburg and McGinn, 1987; Fortmann and Kusel, 1990).

An even more pervasive image of the Northwest forest issue is one of a controversy rooted in economic dependency: the so-called "jobs versus owls" conflict. Such a perspective can be consistent with the image of rural-urban dissension, but is not necessarily so. If attitudes toward forest management arise from a desire to maintain *community* economic well-being and a timber-oriented culture, we would expect to find rural-urban dissension in Northwesters' attitudes. Alternatively, if adherence to a resource management paradigm is associated with *personal* economic well-being, rural-urban differences could simply be an artifact of greater resource dependency in rural areas. In this study, we examine the degree to which rural and urban publics embrace differing forest management paradigms, controlling for personal economic dependence on the timber industry. Data come from a 1992 survey conducted in metropolitan Portland, Oregon, and in rural counties contiguous to the Gifford Pinchot National Forest of Washington.

PERSPECTIVES ON FOREST MANAGEMENT IN POST-INDUSTRIAL AMERICA

Many scholars argue that the public's concern about the management of federal lands is the product of economic and value change accompanying the transition to postindustrial society (Steger et al., 1989; Brunson and Kennedy, 1994). Postindustrial societies are characterized by the economic dominance of the tertiary sector over that of manufacturing and resource extraction; complex nationwide communication networks; a high degree of economic activity based on an educated workforce employing scientific knowledge and technology in their work; and historically unprecedented societal affluence (Bell, 1973; Inglehart, 1990).

It is argued that the advent of postindustrial society has altered individual value structures among some citizens-especially urban dwellers-such that "higher order" needs have supplanted more fundamental subsistence needs as the motivational sources of much societal behavior (Inglehart and Flanagan, 1987; Inglehart, 1990; Yankelovich, 1981). Value changes entailing greater attention to postmaterialist needs are thought to have brought about changes in many types of personal attitudes, including those related to natural resources and the environment (Pierce et al., 1992; Steger et al., 1989). Much empirical research has identified environmentalists as highly educated, wealthy, white collar *and urban* (see Jones and Dunlap, 1992; King 1989:22; Van Liere and Dunlap, 1980).

Concomitant with the development and growth of the urban tertiary sector has been economic and population decline in much of rural America. Urban employment grew 18 percent in the 1980s while rural employment grew only 8 percent. Unemployment and poverty rates were significantly higher, and wages significantly lower, in rural areas than in metropolitan areas (Gorham and Harrison, 1990; Shapiro and Greenstein, 1990). Not coincidentally, more than half of all rural counties lost population during the 1980s and early 1990s while metropolitan counties grew at a rapid rate (Beale and Fuguitt, 1990). Many timber-dependent counties of the Northwest were among those losing population despite net increases in the population of persons aged 65 or over (Hibbard and Elias, 1993).

Economic decline in rural areas can lead to an imperative to increase natural resource extraction among their residents, even as growth in the urban service industry creates a different imperative toward nonmaterial uses and protection of natural environments. Some empirical research supports the proposition that rural citizens are more supportive of natural resource extraction when compared to their urban counterparts (Tremblay and Dunlap, 1978). However, other researchers have found little rural-urban variation in attitudes toward environmental policy (e.g., Christianson, 1992), and rural communities sometimes mobilize *against* natural resource developments (Fortmann and Starrs, 1990). A recent study by McBeth and Foster (1994) found that rural residents in Idaho were more supportive of environmental causes than many observers might have expected. The authors argue that rural environmental concern is "widespread and cross-sectional," and suggest that "environmental groups will find significant sources of political support in rural communities, provided they craft their environmental message in a language consistent with rural attitudes and values" (p. 401). If McBeth and Foster's research is generalizable to other Western rural areas-which they suggest is the case-we should expect to find support for the protection of federal forests in both urban and rural locales.

CONFLICTING NATURAL RESOURCE PARADIGMS

Divergent perspectives on the proper management of natural resources have been evident since the late nineteenth century (Dunlap and Mertig, 1992). At the turn of the century, environmental activists tended to be labeled as "conservationists" or as "preservationists," based on positions taken concerning the management of natural resources. The early conservationist movement was founded mostly on anthropocentric assumptions, aiming to produce what Gifford Pinchot (1907) called the "greatest good for the greatest number [of people] for the longest time." The other, contrasting view of forestry drew from the ideas of John Muir and Aldo Leopold. This approach to forest management was more biocentric in orientation and favored the extension of ethical consideration to all parts of forests, including birds, mammals, plants, insects, and such elements as forest streams and soils.

Brown and Harris (1992), as discussed in Chapter 1, have identified two competing management paradigms-descended from the ideas of Pinchot and Leopold, respectively-as the Dominant Resource Management Paradigm (DRMP) and the New Resource Management Paradigm (NRMP) (see Table 1.1 in Chapter 1). The former paradigm advocates the management of federal forests to produce goods beneficial to humans. The latter paradigm has emerged and grown in popularity in postindustrial society. It has a biocentric view toward forest management that emphasizes maintaining intact all the elements of a forest ecosystem.

Brown and Harris (1992) found evidence of a shift within the USDA Forest Service toward acceptance of the NRMP, reflecting trends within society in general. Orientations toward the NRMP in the Forest Service are associated with the increasing tendency for the agency's line officers to be female, have graduate educations, hold nonforestry degrees, and come from urban backgrounds (Cramer, Kennedy, Krannich, and Quigley, 1993).

PERSONAL AND COMMUNITY RESOURCE DEPENDENCY

We would expect citizens who are dependent on the timber industry to support the DRMP with respect to management of federal forests. However, dependency can be defined in different ways. One can be personally dependent on the timber industry if one's family income is wholly or partially derived from the timber production sector. Or one may tend to support the DRMP if one believes it leads to policies most likely to sustain one's community, either economically or culturally, regardless of one's personal stake in the timber industry. This latter type of dependency is more likely than the former to create strong rural-urban differences in support for a resource management paradigm.

If one's economic livelihood is dependent on resource extraction, surely this would impact attitudes toward the management of public forests (see Chapter 1). Moreover, jobs such as logging have been associated with "occupational cultures," which are likely to reinforce certain attitudes toward forest management (Carroll and Lee, 1990) or forest landscapes (Greider and Garkovich, 1994). However, economic dependence on timber production goes beyond just rural areas. Many urban Westerners work in wood products industries-pulp mills, lumber yards, carpentry, and so on. We can expect this segment of the urban population to have differing orientations toward the environment than the majority of their urban counterparts dependent on the tertiary sector for their economic livelihood.

Persons whose livelihood is not dependent on timber production may nonetheless feel a sense of community dependence on natural resource extraction. Tichenor et al. (1971) argue that attitudes toward environmental issues are directly related to the consequences for the community. These consequences can be economic-if loggers or mill workers lose their jobs, the impact also is felt by store owners whose customers buy less, teachers whose tax base decreases, etc.and so on-or they can be related to changes in the social and cultural conditions brought on by changes in discretionary income, increased anomie, out-migration of younger adults, and other impacts of decline in the timber sector.

Given the cross-cutting nature of environmental concern, economic dependence, and sociocultural dependence on natural resource extraction, we would expect to find both consensus and dissension among rural *and* urban residents in their attitudes toward the management of public forest lands in the West. Figure 6.1 depicts likely patterns of support for resource management paradigms based on the influences of personal and community dependency. If support for the DRMP is primarily a function of personal dependence we should expect to find relatively little difference in attitudes between rural and urban publics. Conversely, if community dependence is a strong motivator we should expect to find greater differences between rural and urban publics and smaller differences between dependent and nondependent individuals, especially in rural areas.

METHODOLOGY AND MEASUREMENTS

Samples: In order to investigate rural and urban attitudes toward federal forest management, opinion surveys were sent to random samples of the public in the greater Portland, Oregon area; the greater Vancouver, Washington area, and rural counties contiguous to the Gifford Pinchot National Forest in southwestern Washington State. All surveys were conducted during September and October 1992. Random samples of names, addresses, and telephone numbers were provided

Figure 6.1
Rural and Urban Support for Natural Resource Paradigms

		Personal Dependence on Timber Industry	
		DEPENDENT	**NONDEPENDENT**
	RURAL	Strongest support for DRMP.	Less supportive of DRMP; moderate support for NRMP.
Community Residence			
	URBAN	Moderate support for DRMP.	Strongest support for NRMP.

by a national survey research company that has comprehensive lists of public telephone directories.[1] Survey design and implementation followed Dillman's (1978) *Total Design Method* and potential respondents were offered a copy of the aggregate results upon completion of the project to encourage responses. All three samples were pooled for the following analyses. Sampling locations and response rates are:

Portland Area Survey: A random sample of the public (both rural and urban) in Washington, Multonomah, Clackamas, and Hood River counties in Oregon. Surveys were sent to 937 prospective respondents and 622 surveys were returned for a 66 percent response rate.

Vancouver Area Survey: A random sample of the public (both rural and urban) in Clark, Cowlitz, Skamania, and Klickitat counties in Washington. Surveys were sent to 943 persons and 609 were returned for a 64 percent response rate.

Rural Washington Survey: A random subsample of residents living contiguous to and within the Gifford Pinchot National Forest. Rural households in Clark, Cowlitz, Skamania, and Klickitat counties were sent 424 surveys and 304 were returned for a 71 percent response rate. This subsample was included to assure a significant number of rural respondents for analysis.

Measures: Respondent dependence on the timber industry was assessed by asking the following question: "Do you or any of your immediate family depend upon the timber industry for your economic livelihood?" Rural and urban location was determined by asking each respondent to describe their place of residency.[2]

A breakdown of several socioeconomic, issue salience and value characteristics for each rural and urban subgroup can be found in Table 6.1. The socioeconomic variables examined include the age of each respondent (only respondents 18 years and older are included in the survey results), a dummy variable for gender (1 = female, 0 = male), formal educational attainment,[3] and an indicator of household income.[4] The issue salience variables include a dummy variable indicating if the respondent visits public forests such as the Gifford Pinchot National Forest,[5] and a measure of self-assessed informedness concerning federal forest policy issues.[6] The value orientation variables include an indicator of self-assessed political ideology[7] (conservative versus liberal) and a dummy variable indicating support for environmental organizations.[8]

Orientation toward the DRMP and NRMP were measured through eight different statements with which respondents were asked to indicate their level of disagreement or agreement (see Table 6.2). The five response categories provided for the statements ranged from 1 = strongly disagree to 5 = strongly agree. The first four items reflect the DRMP while the second set of items reflect the NMRP. These items were drawn from a review of environmental attitude research and the literature of environmental ethics.[9]

FINDINGS

Table 6.1 reports the distribution of responses for the various socioeconomic, value, and issue salience characteristics for each of the subgroups. To simplify the discussion of results, the following acronyms will be used for the subgroups:

RD = Rural Dependent   **UD = Urban Dependent**
RND = Rural Nondependent   **UND = Urban Nondependent**

The youngest subgroup is the UND, followed by UD, RND, and lastly RD. This is in line with the previous discussion on population loss in rural areas as younger cohorts flee to the city for economic or other reasons. With the exception of RD, the other three groups are closely balanced between males and females. The RD sample is disproportionately male. This may accurately reflect the population, given the traditionally male dominance of natural resource extraction jobs in rural areas, or it may reflect a rural cultural presumption that males are better qualified to express attitudes toward natural resources. As would be expected, formal educational attainment and household income is highest among urban respondents with the UND subgroup having the highest incomes and educational levels.

In regard to the two issue salience indicators included in the study, we find that rural respondents are slightly more likely to visit federal forests than their urban counterparts. However, at least 60 percent of urban respondents reported visiting federal forests for leisure and recreation. Both rural and urban respondents who are timber dependent consider themselves more informed on federal forest issues than their nondependent counterparts.

The distribution of responses among the four subgroups for the subjective political orientation question indicates that the most liberal subgroup is UND and the most conservative is RD. Only 2 percent of the RD subgroup identified

Table 6.1
Socioeconomic, Value, and Salience Characteristics of Rural and Urban Publics

	RURAL		URBAN	
	Dependent	Nondependent	Dependent	Nondependent
	mean (s.d.)	mean (s.d.)	mean (s.d.)	mean (s.d.)
Socioeconomic				
Age[a]	52.05 (15.3)	49.84 (15.2)	48.61 (17.0)	46.77 (16.4)
Gender[b]	.40	.51	.50	.49
Education[a]	4.38 (1.15)	4.94 (1.25)	4.98 (1.26)	5.52 (1.54)
Income[a]	4.53 (2.16)	5.48 (2.09)	5.68 (2.11)	5.67 (2.12)
Salience:				
Visitor[b]	.67	.64	.62	.60
Informed[a]	3.36 (1.07)	2.85 (0.95)	3.08 (0.96)	2.87 (0.94)
Values:				
Ideology[a]	4.30 (1.46)	4.20 (1.31)	4.17 (1.18)	3.92 (1.32)
Green[b]	.02	.08	.11	.15
n =	175	295	249	618

a. F-test significant at .01.
b. Chi-square significant at .01.

themselves as passive or active members of environmental groups while 15 percent of the UND subgroup indicated they were members.

Table 6.2 shows responses to the eight attitude items. Mean responses greater than 3.0 indicate overall agreement with a statement, while means below 3.0 indicate disagreement within each subgroup. After the first four items scores were reverse-coded so that higher numbers reflected support for the NRMP and lower numbers reflect support for the DRMP, the responses were summed to form an additive index ranging from 8 (strong support for the DRMP) to 40 (strong support for the NRMP). Reliability coefficients (Cronbach's Alpha) for the index are reported at the bottom of the table and range from .852 to .878, suggesting that respondents were very consistent in their response patterns for the additive index.

When examining the mean scores for the individual items and the additive index, we find that the groups most supportive of a New Resource Management Paradigm are the rural and urban nondependent subgroups, while rural and urban dependent respondents are significantly less supportive. This supports the proposition that support for the NRMP crosscuts urban and rural populations when controlling for dependency on the timber industry. The rural dependent subgroup, however, is the least supportive of the NRMP and therefore the most supportive of the DRMP.

As the bivariate results in Table 6.2 indicate, there is a statistically significant difference between the four subgroups in their support for the NRMP. However, other factors such as the socioeconomic characteristics, issue salience, and value indicators presented in Table 6.1 may also explain the variation in support for the additive paradigm index. Therefore, ordinary least squares estimates for the index are presented in Table 6.3 to examine the independent impact of the four subgroups on support for the NRMP. A series of dummy variables were created to assess subgroup membership (RD: 1 = RD, 0 = else; RND: 1 = RND, 0 = else; UD: 1 = UD, 0 = else; UND: 1 = UND, 0 = else). The multivariate statistical procedures employed require that for prediction equations entailing multiple dummy variables for particular measures, one of the dummy variables must be omitted for the equation to be estimated (Kleinbaum and Kupper, 1978). Consequently, in the forthcoming multivariate analyses the dummy omitted will be RD (Rural Dependent).

The F-test results indicate that the OLS model presented in Table 6.3 is statistically significant. The adjusted R^2 for the model is a modest .25. However, when we control for independent effects of the socioeconomic, issue salience, and value variables, all three dummy variables assessing rural-urban residence and timber dependency have a statistically significant impact. These results suggest that there are indeed statistically significant differences in these groups' support of the NRMP index. However, this support transcends a rural-urban dichotomy when controlling for dependence on the timber industry.

When examining the standardized coefficients in the model, however, we find that other variables are more important for explaining variation in NRMP support than membership in the rural and urban subgroups. Age, education, and the two value indicators (ideology and green) are strongly related to index scores. These results indicate that other factors may help to drive dissension and consensus concerning the management of federal forests in the Pacific Northwest.

Table 6.2
Rural and Urban Orientations Toward Management of Federal Forest Lands

	RURAL		URBAN		
	Depend.	Nondep.	Depend.	Nondep.	
	mean	mean	mean	mean	
	(s.d.)	(s.d.)	(s.d.)	(s.d.)	_F-test_
a. The economic vitality of local communities should be given the highest priority when making federal forest decisions.	3.85 (1.28)	3.33 (1.34)	3.49 (1.33)	3.03 (1.31)	21.83***
b. Some existing wilderness areas should be opened to logging.	3.33 (1.56)	2.43 (1.33)	2.86 (1.41)	2.38 (1.31)	27.23***
c. Endangered species laws should be set aside to preserve timber jobs.	3.69 (1.34)	2.77 (1.36)	3.26 (1.18)	2.60 (1.21)	36.08***
d. Federal forest management should emphasize timber and lumber jobs.	3.60 (1.34)	2.91 (1.36)	3.29 (1.18)	2.76 (1.21)	26.80***
e. Clear-cutting should be banned on federal forest land.	2.70 (1.46)	3.50 (1.56)	3.14 (1.53)	3.84 (1.31)	37.06***
f. More wilderness areas should be established on federal forest lands.	2.22 (1.29)	3.39 (1.45)	2.95 (1.31)	3.64 (1.20)	64.25***
g. Greater efforts should be made to protect the remaining "Old Growth" forests.	2.69 (1.49)	3.70 (1.36)	3.24 (1.48)	3.94 (1.27)	48.27***
h. Greater efforts should be given to wildlife on federal forest lands.	2.85 (1.13)	3.84 (1.11)	3.57 (1.09)	3.75 (1.08)	37.05***
_n=_	175	295	249	618	
Additive index mean:	19.86	27.09	24.57	28.42	65.31***
Additive index s.d.:	(7.65)	(8.14)	(7.54)	(7.08)	
Cronbach's Alpha:	.852	.878	.855	.858	

Note: The scale used for the individual items was 1 = strongly disagree to 5 = strongly agree. For the additive index, items **a** through **d** were recoded so that higher numbers reflect the New Resource Management Paradigm and lower numbers reflect the Dominant Resource Management Paradigm; *** Significant at $p < .001$.

Table 6.3
Ordinary Least Squares Estimates for the New Resource Paradigm

	b	B
AGE	-.07***	-.14
GENDER	.71*	.05
EDUCATION	.79***	.14
INCOME	-.04	-.01
VISITOR	.11	.02
KNOWLEDGE	.31*	.05
IDEOLOGY	-.96***	-.18
GREEN	6.11***	.30
RURAL-NON	.88*	.06
URBAN-DEP	1.86***	.10
URBAN-NON	1.08***	.11

$$R^2 = .26$$
$$\text{Adjusted } R^2 = .25$$
$$F = 60.646***$$

* Significant at p < .05; ** Significant at p < .01; *** Significant at p < .001

DISCUSSION AND CONCLUSIONS

The media have often depicted of the Northwest forestry debate as a simple rural-urban value conflict summed up in the catch-phrase "jobs versus owls." Such a polarized view may be nurtured and exploited by political operatives hoping to reinforce loyalty for their cause by painting the issue in black-and-white terms. Sociological analysis would suggest that the popular view is too simplistic. Rural resource-dependent communities are changing, and rigid support for resource extraction, if it ever existed, is no longer the norm. Increasingly, the environmentalist voice is heard in rural communities (Fortmann and Kusel, 1990), and not simply because urban expatriates are moving to such places. Studies are finding that new and long-standing residents of rural communities may hold similar views about issues such as clear-cutting (Blahna, 1990) or protection of air and water quality (McBeth and Foster, 1994).

In this study we predicted that support for a resource management paradigm would not simply be a matter of urban or rural residence, but would be associated with measures of dependency. Moreover, dependency on resource extraction could be personal, as when a family's income derives from the timber industry, or it could derive from dependence on the continuation of a community economy, culture, and social structure that is intertwined with the timber industry.

We found evidence that personal dependency influences attitudes toward the NRMP. Persons whose livelihood depends on the timber industry were less supportive of the NRMP independent of urban or rural residence. Urban dependent residents were, in fact, less likely than rural nondependent residents to support the new paradigm. This suggests that personal dependency is more influential on support for a resource management paradigm than rural or urban residency.

Evidence for the influence of community dependency is less strong. Rural dependent respondents expressed attitudes that were clearly in disagreement with the NRMP while urban dependent respondents expressed attitudes that were essentially neutral. This may be because there is greater opportunity in urban areas for adjustment to shifting economic conditions. Or it may reflect, as Carroll and Lee (1990) suggest, the tendency for rural cultures in the Northwest to be almost inextricably connected with natural resource extraction. Nonetheless, rural nondependent respondents were only slightly less likely than their urban nondependent counterparts to support the NRMP, suggesting that community dependency is not a strong influence on that subgroup's attitudes toward a resource management paradigm.

Finally, we found that residence and personal dependency are not sufficient to explain orientations toward a resource management paradigm. Age, education, environmental group affiliation, and political ideology all were more influential than subgroup membership on support for the NRMP. Younger cohorts are more supportive of the NRMP than their older, less educated neighbors. Just as the Forest Service has shifted in orientation toward the NRMP (Brown and Harris, 1992; Cramer et al., 1993), we might expect a similar trend in rural Pacific Northwest communities as these younger cohorts move into leadership roles.

NOTES

1. Previous research (Leuthold and Scheele, 1971) has suggested that samples drawn from municipal telephone directories will tend to underrepresent some racial minorities (e.g., African Americans); those individuals with highly mobile occupations; and lower income, less educated people.

2. Rural and urban residency was determined from the pooled samples by asking each respondent to describe her or his place of residence. Those indicating they live in a rural area or small city (less than 2,000 population) in a rural location were classified as "rural." All other respondents were included in the urban category.

3. The question used was, "What is your highest level of education?" The following response categories were provided: (1) never attended school, (2) some grade school, (3) completed grade school, (4) some high school, (5) completed high school, (6) some college, (7) completed college, (8) some graduate work, and (9) an advanced degree.

4. The question used was, "Would you mind indicating your approximate annual family income before taxes?" The following response categories were provided: (1) less than $7,000, (2) $7,000 to $9,999, (3) $10,000 to $14,999, (4) $15,000 to $19,999, (5) $20,000 to $24,999, (6) $25,000 to $29,999, (7) $30,000 to $49,999, and (8) $50,000 and above.

5. Respondents were asked if they ever visit federal forests such as those managed by the U.S. Forest Service. Those answering "yes" are given a 1 and those answering "no" are coded as 0.

6. Respondents were asked "How well informed would you say you are concerning federal forest land issues?" The response scale ranged from 1 = not informed to 5 = very well informed.

7. The question and scale used to ascertain subjective political ideology was, "On domestic policy issues, would you consider yourself to be?" The response scale ranged from 1 = very liberal to 7 = very conservative.

8. Those respondents indicating that they *belong* to an environmental group (whether active or not) were given a 1 and those without a membership or in opposition were coded 0.

9. Many of the forest policy statements were drawn from a 1990 University of California, Davis, questionnaire on national forest policy practices (Sabatier et al., 1990), and suitably reworded for our study. The remainder were constructed from other discussions of forest policy (see DeBonis, 1989).

Chapter 7

County Government and the Public Lands: A Review of the County Supremacy Movement in Four Western States

Stephanie L. Witt and Leslie R. Alm

This chapter examines the role of county governments in conflicts over the public lands and environmental policy in the western United States. The importance of county government in examining these issues is crucial, as counties are at the forefront of a growing local versus federal conflict known as the County Supremacy Movement. This movement and its employment of "wise-use" or county supremacy ordinances[1] marks a recent development in natural resource and environmental policy in the West. This study compares urban counties, rural counties, and those counties that have passed county supremacy ordinances, using aggregate data gathered from surveys and interviews.

COUNTY GOVERNMENT

Several recent studies have documented an increase in interest in county government (DeSantis and Renner, 1994; Cigler, 1994; Berman, 1993). One study has even gone so far as to suggest that counties, "may become THE local governments of the future" (Menzel, Marando, Parks, Waugh, Cigler, Svara, Reeves, Benton, Thomas, Streib, and Schneider, 1992, emphasis in original). Counties are generally held to be increasing in importance because of additional responsibilities given to them within the intergovernmental system (Waugh and Streib, 1993). Increased responsibility for service delivery is particularly relevant for metropolitan counties, which must provide urban-level services.

Rural counties, however, face a different set of difficulties. Their interests are not at all unitary with urban counties. Cigler (1994) reports that many state associations of counties have separate caucuses for urban and rural counties, and some associations have split away from their state Association of County Officials organizations. She notes that these conflicts are often over state funding issues.

Other key differences between urban and rural counties include the decline in rural economies and the relatively greater dependence of county governments, particularly in the rural West, on federal monies tied to natural resource management. Rural areas also have lower per capita incomes than urban areas in the West (Alm and Witt, 1995). Cigler's compiled list of structural economic changes that have hurt rural communities includes a shift from resource and manufacturing industries to service industries, and a change in the role of natural resources from supporting extractive industries to recreational uses. These changes have resulted in higher levels of poverty among rural residents and, in many counties, a loss of population (Cigler, 1993).

Rural counties in the West are further distinguished from their counterparts by a reliance on federal compensation to counties for tax-exempt federal lands. The two major sources of this type of federal money for state and local governments are natural resource payments and payments-in-lieu-of-taxes (PILTs) (Idaho Association of Counties 1993).[2] Advocates of this system say these payments are necessary to offset the costs of the tax-exempt status and financial burdens of federal land ownership on the county (Fairfax and Cawley, 1991).

Federal land ownership is vast in the West. Nearly 64 percent of Idaho's land, for example, is held by the federal government (Idaho Association of Counties, 1993). For many counties, revenues derived from these holdings are a key part of their revenue base. The statement of the Idaho Association of Counties' Public Lands Committee notes: "In counties with a high percentage of public land, federal and state decisions dictate social and economic conditions" (Idaho Association of Counties, 1993: vii).

Naturally, changes in federal land management practices that hurt the local economy and/or decrease the receipts from public lands would especially impact rural Western counties. This situation places the Western county in a direct, and often confrontational relationship with the federal government and its land agencies. While several studies have addressed the relationship between county and state governments (see Cigler, 1994; Waugh and Streib, 1993; Waugh, 1988), the relationship between counties and the federal government has largely been ignored. This study begins to fill that gap by focusing on Western rural counties at the forefront of a county-government-based movement to assert county supremacy over federal agency decisions in regard to land use decisions.

THE "WISE-USE" ORDINANCES AND THE COUNTY SUPREMACY MOVEMENT

Counties are at the center of recent environmental conflicts in many states, including the four Western states that are the focus of this chapter: Colorado, Idaho,

Oregon, and Washington. These counties have passed land use ordinances that assert county joint sovereignty over federal lands within their borders. Because of their attempt to make federal land use decisions subject to county approval, this movement is sometimes called the "county supremacy" movement and is considered to be part of the "wise-use" movement. Catron County, New Mexico was the first to institute a wise-use ordinance (Clifford 1993). Estimates of the number of counties adopting or debating adoption of the Catron county model vary, but range between 150 and 500 counties nationwide (National Federal Lands Conference [NFLC] 1995; Clifford, 1993; Reed, 1993-94; Wilderness Society, 1992). This chapter hopes to add clarity to this debate by examining the extent of this movement in four Western states that are part of our study. Although likened to the Sagebrush Rebellion of the early 1980s (Arnold, 1994; Reed, 1993,94), this county-based movement is not limited to the West. According to the NFLC, a pro-wise-use ordinance group, counties in New York, Wisconsin, and Virginia have also investigated county supremacy ordinances (NFLC 1995).

The term wise-use is derived from Gifford Pinchot's definition of conservation as the wise-use of resources (Cawley, 1993:166). Perceiving that environmentalists seek preservation of public lands that will destroy local economies dependent on resource extraction and recreational activities, the wise-use movement advocates multiple uses of public lands (Erm, 1993, 94). The movement consists of a variety of interest groups that seek to preserve multiple uses: farmers, miners, timber industries, property-rights groups, off-road vehicle enthusiasts, and fishermen (Erm, 1993, 94; Cawley, 1993). The large percentage of federal land in Western states contributes to the popularity of the wise-use movement in the West. As Reed notes, "over one-half of the land ownership in the 12 Western states remains with the Federal government compared with only 4 percent in the other 37 continental states" (1993, 94: 526). Or, put differently, "about 93 percent of the total federal estate" is located in twelve Western states (Cawley, 1993: 2).

The county supremacy ordinances take several forms. Many are modeled after the original Catron County, New Mexico, Interim Land Use Plan and are written in the form of an ordinance. Others include much of the same language, especially the preamble paragraphs asserting the county's legitimate claims to sovereignty, yet are written as resolutions. Others include language regarding the equal footing doctrine, an argument that asserts that federal ownership and control of public lands in Western counties is illegitimate because public lands did not exist at the founding of the country with the 13 original states and, since then, all other states have entered with "equal footing" (Arnold, 1994; Erm, 1993-94). Other counties have begun designating jeep trails as county roads to keep them open for development and to prevent further designation of wilderness areas (Arrondale, 1994; Meacham, 1994). Themes common to all of the county supremacy strategies are a general distrust of federal land management practices and a desire to protect local economic uses of the natural resources on public lands. An important feature of the county supremacy movement is the involvement of elected county officials, with the focus on the county as a unit of government that protects local interests.

The county supremacy ordinances modeled after the Catron County ordinances claim that federal land "must be managed to maintain customary local uses" (Arrondale, 1994: 2; Hungerford, 1995). Key to this strategy is a claim developed by Wyoming attorney Karen Budd Falen (who once worked with Interior Secretary Watt), that federal environmental laws such as the National Environmental Protection Act "require federal agencies to consult local governments and preserve local communities' 'custom and culture' when they set policy on public lands" (Arrondale, 1994: 2). Reed points out that the custom and culture that wise-use groups assume is predominant are almost entirely those of the extraction and resource-dependent industries such as logging, mining, ranching, and farming (1993, 94: 549). Several ordinances contain lengthy dispositions on the obligations that federal laws place on land management agencies (see for example the *Owyhee County Interim Comprehensive Land Use and Management Plan for the Federally and State Managed Lands in Owyhee County* [Owyeehee County, Idaho, 1993]). County Supremacy ordinances also require consultation with county governments before federal land use changes are made by referencing federal statutes such as the Federal Land Policy and Management Act of 1976 (FLPMA) and the Forest and Rangeland Renewable Resources Planning Act of 1974 (RPA) (see Hungerford, 1995 for a lengthier treatment of these requirements).

Proponents of the wise-use ordinances see them as a way to protect property rights; that is, the right to make a living using the public lands (Clifford, 1993). Federal land use decisions that circumscribe the ability of local residents to continue to make a living off of the land, therefore, are perceived by wise-use advocates to be an unconstitutional "taking" (Erm 1993, 94). Assertions regarding the importance of the Fifth Amendment to the U.S. Constitution and the application of the Fifth Amendment to counties are common in the supremacy ordinances (Hungerford, 1995). Many counties contemplating county supremacy ordinances consider their adoption necessary to preserve "a way of life" (Arnold 1994). Counties bear the brunt of federal public land management decisions that curtail uses critical to the local economy. Not only does the local economy suffer, but direct receipts to the county of federal reimbursements for timber, mining, and grazing lands may be reduced. This connection is highlighted in a quote from a National Association of Counties (NACo) Public Lands Steering Committee member: "More and more, the long-term impacts resulting from environmental fanaticism in our nation are having a devastating effect on the economy, our schools and roads" (Arnold 1994).

Many rural counties in the West have been experiencing a net loss in jobs and population as the importance of resource-based industries declines (Cigler 1993). Further federal attempts to restrict access and activity on public lands exacerbates this trend. A button distributed by two wise-use counties at the recent meeting of the Idaho Association of Counties highlights these realities. It reads: "Idaho's Endangered Species: Working People." NACo concern over the economic effects of federal endangered species protection is evidenced by that association's designation of some affected areas as "endangered communities." An endangered community is defined by NACo as "a community directly dependent on natural resource utilization for survival and whose economy is directly affected by public land multiple use policies" (Kolar, 1993).

Because of their importance to rural residents and their unique relationship with the federal government in regard to public lands, counties have become a focal point of the wise-use movement. In spite of their growing popularity among county commissions, however, the ordinances and strategies of the county supremacy movement have found little success in the courts or among state Attorneys General (*Boundary Backpackers v. Boundary County,* 1994; Hungerford, 1995; Reed, 1993–94; Clifford, 1993).[3] The Washington State Attorney General's opinion on a wise-use ordinance passed in Walla Walla County simply stated:

1. A county lacks authority to require any agency of the United States to follow county policies or procedures in land use decisions or environmental regulation, except where Congress has specifically directed federal agencies to conform to local law

2. A county lacks authority to require any agency of the state of Washington to follow county policies or procedures in land use or environmental regulation, except where state law, expressly or by necessary implication, Requires state agencies to conform to county procedural or substantive requirements as to a particular agency decision (Gregoire, 1994)

Similar opinions have been issued in New Mexico and Idaho, and informal opinions have been written in Nevada and Montana (Mazurek, 1993). This fact seems to have little effect on the interest displayed by disgruntled county officials. One group of county commissioners interviewed for this study acknowledged that they knew before passage that their Catron-style land use ordinance would probably be found unconstitutional, but felt it was an important enough symbolic action that they passed it anyway.

QUESTIONS FOR ANALYSIS

Previous research has found that there are differences in attitudes about environmental issues between urban and rural residents. In analyzing environmental policy in the West, many researchers have pointed to the "New West," with its emphasis on preservation, versus the "Old West," characterized by multiple use of resources (Hays, 1991; Etlinger, 1994). This division among westerners is often characterized as an urban versus rural phenomena (Thomas, 1991; Buttel, 1992; Alm and Witt, 1995). This dovetails with previous research that has found that urban residents are more likely to hold environmentalist beliefs (Jones and Dunlap, 1992; Lowe and Pinhey, 1982; Tremblay and Dunlap 1978). Urban and rural counties also spend differing amounts on environmental projects (Alm and Witt, 1995). Furthermore, as described in the preceding sections, urban and rural counties have differing agendas and sets of economic and intergovernmental challenges. Western rural counties' unique environmental relationship with the federal government is conflictual, often resulting in ordinances that assert county supremacy over federal land decisions. This results in increased acrimony between county and state governments.

This study uses aggregate data as well as survey and interview data gathered from counties in Colorado, Idaho, Oregon and Washington to address several questions. First, are there substantial differences between urban and rural counties? Second, is the level of conflict over environmental policy higher in rural counties dependent on natural resources? Third, are the relationships between rural county officials and the state and federal government different from those of urban county officials? Finally, the subset of counties that have passed county supremacy ordinances is examined in comparison to the other counties. It is to be expected that County Supremacy counties include a larger percentage of public lands, are more dependent on resource extraction industries, and have higher levels of conflict with the federal government as well as their own state.

DATA AND METHODS

The data utilized in this study are derived from several sources. Each of these sources is described briefly below:

Survey: A survey instrument was sent to county commissioners in Idaho, Oregon, Washington, and Colorado. The survey of Idaho Commissioners was conducted in the fall of 1994. The survey of Washington, Oregon, and Colorado county commissioners was conducted in the summer of 1995.[4] A total of 268 county commissioners out of 595 responded to the survey for a return rate of 45 percent. Commissioners from 149 of the 182 counties in the four states responded (82%).[5] The survey asked county commissioners to assess the level of conflict in their county regarding environmental issues, to assess their working relationship with state and federal governments on environmental issues, and to indicate whether their county had considered or passed a county supremacy ordinance.

Aggregate Data: Information on county finances, employment figures, and demographic data were obtained from U.S. census reports and from individual state profiles of their counties. This research project also utilizes the Idaho Department of Commerce's definition of *rural* as those counties that do not have a city of twenty thousand or greater population (Idaho Department of Commerce, 1994). This contrasts with the U.S. Census definitions of *urban* and *rural*, which distinguish urban counties as those having at least 100,000 people with at least one central city of 50,000 population. While the Idaho definition's level of population is significantly lower than the U.S. census definition, we feel it more accurately reflects the population dispersions in the western United States (California excluded). This urban and rural breakdown results in 189 counties being classified as rural and 79 as urban in the four states included in our study.

ANALYSIS

Table 7.1 utilizes aggregate data to assess the extent of differences between rural and urban counties in the four-state sample. As expected, based on Cigler's (1993) review of the rural economic decline, the rural counties have lower percapita personal incomes ($16,058 versus $17,151), more families below the poverty line (11.47% versus 8.54%), and lower percent growth in housing (19.23% versus 20.83%). Rural counties have much higher levels of federal land ownership within their boundaries (41.01% versus 27.90%), and have a greater percentage of their budgets derived from federal natural resource reimbursements (10.95% versus 3.41%). The reliance of those rural counties on extractive industries is demonstrated by the percentage of employment in extraction (14.92% for rural versus 4.87% for urban). The rural-urban differences in percent of federal land, percentage employment in extraction, percentage of county budget from federal natural resource payments, percentage of families below the poverty line, and percentage urban are all statistically significant.

Table 7.1
Aggregate Differences Between Rural and Urban Counties in Idaho

	Rural	**Urban**	**t-test**
Percent of federal land	41.01	27.90	3.15[b]
Percent employment in extraction	14.92	4.87	4.91[a]
Percent budget from federal land funds	10.95	3.41	3.26[a]
Percent of families below poverty line	11.47	8.54	5.05[a]
Percent housing growth	19.23	20.83	-1.01
Percent urban	25.95	76.14	-16.45[a]
Per capita personal income	16,058	17,151	-1.74
Spending on the environment in $1,000s	395.60	6,662.28	-2.34[b]
	n = 136	n = 38	

Note: These data were developed by the authors from U.S. Census data and Idaho Department of Commerce, *County Profiles of Idaho* (Boise: Economic Development Division, Idaho Department of Commerce 1994).
a. significant at p < .01
b. significant at p < .05

The survey of county commissioners (see Table 7.2) is utilized to assess perceptions about their county's relationship with the federal government.[6] While 25.7 percent of the rural commissioners felt that the relationship was "poor," only 18.9 percent of the urban commissioners felt that way. Further, 40.5 percent of the urban commissioners indicated that their relationship with the federal government was "very good" or "outstanding," while only 30.8 percent of the rural commissioners did. In general, it seems that rural commissioners report more trouble in their relationship with the federal government than their urban counterparts.

Table 7.2
County Commissioner Attitudes About Relationship with the Federal Government

	Rural Commissioners	Urban Commissioners
Rating of Relationship		
Poor	25.7% (45)	18.9% (14)
Good	43.4% (76)	40.5% (30)
Very Good, Outstanding	30.8% (54)	40.5% (30)
	n = 175	n = 74

Note: These data are derived from the authors' 1994, 1995 surveys of county commissioners in Colorado, Idaho, Oregon, and Washington.

Table 7.3 displays responses of county commissioners concerning their county's relationship with the state agency responsible for environmental quality.[7] In this case, about equal percentages of rural and urban county commissioners describe the relationship with the state environmental agency as "poor" (26% versus 25.6%). However, while 34.6% of urban county commissioners described their relationship with the state environmental agency as "very good" or "outstanding" only 23.7% of rural county commissioners did.

Table 7.3
County Commissioner Attitudes About Relationship with State Environmental Quality Agency

	Rural Commissioners	Urban Commissioners
Rating of Relationship		
Poor	26.0% (47)	25.6% (20)
Good	50.3% (91)	39.7% (31)
Very Good, Outstanding	23.7% (43)	34.6% (27)
	n = 181	n = 78

Note: These data are derived from the authors' 1994, 95 surveys of county commissioners in Colorado, Idaho, Oregon, and Washington.

Commissioners' assessment of the level of conflict over environmental policy in their county is displayed in Table 7.4.[8] As expected, the level of policy conflict is higher in rural than in urban counties. For example, 25.9 percent of rural county commissioners said that the level of conflict was "high," while only 20.3 percent of the urban commissioners perceived the level of conflict to be high. While 30.8 percent of rural county commissioners think that there is no conflict or that the level of conflict is "low," 48.1 percent of urban county commissioners perceive that their county's level of conflict over environmental issues is low or nonexistent.

Given the growing importance of the county supremacy movement, the counties within the four states that have passed county supremacy ordinances were compared to the other counties.[9] Table 7.5 presents a breakdown of the counties who have passed county supremacy legislation by state. The results of our four-state study indicate that 26, or 17.3 percent of the 150 counties from which we have data, have passed some type of county supremacy ordinance or resolution (see Table 7.5). There are a total of 182 counties in Oregon, Washington, Colorado, and Idaho. Idaho, Oregon, and Washington counties have passed county supremacy legislation at similar rates of 21.6, 21.9, and 25 percent respectively. Only 4.4 percent of responding Colorado counties, on the other hand, reported passing county supremacy legislation. Activity involving county supremacy ordinances and resolutions is actually much higher when information about testimony consideration

Table 7.4
County Commissioner Attitudes Regarding the Level of Environmental Conflict

	Rural Commissioners	Urban Commissioners
Level of Conflict		
No Conflict	6.5% (12)	7.6% (6)
Low	2.3% (45)	4.5% (32)
Average	42.2% (78)	31.6% (25)
High	25.9% (48)	20.3% (16)
	n = 185	n = 79

Note: These data are derived from the authors' 1994, 95 surveys of county commissioners in Colorado, Idaho, Oregon, and Washington.

is included. Fifty-five percent of the responding counties in Oregon, Washington, and Colorado indicated that they had heard testimony or considered passing county supremacy legislation.[10]

Several of the characteristics noted as important to the rise of the county supremacy movement were included in a comparative analysis of the county supremacy and other counties in Table 7.6. Specifically, difference of means tests on the percentage of federal land in the county, the percentage of the county's budget derived from federal natural resource paybacks, the percentage of jobs in extractive industries, and the county's spending on the environment for county supremacy and noncounty supremacy counties were performed.

As expected, the percentage of federal land was higher in the county supremacy counties (49.15 percent versus 36.02 percent; p < .01). The percentage of the county budget derived from federal natural resource payments was also much higher in the county supremacy counties (21.28 percent versus 8.18 percent; p<.01). The percentage of jobs in extractive industries (e.g., timber) was slightly higher in the

Table 7.5
County Supremacy Counties by State

State	Passed Supremacy Legislation	Did Not Pass Supremacy Legislation
Colorado	4.4% (2)	95.6% (43)
Idaho	21.6% (8)	78.4% (29)
Oregon	21.9% (7)	78.1% (25)
Washington	25.0% (9)	75.0% (27)

Note: Information from Colorado, Oregon, and Washington are derived from the author's survey of county commissioners. The listing of Idaho supremacy counties is from the Idaho Attorney General's Office.

county supremacy counties (14.06 percent) than in the other counties (11.53 percent), but this difference was not statistically significant. Average environmental spending was lower in the county supremacy counties ($550,110) than in the other counties ($2,315,520). These findings point to key structural differences among rural counties that may make them fertile ground for the county supremacy movement organizers.

Attitudes among county commissioners from county supremacy and the other counties were compared to determine whether relationships with the federal and state governments were different for these two groups. Table 7.7 demonstrates that county supremacy counties have a higher level of conflict over environmental issues than other counties. To illustrate, 44.4 percent of the county supremacy county commissioners said their county's level of conflict was "high," while only 20.1 percent of the other county commissioners made that conclusion. On the other hand, 24.5 percent of the county supremacy county commissioners indicated that they had "low" or "no" levels of conflict over environmental policy in their county, compared to 38.3 percent of the other county commissioners. The level of conflict in the wise-use counties was highlighted during one interview with a long-time county resident. He confided that his son had been "beat up" at school after he (Dad) had casually remarked at a neighborhood barbeque that "We don't need another hydroelectric dam in the Selkirks." The level of conflict, unfortunately,

Table 7.6
Aggregate Differences Between County Supremacy Versus Other Counties in Colorado, Idaho, Oregon, and Washington

	Supremacy Counties	Other Counties	*t*-test
Percent federal land in county	49.15	36.02	2.32*
Percent of county budget from federal natural resource and PILT payments	21.28	8.18	2.62*
Percent of jobs in extraction	14.06	11.53	1.04
Environmental spending in $1,000s	550.11	2,315.52	-.89
	n = 26	n = 148	

Note: These data were compiled by the authors using U.S. Census data and Idaho Department of Commerce, *County Profiles of Idaho* (Boise: Economic Development Division, Idaho Department of Commerce 1994).
* significant at p < .01

has recently extended beyond the school yard. U.S. Forest Service Offices in Nevada have been bombed, and the Idaho State Office of the Bureau of Land Management (BLM) had recently issued an Instruction Memo regarding "County Supremacy Movement Safety Guidance" (Kanamime, 1995; U.S. Department of Interior, 1995). Among other things, the memo instructs BLM employees to travel in pairs whenever possible and to not leave the BLM compound without radio communication.

Commissioners from county supremacy counties have a slightly poorer relationship with the federal government than commissioners from the other counties, as shown in Table 7.8. While 30.2 percent of the county supremacy county commissioners described their working relationship with the federal government as "poor," only 22.3 percent of the other county commissioners had this view. Similar percentages of commissioners from county supremacy and the other counties report that their relationship with the federal government is "outstanding" or "very good."

Table 7.7
County Commissioner Attitudes Regarding Level of Environmental Conflict

Level of Conflict	Supremacy Commissioners	Other Commissioners
No conflict	6.7% (3)	6.8% (15)
Low conflict	17.8% (8)	31.5% (69)
Average conflict	31.1% (14)	40.6% (89)
High conflict	44.4% (20)	20.1% (44)
	n = 45	n = 219

Note: These data are derived from the authors' 1994–95 surveys of county commissioners in Colorado, Idaho, Oregon, and Washington.

Table 7.8
County Commissioner Attitudes Regarding Relationship with the Federal Government

Rating of Relationship	Supremacy Commissioners	Other Commissioners
Poor	30.2% (13)	2.3% (46)
Good	34.9% (15)	44.2% (91)
Very Good, Outstanding	34.9% (15)	33.5% (69)
	n = 43	n = 206

Note: These data are derived from the authors' 1994–95 surveys of county commissioners in Colorado, Idaho, Oregon, and Washington.

The distinction between county supremacy counties versus the other counties sharpens further when attitudes about the working relationship with the state environmental agency are examined. Table 7.9 shows that more county supremacy county commissioners (40.9%) perceive their working relationship with the state environmental agency to be "poor" than do the other county commissioners (22.8%). It should be noted that many county supremacy ordinances apply to the states as well as to the federal government (Hungerford, 1995). This antagonism may be reflected in these survey results.

Table 7.9
County Commissioner Attitudes Regarding Relationship with State Department of Environmental Quality

Rating of Relationship	Supremacy Commissioners	Other Commissioners
Poor	40.9% (18)	22.8% (49)
Good	34.1% (15)	49.8% (107)
Very Good, Outstanding	25.0% (11)	27.4% (59)
	n = 44	n = 215

Note: These data are derived from the authors' 1994–95 surveys of county commissioners in Colorado, Idaho, Oregon, and Washington.

CONCLUSION

There are important differences between urban and rural counties. Rural counties have higher levels of families in poverty, lower per capita incomes, and lower rates of housing growth than urban counties. Rural counties also have higher percentages of federal lands and jobs based in extraction. Compared to urban counties, the rural counties spend substantially less on environmental programs. Rural county commissioners perceived conflict over environmental issues to be high in their counties compared to their urban counterparts. Their relationships with both the state and federal governments are perceived to be worse than those of urban county commissioners.

When looking at Western counties, however, it is important to look at the subset of counties (almost exclusively rural) that have passed county supremacy legislation. Distinctions apparent in comparisons of urban and rural counties sharpen when comparing county supremacy and noncounty supremacy counties. In particular, the percentage of federal land in the county supremacy counties is much higher, the percentage of their budget derived from federal resource payments is higher, and spending on the environment is lower than among noncounty supremacy counties. Furthermore, the level of conflict over the environment appears to be higher in the county supremacy counties and the relationship with the federal government may be worse than among the other rural counties. It may be that the county supremacy movement is leading some rural counties to move even further away from the perceived environmentalism of urban counties.

If county governments in general were once referred to as "the forgotten governments" (Marando and Thomas, 1977), then rural counties must surely be the most forgotten of them all. However, rural county governments, especially in the West, are taking the lead in the important policy issues involving the environment and the management of public lands. Struggling to deal with their "love-hate" relationship with the federal government-in which they rely on federal resource payments yet chafe under federal land use decisions-counties have begun to assert their own powers.

The legal success of the county supremacy movement is doubtful. An early state court decision, *Boundary Backpackers v. Boundary County*, (No. CV93-9955 [Idaho 1st Jud. Dist. Ct., Jan. 27, 1994]), struck down that Idaho county's ordinance. Further, the federal government has gone on the offensive by filing suit against Nye County, Nevada, in Federal District Court (Ostrow, 1995). There is some evidence that the judicial proceedings are dampening the county supremacy effort. Out of 14 counties that had indicated they were considering adoption of ordinances in the summer of 1995, six had decided against it by December, 1995. In one case in Oregon, the commissioners refused to adopt as an ordinance a county supremacy initiative that had been approved by the county's citizens (Witt and Alm, 1996). At the same time, several federal land management agencies have tried to improve coordination of decisionmaking with county governments. This may be a sign that the effort is achieving some measure of success.

On the other hand, the fact that many other western counties have the same characteristics of the county supremacy counties in these four states, and that counties all over the West have significant federal land holdings within them, may mean that the county supremacy movement is just getting started. A Republican Congress more sympathetic to calls for state and local control may also prove helpful for advocates of both wise-use and county supremacy measures. Whatever the outcome at the Congressional level, it is clear that counties have reintroduced themselves as important players in the management of western public lands.

NOTES

1. There is substantial disagreement about what to call these ordinances and the movement associated with them. They are variously referred to as: wise-use (Erm, 1993, 94), custom and culture (Hungerford, 1995), county supremacy ordinances (Reed, 1993, 94), and county control ordinances (Hart, 1995). This chapter will refer to them as county supremacy ordinances.

2. Sources for the Federal Resource Programs entitlement payments to counties are derived from mineral leases and permits (30 U.S.C. 355); the Taylor Grazing Act (43 U.S.C. 315i); national forest revenues (16 U.S.C. 500); and payments in-lieu-of-taxes (31 U.S.C. 6901, 6907). Listing of statutes provided by the Idaho Association of Counties (1993).

3. A full discussion of the constitutional issues involved in the county supremacy movement's land use ordinances is beyond the scope of this chapter. A review of the legal issues (pro and con) can be found in Reed (1993, 94) and Erm (1993, 94). See also Hungerford (1995) and Hart (1995).

4. The surveys were conducted at different times because Idaho was included in the first phase of our study in 1994. An additional grant from Boise State University's faculty research program allowed the addition of Washington, Oregon, and Colorado in 1995. The Association of Idaho Counties and the Washington Association of Counties both allowed access to their annual meetings and provided assistance in collecting surveys. We are grateful for their help and advice.

5. The percentage of the counties represented by the responding commissioners were: 84% from Idaho, 70% from Colorado, 92% from Washington, and 89% from Oregon.

6. The survey question was: "In regard to environmental policy issues, how would you characterize the working relationship between your county and the Federal government?"

7. The survey question was: "In regard to environmental policy issues, how would you characterize the working relationship between your county and the state agency responsible for environmental quality?"

8. The survey question was: "In some counties there has been conflict between groups organized around environmental-recreational issues and local governments. How would you characterize the level of conflict over these issues in your county?"

9. County supremacy counties were identified in Oregon, Washington, and Colorado based on responses from county commissioners in our mail survey that their county had passed legislation of this type. Idaho county supremacy counties were identified by the State Attorney General's Office. Follow-up calls requesting copies of the ordinances or resolutions were made to all county supremacy counties in all four states.

10. The results on testimony and/or consideration of county supremacy legislation do not include Idaho because the survey of Idaho county commissioners was done earlier, and did not include the same county supremacy question.

Chapter 8

The County Supremacy Movement and Public Lands in Oregon

Christopher A. Simon

The origins of the county supremacy movement and the "wise-use" movement are often traced to the animus that developed between Western ranchers, timber workers, and conservation-minded federal land managers during the "Sagebrush Rebellion" of the late 1970s and early 1980s (Erm, 1993/94). Academic and popular literature attribute the reemergence of hostilities-directed primarily towards the U.S. Forest Service, U.S. Park Service, and Bureau of Land Management-to a plethora of changes occurring in the West. Land use policy changes for ranchers and timber workers (Falen and Budd-Falen, 1993/94), greater support for environmentalism in urban centers (Helvarg, 1994), socioeconomic decline in rural counties (Reed, 1993), and rising property taxes in rural counties (Dearborn, 1993) are among the multitude of factors that are plausibly related to the passage and continued support for wise-use and supremacy ordinances in Western counties.

During the years, eight Oregon counties that have considered-either via popular county-level initiative or by means of commission action-county supremacy and wise-use ordinances in the 1990s (See Appendix for the text of some of these initiatives). The counties are geographically dispersed, so it is not clear that the issue can be ascribed to some form of sectionalism in rural central and eastern Oregon. This study seeks to analyze socioeconomic variables that are often associated with county supremacy and wise-use ordinances to determine if there are noteworthy similarities among the counties that have either entertained or passed these ordinances and other Oregon counties.

RURAL WESTERN COUNTIES: A CHANGING DYNAMIC

The county supremacy and wise-use movements in the West are often attributed to the increasingly contentious nature of interest group politics attendant to significant modifications in federal land use policy (Culhane, 1981). In recent years, grazing rights and timber harvest access on federal lands have been the subject of acute debate between ranchers and timber interests, who are dependent on the publicly owned rangeland for their cattle operations and forest-supplied raw materials, and environmentalists concerned about either the preservation or conservation of natural resources for long-term communal benefit (Falen and Budd-Falen, 1993/94; Richardson, 1993).

The persistent movement toward incorporating environmental concerns into public land use plans and the conscious goal of developing sustainable uses of federal land and timber has been seen as the cause of economic decline in the wood products industry, which depends heavily on federal forest lands for its raw materials. Greater attention focused on the threatened extinction of wildlife and the deleterious effects of timber harvesting practices on the ecosystem in general have meant that many rural counties are facing the need to develop new economic activities to maintain their communities. The careful management of timber as a viable and long-term resource has become a concern for both environmentalists and timber industry workers. The concerns of the environmental groups are often more universalistic (see Nash, 1992), while the timber workers, ranchers, and their dependents are usually preoccupied with the maintenance of a way of life and a particular industrial base in their communities (Helvarg, 1994; Dietrich, 1992).

Distinctions between the values of economic and environmental interests are evident in analyses comparing the attitudes of rural denizens with urbanites. Survey findings generally support the hypothesis that individuals who reside in rural areas are less likely to be closely attuned to the relationship between the myriad of industrial pollutants and the degradation of environmental quality than are individuals who dwell in urban and suburban areas: "Pollution concern and residence are highly associated at the community level" (Tremblay and Dunlap, 1978: 484, 489).

The competition of interests between environmentalists, agriculturalists, and wood products workers has resulted in instances of protest on both sides. Dietrich (1992) documents the friction that existed between timber workers and environmentalists on the Olympic Peninsula in Washington, concluding that the long-term presence of the timber industry in the region became an integral part of a unique and highly insular community existence and related value structure. Helvarg (1994) tends to confirm Dietrich's (1992) conclusions in a similar case study analysis of environmental protest movements in Northern California. Helvarg (1994) observed that citizens of rural timber-dependent communities were often unable to understand or appreciate the concerns of environmental activists, viewing them as agitators and troublemakers.

Land use policy changes are often cited as a source of frustration for ranchers and timber interests in rural Western counties (Richardson, 1993). The increased scope and reach of environmental law in the 1960s and 1970s, and the subsequent changes in land use policy and administrative practices have been the source of prolonged and acute tension between federal and county governments and their citizens. Competing interests seek to shape land use policies, often giving short shrift to the needs of the community at large (Plotkin, 1987). While land use policy makers must seek to develop balanced outcomes, it is not clear that the forces of pluralism accommodate this need. Furthermore, the political dynamics at play may work against effective land use policy making and regulation (Tarlock, 1993).

The result of shifting land use policies from greater environmental concern during the Carter and Clinton administrations to the more limited concerns expressed by the Reagan and Bush administrations, has resulted in changing policy objectives and an inconsistent policy atmosphere. Rangeland, timber harvesting, and mining reforms during the Clinton administration have been associated with a changing federal-local relationship and with potential economic and social instability and decline in rural communities. In some instances, such as in Nye County, Nevada, federal officials were harassed and/or threatened with arrest by county officials.

While these broad characterizations of rural and urban counties in the West are sometimes disputed, they do apply generally-although it is necessary to heed the wisdom of not generalizing too strongly about rural dwellers as a group (Machlis and Force, 1988: 226). Environmental beliefs, opinions, and values among rural denizens are not uniform. Evidence in the rural sociology literature indicates that agricultural interests value rurality for quite different reasons from those of "ruralists," people who reside in rural areas but who may be employed and active in nonagricultural enterprises (Buttel and Flinn, 1977: 549). The exploratory factor analysis conducted by Buttel and Flinn (1977) tends to indicate that agriculturalists are concerned with the maintenance of a value structure unique in rural areas, while ruralists tend to focus on the benefits of not living in congested urban areas. While the focus of nonagriculture ruralites and agriculturalists may be different, it is quite possible that, ultimately, these seemingly different opinions and beliefs reflect a shared set of core values associated with independence from federal and state government regulation-albeit for different reasons-on the citizen, and perhaps the county government *in toto*. The desire on the part of rural citizens for independence from real or perceived government intrusion is consistent with historical accounts of American political culture in the West (Nash, 1992).

In the mid-1980s, a nationwide farm recession effectively weakened farming-dependent county governments' ability to raise revenue. Lawson (1986) found that agriculture-based counties were more reliant on property taxes, which were at the mercy of declining property assessments. Additionally, these counties were more likely to receive larger infusions of federal general revenue-sharing moneys at that time of the study than were the nonagricultural counties that were analyzed (Lawson, 1986: 22). Rural counties, perhaps due to demonstrated levels of deep-seated economic impairment, are more likely to receive federal grant resources (Martin and Wilkinson, 1984:386). Nevertheless, the intergovernmental relationship between the federal government and these farming-dependent counties, while fiscally beneficial to counties, often breeds antagonism from the local jurisdictions.

Seven years after Lawson's (1986) study, Dearborn (1993) found that property taxes, despite fluctuating assessments, have increased in terms of an aggregate state-level analysis. In the case of Oregon, property taxes increased an average of 141.1 percent during the period 1980 to 1990 (Dearborn, 1993); nationally, the average increase was approximately 128 percent. Given these seemingly contradictory findings, it is possible that for economic reasons, rural counties may have reacted to rising property taxes by calling into question the utility and benefit of federal lands, which are not subject to taxation by local governments. For rural county governments and their citizens, the development of federal lands in rural counties might appear to be a short-term method of dealing with rising property tax assessments.

Sociological studies indicate that many rural counties in the West have experienced and continue today to experience rapid and often disruptive socioeconomic changes (Machlis and Force, 1988). In addition to the declining employment in agriculture, and the wood-products industries, increases in rural poverty rates have been documented in Government Accounting Office reports. Many rural counties are also experiencing rapid and possibly socially disruptive population shifts (Reed, 1993/94: 528).

Rising levels of socioeconomic disadvantage and large population shifts in rural counties may have a deleterious effect on community stability. Evidence in the literature indicates that rural county governments increasingly operate under serious fiscal constraints, while facing population changes and the rise of crime, poverty, and families at risk. For ruralists, agriculturalists, and the county government officials representing them, problems traditionally associated with urban areas are now an increasing concern for rural communities. County supremacy and wise-use initiatives might reflect citizen frustration associated with the rise of these social problems and the widespread belief that the ability of state and federal intervention to help solve these problems is increasingly limited.

Land use regulation, increasing evidence of the growth of traditionally urban problems in rural counties, and perceived threats to the stability of rural communities are all conditions attributed to the growing tensions facing the federal-local relationship in many rural Western counties (Dowdle, 1984). The alternative offered by county supremacy and wise-use initiative advocates, however, does not appear to be solidly grounded in constitutional principle. Given the current fiscal crises facing many county governments, the evidence in the literature indicates that is not likely that the devolution of power and authority would result in more equitable outcomes for all competing interests. It is not likely that the level of competition among interest groups will decline, nor will competition cultivate greater equality amongst interests (Berry, 1989).

COUNTY SUPREMACY AND WISE-USE INITIATIVES: A LEGAL ANALYSIS

County supremacy and wise-use initiatives represent two distinct approaches within what legal scholars consider to be the renewed Sagebrush Rebellion (Reed, 1993/94: 527). Both initiatives have the intended effect of increasing the influence of local governments and well-positioned local interests in rural Western counties in the area of federal landuse planning. Viewed in terms of interest group pluralism, the movement has been attributed to rural agribusiness, mining, and timber interests whose influence at the federal level declined when a Democratic presidential administration appeared to adopt an environmental agenda.

The origins of the county supremacy movement can be traced to the Catron County, New Mexico, ordinances claiming a preeminent status for county "way of life" values in land use decisions (Washington Association of Counties Meeting, 1993). Ranchers in Catron County were angered by federal grazing policies that would increase fees and limit the number of animal units allowed on federal lands. Proponents of the county supremacy movement tend to support the notion that local planning boards could better regulate land use in a manner that would create sustainable economic growth and manage natural resources, although evidence that wholly positive outcomes would occur remains unclear (Gramling and Freudenberg, 1990: 554, 555; McCurdy, 1984).

At a meeting of the Washington Association of Counties in May 1993, a spokesman for the county supremacy movement in Nye County, Nevada, indicated that local initiatives for county supremacy were the product of frustration over limited property tax bases in counties that contain large federal land holdings. He argued that these extensive land holdings placed these rural counties on an unequal footing with counties in the original thirteen states; the federal government has only limited land holdings outside the West. Additionally, he argued further that large federal land holdings in the counties had a negative effect on the property tax base, reduced the efficacy of local governments to serve their citizens' needs, and depressed local economies (Washington Association of Counties Meeting, 1993).

Karen Budd-Falen, the legal architect of the Catron County ordinances, defends grazing rights on federal lands and maintains that federal actions are frequently at odds with administrative regulations; she also claims that federal agency actions are based on an unconstitutional reading of federal authority. According to Falen and Budd-Falen (1993/94: 506, 508), grazing on federal lands is not a properly construed "privilege;" rather, it is legally a property right that cannot be reduced or eliminated without due process. Land holdings and grazing rights existed prior to U.S. intervention in the West, and these property rights were guaranteed in the Treaty of Guadelupe Hidalgo (Falen and Budd-Falen, 1993/94: 513). They conclude that any alterations in federal land use policy that have a deleterious effect on grazing interests constitute a form of land taking, which must be conducted in a manner consistent with the Fourteenth Amendment (Falen and Budd-Falen, 1993/94: 524).

Proponents of the ordinances also incorporate the Tenth Amendment into their argument (Falen and Budd-Falen, 1993/94). Consistent with the dual federalism model, supporters of these ordinances argue that federal land holdings represent a violation of the Reserved Powers Clause. This argument has not been given much credence in recent Supreme Court decisions, such as *Garcia v San Antonio Metropolitan Transit Authority*, 105 S.Ct. 1005 (1985). While this case was more directly concerned with state immunity from federal applications of the Commerce

Clause, Chief Justice Rehnquist's dissenting opinion indicated that the implications of the majority decision would be more directly related to the efficacy of the Tenth Amendment. Chief Justice Rehnquist concluded that by overturning *National League of Cities v. Usery,* 96 S.Ct. 2465 (1976), Justice Brennan's opinion generally ignored the need for a Court-defined scope of State immunity which was implicit in the case. For this reason, the applicability of the Tenth Amendment as a viable constitutional justification for county supremacy initiatives or ordinances is quite possibly a moot point. The recent district court decision setting aside the Nye County, Nevada, ordinances represents further support for this conclusion (McCoy, 1996: B10).

The legal reasoning supporting the county supremacy and wise-use movement has been criticized by a number of legal scholars (Erm, 1993/94; Reed, 1993/94). Falen and Budd-Falen's (1993/94) property right claim may not be clearly defined by the Court, effectively weakening their constitutional claims. Court decisions tend to support the argument that local or state control over federal land use planning is limited by the federal government, reaffirming the Supremacy Clause in this area (Reed, 1993/94: 547). wise-use ordinances, requiring federal land use plans to be consistent with local "custom and culture," were rejected in *Boundary Backpackers v Boundary County* (1994) on the basis that their provisions violated the Supremacy Clause as well as being inconsistent with Dillon's Rule[1] (Erm, 1993/94: 655).

Tracing Supreme Court decisions since the 1820s, Waugh (1988) finds that while *Coyle v Smith* (1911) may represent a limitation on federal imposition on state sovereignty, it was not intended to justify state- or county-imposed limitations of federal land management policy in the West. Earlier Court interpretations affirmed the power of the national government to manage and retain sovereign authority over federal lands. The Court decision in 1911 did limit the ability of Congress to impose certain admission requirements on prospective states that would effectively limit state sovereignty after admission (Waugh, 1988: 61). The Court decision in *Coyle* is possibly (mis)applied by county supremacy and wise-use proponents, using logic similar to that of the nullification advocates in the ante-bellum South (Merriam, 1903: 269, 270).

THE INITIATIVE AND THE OREGON SYSTEM

While direct democracy has been a part of the American political process since the New England town meetings, it has not been supported consistently. John Adams and James Madison, representing different visions of good government, both tended to reject the notion of direct democracy. There was a degree of apprehensiveness regarding pure democratic systems due to the possibilities for factional control of government by what were viewed as the uneducated masses. Madison preferred representative democratic institutions, concluding that the possibility for factional control could be limited if factionalism was divided by different levels of government, separation of powers, and the use of staggered terms of office (Madison, 1982: 42-49).

The popular initiative, despite the occasionally vague and/or nefarious outcomes that it may produce, has the potential to be a powerful linkage mechanism between citizens and their government (Schmidt, 1989: 25; Cohen, 1971: 88, 89). In the late nineteenth century, the popular initiative emerged as a favored reform of the populist movement and was supported by agrarian associations in rural areas and socialist organizations in urban centers (Cronin, 1989: 53).

Direct democracy instruments can be misused by powerful interests who seek to advance their own narrow objectives, occasionally at the expense of the general public (Barnett, 1915: 21). Critics attribute the adoption of California's Proposition 13, and more recently Ballot Measure 5 in Oregon, to costly interest group misinformation campaigns that obscured the negative effects of particular measures on long-term planning and on the provision of essential public goods and services (Lunch, 1994). Voter preferences on specific issues often may reflect a general frustration with government, with political parties, with prevailing socioeconomic conditions, and with changes occurring within society as a whole or particular segments of it (Zimmerman, 1987: 34).

Schmidt (1989: 34, 40) counters the arguments of the critics, concluding that initiative measures are often more clearly written than legislatively drafted measures, potenially represent a balance between the left and the right, and are generally supplements to-not replacements for-deliberative legislative action. Schmidt (1989: 40) concludes that most of the criticisms leveled at the initiative process reflect limited faith in the abilities of the voter, which he argues is a largely misguided concern.

The persistent William Simon U'Ren has been identified as the most prominent figure in the movement to establish what is known as the "Oregon system"--the initiative, referendum, and recall petition process in that state. U'Ren has been characterized as a populist reformer closely associated with the Grange Movement in western Oregon. U'Ren and his Direct Legislation League disdained the corruption that occurred in the state legislature and viewed the initiative as a method of bypassing that established institution of government (Schuman, 1994: 948; Keisling, 1992: 367).

The adoption of the initiative process in Oregon can be attributed to forms of political intrigue which are similar to those often cited by populists and the Progressives as sources of dominant political party corruption (LaPalombara, 1950:6-8). The state legislature was controlled by a Republican majority, but divisions within the ruling party necessitated a unique appeal to Populist and other third party legislators. Pro-gold standard Republicans needed these legislators' support in order to reelect incumbent Senator John Mitchell. U'Ren and others agreed to the alliance in return for Republican support for the initiative reform. An amendment to the state constitution establishing the popular initiative was referred to the People and ratified in 1902 (Eaton, 1912:4). In 1906, the use of the initiative was extended to local governments within Oregon (Beard and Shultz, 1912: 81).

FOCUS OF RESEARCH

While the legal arguments supporting county supremacy and wise-use initiatives are considered specious by some legal scholars (Reed, 1993/94), the social and economic environmental conditions that exist in counties in which they are initiated and passed remain a largely unexplored research area. As discussed earlier, the sparse literature available suggests that these movements are related to changing socioeconomic conditions in counties in the West. Timber dependent counties are experiencing socioeconomic changes as the wood products industry declines. Counties that are heavily reliant on wood products and agricultural industries may find it difficult to retool and retrain for a new economic base. The counties that have witnessed the passage of county supremacy or wise-use initiatives might be experiencing greater increases in socioeconomic distress than other counties-in this case, in the State of Oregon.

In this study socioeconomic disadvantage will be measured in terms of change in average median family income, percentage of county residents possessing college degrees, poverty rate, and unemployment rate for the county supremacy and wise-use movement counties as compared with the other 28 counties in Oregon. It is hypothesized that counties in which these initiatives appeared on the ballot are experiencing more rapid change toward socioeconomic disadvantage than other counties in Oregon.

The decline in the wood products industry in the West has also been cited as a source of federal-local tensions in rural counties. As the wood products industry recedes in timber-dependent counties, it is hypothesized that tensions between land-use planners and wise-use advocates will increase. This hypothesized explanation for county supremacy and wise-use initiatives is consistent with case studies of rural timber-dependent regions in the West (Helvarg, 1994; Dietrich, 1992). It is expected that the decline in the wood products industry as a proportion of the rural workforce is greater in counties that have entertained county supremacy or wise-use initiatives than in the other Oregon counties.

Rapid change in rural communities has also been cited as a source of concern for agriculturalists and ruralists (Buttel and Flinn, 1977). Increases in violent crime in Oregon's rural counties have resulted in elevated demand on county and city law enforcement agencies. Rural poverty has resulted in a greater demand on county social and health services. While tax increases may reflect increased demand on government services, they might also be a source of concern in rural counties. Oregon's Ballot Measure 5 in 1990, while not supported as widely in rural counties as elsewhere, is evidence that tax revolt via the initiative process might offer a partial explanation for county supremacy initiatives.

Based on interviews conducted with federal, state, and county administrators and two elected county officials in Crook County, Oregon, it is hypothesized that the growing presence of federal officials is the source of federal-local tensions. In Crook County, this increased federal employment has coincided with new federal facilities and new and improved office technology. While the county officials generally claimed that they are on good terms with federal officials, three of the five county officials who were interviewed made negative comments regarding the changing federal presence. The three county officials perceived that they were working with the federal officials from a position of disadvantage.

It is hypothesized that in recent years the growth in the rate of federal employment in the counties that have formally considered county supremacy or wise-use measures via the initiative process has been significantly greater than in the counties that have not considered these measures. If we fail to reject this hypothesis, then further analysis should be conducted to determine if the federal-local tensions that appear to exist between county officials and federal officials are related to the passage of county supremacy or wise-use initiatives. County officials might offer cues to voters or simply reflect voter stances on federal-local relations.

It is possible that the condition of federal-local relations might be affected by federal grant activity. County officials often complain that the federal government issues mandates, but does not offer financial support to execute these federal policies. Local governments often compete with each other for federal grant money, creating the potential for local-local tensions as well as federal-local conflict. It is hypothesized, therefore, that county supremacy or wise-use initiatives may be related to a slower rate of growth in federal grant money per capita.

METHODS AND DATA EMPLOYED IN STUDY

This study analyzes the population of Oregon counties (N = 36); the eight counties that either have enacted or considered county supremacy or wise-use ordinances receive particularly close attention. The limited number of cases available makes logistic regression modeling impractical. Analysis of variance will be used to compare the difference between two groups of Oregon counties, (1) counties that have considered or passed the ordinances, and (2) counties that have not done so.

The data employed in this study are drawn from three principal sources. The *County and City Databook* for 1988 and 1994 provided pertinent information on socioeconomic conditions within the county, as well as information regarding rate of federal employment and federal receipts. Data on wood products employment, payroll, and the number of businesses in the counties were gathered from *County Business Patterns, Oregon.* Presidential election data for 1980, 1984, and 1992 were gathered from the *America Votes* series. The data collected represents a comparison between socioeconomic conditions in the early to mid-1980s with the conditions in the first three years of the 1990s.

Due to variations in the reported data, not all information for the early 1980s or the early 1990s come from two particular years. This should not pose a problem because the study does not employ time series analysis. Rather, the focus of this study is on relative change between counties that have considered or passed county supremacy or wise-use ordinances and the other 28 counties in Oregon to determine if variations in socioeconomic change and presidential vote are in evidence. Variations between the two groups analyzed will be the basis of future comparative case study analyses.

FINDINGS

The Oregon counties that have considered or passed county supremacy or wise-use initiatives are significantly more dependent on the wood products industry than the remaining counties. In 1986, the wood products industry accounted for (on average) nearly 30 percent of the jobs in the eight counties, compared with approximately 13 percent of jobs in other Oregon counties. The significant gap continued to exist in the early 1990s as well, with approximately 20 percent of the workforce in the county supremacy and wise-use counties employed in the wood products industry.

Based on evidence in the rural sociology and political science literature, it was hypothesized that the increase in socioeconomic disadvantage in Oregon counties that have either considered or passed county supremacy or wise-use initiatives would be greater than in counties that have not considered these measures; the data collected and scrutinized failed to support this hypothesis. On average, there was no statistical difference in change in per capita income. Counties that considered or passed county supremacy or wise-use measures witnessed a 12.4 percent decline in per capita income (in real dollars) between 1980 and 1990; the per capita income in counties that did not consider or pass such measures declined on average 14.7 percent during the same period.

Table 8.1
County Workforce Dependency on Wood Products Industry

	Percentage of Workforce in Wood Products-1986	
	Mean	**s.e.**
No Initiative (n = 23)	12.6	0.19
Initiative (n = 7)	29.6	0.38
F-test probability	0.0002***	

	Percentage of Workforce in Wood Products-1992	
	Mean	**s.e.**
No Initiative (n = 27)	8.4	0.15
Initiative (n = 7)	19.7	0.53
F-test probability	0.006***	

* p < 0.10; ** p < 0.05; *** p < 0.01

Table 8.2
Socioeconomic Change in Oregon Counties

Percent Change in Per Capita Income-1984, 1990

	Mean	s.e.
No Initiative	-12.74	0.63
Initiative	-14.73	1.27

F-test probability	0.15

Percent Change in Poverty Rate-1979, 1992

	Mean	s.e.
No Initiative	27.18	5.20
Initiative	13.77	12.89

F-test probability	0.27

Percent Change in College Educated-1980, 1990

	Mean	s.e.
No Initiative	12.92	2.25
Initiative	15.41	5.96

F-test probability	0.64

Percent Change in Unemployment Rate-1986, 1992

	Mean	s.e.
No Initiative	-93.01	0.40
Initiative	-91.41	0.44

F-test probability	0.05**

$* p < 0.10; ** p < 0.05; *** p < 0.01$

The change in the poverty rate between 1979 and 1992 yielded a smaller increase in poverty for the counties considering or passing the measures compared with the counties that did not consider the measures. Poverty increased 13.8 percent in the former group, while the rate of increase in the latter group of counties was 27.2 percent. Unemployment rates for all counties dropped on average 92.7 percent. It is likely that this sharp decline in the unemployment rate reflects a social artifact--the emergence of Oregon from economic recession of the early 1980s. The decline in the unemployment rate in the counties that considered or passed county supremacy or wise-use initiatives was on average marginally less than in the other Oregon counties (p=0.05).

The percentage of college-educated residents in the counties that considered or passed supremacy or wise-use initiatives has on average increased by 15.4 percent, which is 2.5 percent higher than the increase in the other 28 counties. This, however, does not represent a statistically significant difference. On average, counties considering or passing county supremacy or wise-use initiatives in Oregon have not experienced a significantly greater increase in socioeconomic disadvantage when compared with other Oregon counties.

A second explanation for the rise of county supremacy and wise-use initiatives is related to rapid social change. Rapid population growth and crime, for instance, might affect community stability, especially in rural counties. On average, the counties that have either considered or passed the supremacy or wise-use initiatives experienced a marginal decrease in their population-a 0.1 percent decrease between 1980 and 1992. Note, however, that there was large variation across the county supremacy and wise-use counties, ranging from a 4.9 percent population decrease to a 15.4 percent increase. The average population increased 9.5 percent for the other counties in Oregon. The evidence is not clear that rapid population growth (or decline) is consistently associated with county supremacy or wise-use initiatives in Oregon.

Crime rates for counties considering the wise-use measures increased on average 8.2 percent, compared to an increase of 0.6 percent for the other Oregon counties for the period between 1985 and 1992. The difference between the two groups in terms of the change in violent crime rates was insignificant-with the rate dropping for both groups.

For the period 1982, 1992, the change in per capita taxes yielded a smaller average rate of increase for counties that have passed or considered county supremacy or wise-use initiatives compared to other Oregon counties. The average increase in taxes for the counties that proposed or passed the ordinances was 31.6 percent, compared with the other 28 Oregon counties, whose average increase in taxes was 77.3 percent. The variation within both groups was large, and the variance across groups was not significant. Based on changes in taxes over a ten-year period, there is no clear evidence that the counties that considered or passed county supremacy or wise-use initiatives are experiencing an accelerated increase in taxes. The tax revolt phenomenon does not appear to be an explanation for the county supremacy movement in Oregon.

The decline in the timber industry is often cited as an explanation for county supremacy and wise-use initiatives. As addressed earlier, protests in communities in the West have been attributed to environmental policy changes that limit timber harvests (Fortmann, 1988). The employment rate for wood products employees in Oregon counties considering or passing county supremacy or wise-use initiatives

Table 8.3
Changes in County Population and Crime

Percent Change in Population-1980, 1992

	Mean	s.e.
No Initiative	9.53	2.45
Initiative	-0.14	2.34
F-test probability	0.05**	

Percent Change in Crime Rate-1985, 1992

	Mean	s.e.
No Initiative	0.61	5.00
Initiative	8.21	11.82
F-test probability	0.50	

Percent Change in Violent Crime Rate-1985, 1992

	Mean	s.e.
No Initiative	-0.47	9.37
Initiative	-17.58	13.91
F-test probability	0.38	

* $p < 0.10$; ** $p < 0.05$; *** $p < 0.01$

Table 8.4
Change in Taxes in Counties, Per Capita

Percent Change in Taxes Per Capita-1982, 1992

	Mean	s.e.
No Initiative	77.31	26.16
Initiative	31.56	18.20
F-test probability	0.37	

* $p < 0.10$; ** $p < 0.05$; *** $p < 0.01$

has declined at a rate *significantly lower* than for counties not considering these initiatives (p < 0.01). Counties considering or passing county supremacy or wise-use initiatives have experienced an average 76.8 percent decline while other Oregon counties on average have witnessed a 91.4 percent decline in their wood products employment rate. In this instance, the hypothesis that counties considering supremacy or wise-use initiatives are experiencing significantly larger decreases in their wood products industry must be rejected.

The change in the federal employment rate between 1984 and 1990 was significantly different for the counties that considered the measures when compared with the counties that did not. The federal employment rate for counties that either considered or passed the measures experienced an average increase in the federal employment rate of 184.4 percent, compared to a 25.96 percent increase in other Oregon counties (p = 0.06). This increase could be explained by both an increased number of federal employees and declining overall population in the counties that have passed or considered these measures. Federal grants, measured in dollars per 1,000 citizens, increased on average 68.8 percent in the counties that considered the measures, compared to 44.4 percent for other Oregon counties (p = 0.02).

A comparison of the counties that have considered or passed county supremacy or wise-use initiatives in terms of their aggregate voting record in the 1980, 1984, and 1992 presidential elections yielded significant results. The Reagan administration is widely acknowledged to have been openly hostile to environmentalists and their policy agenda (Richardson, 1993). It could be hypothesized, therefore, that counties that have considered county supremacy or wise-use measures would have a higher percentage of their voters supporting Reagan in 1980 and 1984. Additionally, it is hypothesized that support for Bush would be significantly greater in county supremacy or wise-use counties than in the other counties in Oregon. The Clinton campaign indicated a greater interest in environmental protection than did the Bush campaign (see Gore, 1992).

The counties that have considered or passed county supremacy or wise-use initiatives do seem to show greater support for Reagan, with 63.3 percent of the voters supporting the Republican nominee in 1980 (p = 0.05). The 1984 presidential votes of the counties that have considered or passed such initiatives are not statistically different from the other Oregon counties. However, in the 1992 presidential election Bush received greater support in the county supremacy or wise-use counties than he did in the other counties in Oregon (p = 0.03).

CONCLUSION

Statistical comparisons of social, demographic, and political correlates for those counties that have either considered or passed county supremacy or wise-use initiatives in the State of Oregon yield somewhat mixed results. On average, the eight counties analyzed in this study do not appear to be experiencing significantly different social and economic changes when compared with the other 28 counties in the state.

Table 8.5
Federal-Local Relationship and Wood Products

Percent Change in Federal Grants-1986, 1992

	Mean	**s.e.**
No Initiative	44.39	4.37
Initiative	68.78	11.17
F-test probability	0.02**	

Percent Change in Federal Employment-1984, 1990

	Mean	**s.e.**
No Initiative	25.97	8.53
Initiative	184.44	15.44
F-test probability	0.06*	

Percent Change in Wood Products Employment-1984, 1992

	Mean	**s.e.**
No Initiative	-91.47	1.25
Initiative	-76.78	5.70
F-test probability	0.01***	

* p < 0.10; ** p < 0.05; *** p < 0.01

On average, social change indicators do seem to point to slightly negative population growth in the eight Oregon counties. On average, per capita income is depressed throughout Oregon, which is also reflected in a general increase in the poverty rate. The crime rate is not statistically different for the counties that have considered or passed county supremacy or wise-use initiatives.

One of the most interesting findings was that the decline in the wood products industry in the eight counties was significantly *lower* than in the counties that have not considered county supremacy or wise-use measures. Additionally, the increase in federal grant dollars per capita increased in the eight counties at a rate significantly higher than in the other Oregon counties. While this finding appears to dispel the conclusion that the wood products industry in these eight counties is declining at a much more rapid pace than in other counties, it is important to note

Table 8.6
County Presidential Election Results

Percent Voting for Reagan-1980

	Mean	s.e.
No Initiative	58.17	1.31
Initiative	63.60	2.11
F-test probability	0.05**	

Percent Voting for Reagan-1984

	Mean	s.e.
No Initiative	59.12	1.34
Initiative	64.20	2.25
F-test probability	0.12	

Percent Voting for Bush-1992

	Mean	s.e.
No Initiative	34.54	1.05
Initiative	39.45	1.75
F-test probability	0.03*	

* $p < 0.10$; ** $p < 0.05$; *** $p < 0.01$

that these counties are economically more timber dependent. Any decline in the wood products industry, therefore, may have a much greater relative impact on the counties that have considered or passed county supremacy or wise-use ordinances than in Oregon's remaining counties.

Federal employment in the eight counties considering the wise-use measures dramatically increased between 1984 and 1990. Interviews with county officials in Crook County-one of the counties that have had a county supremacy initiative on their ballot-tends to support the argument that the increase in federal employment rate is a source of tension for local government officials.

While the eight Oregon counties did not appear to have experienced significantly different social or economic change from other Oregon counties, the decline in the wood products industry is likely to have had a much greater impact due to their narrower economic base. Field research should be conducted to determine if citizens in the eight counties are more sensitive to socioeconomic change than those in other counties in Oregon. Socioeconomic change affects different communities--especially rural communities--quite differently from more urbanized population centers.

Finally, further field research needs to be conducted to determine the nature of the federal-local relationships. The sizable increase in federal employment rate might be a source of tension between federal and county officials. As some officials in Crook County, Oregon, indicated during personal interviews, it is very likely that the increased federal presence contributes to a sense of diminished local efficacy among both county officials and citizens.

APPENDIX: Examples of County Supremacy Ordinances

Crook County, Oregon (1995; Turnout = 39%; In-Favor = 41%; Failed)

"Shall the people of Crook County interpret the United States Constitution to make some public lands unconstitutional?"

Grant County, Oregon (1995; Turnout = 53%; In-Favor = 72%; Passed)

"Shall the people of Grant County refuse to recognize Federal management of certain public lands?"

Union County, Oregon (1994; Turnout = 68%; In-Favor = 50%; Passed)

"Shall the People of Union County declare that the Federal government lacks constitutional authority to possess land in Union County?"

NOTE

1. Dillon's Rule established the precedent that local governments may exercise only those powers explicitly granted to them by the state. Federal courts have consistently upheld the dependency of localities on the state since Iowa Judge John Dillon first laid down Dillon's Rule in 1868.

Chapter 9

Changing Political Geometry: Public Lands and Natural Resources in Nevada

Kelly DeVine and Dennis L. Soden

In the past, the traditional iron triangle of land-users (ranching and mining interests), supportive congressional representatives, and "captured" agencies (U.S. Forest Service, Bureau of Land Management) dominated the way in which land and natural resource use decisions were made (see for example, McCool, 1988; Soden, 1995a). The primary focus of their collective effort was the development of patterns of resource use and exploitation, with the active involvement of the industries and communities that depended on the productive use of those resources (Gaventa, 1980; Soden, 1989). Miners and grazers, however, no longer dominate the economies or the politics of the West as they have in the past. With the rise in concern for environmental protection, new parallel concerns about the long-term unintended consequences of resource use have begun to complicate matters. Similarly, policies encouraging low-cost leasing of federal properties and incentives to conduct exploratory mining and similar activities have come under scrutiny. As a consequence of these developments the traditional legs of the iron triangle are being reconfigured.

This chapter explores these new developments and challenges to federal lands policy and resource use, focusing on the evolving array of players and rights claimed in the Nevada setting. From one perspective Nevada, a state in which the federal government owns 87 percent of all lands, has been highly controlled by the Bureau of Land Management (BLM) and the U.S. Forest Service (USFS), and to a lesser degree by other federal agencies such as the Department of Defense (DOD) and Department of Energy (DOE). From another perspective, however, extractive industries and ranching have added much to the state's economy and produced a strong set of local interests to offset federal influence (Hulse, 1991). From still another perspective, it has been the tourist, gaming, and urban-centered industries that have far outstripped the contribution of the extractive industries to the state's economy and owe little of their vibrancy or continuity to the aforementioned agencies (Moehring, 1989; Soden and Herzik, forthcoming).

Clearly these historical patterns are undergoing noteworthy changes. The Sagebrush Rebellion of the early 1980s challenging federal prerogatives has resurfaced, and has joined forces with the growing Property Rights Movement, which is fighting against both the perceived and the real burdens of governmental regulation. Environmental interest groups also have achieved a foothold in the state and are pursuing their protection-oriented agenda, which features an emotional preference for a strong federal government role in the regulation of public lands. Added to these traditional adversaries are the growing population centers such as Clark County, home to Las Vegas (the fastest-growing metropolitan area in the country) and the Carson-Washoe counties area, home to burgeoning Reno. These areas, while showing little or no awareness of the extractive industries and ranching activities that have utilized federal lands for decades, look to the BLM and the USFS to safeguard the recreational values of the vast public lands close to their communities. At times, these groups are finding themselves joined against government policies at the national, state, and local levels alike, as has been the case with respect to the proposed nuclear repository at Yucca Mountain (Herzik and Dobra, 1994) and in determining future land uses for the Nevada Weapons Test Site (Conary and Soden, 1996). The result of all these developments is a breakdown of the traditional iron triangles. Increasingly, the norm is shifting alliances that vary from issue to issue based more on practical political considerations and single-issue politics than on any underlying agreement on the overarching policy direction at stake.

Our analysis suggests that the multiple agendas of resource use and protection may come together in a new political dimension based on regional dynamics, but will be far from a revolution in federal lands policy in the State of Nevada. We suggest that the ultimate result of change will lend itself to shifting alliances and, perhaps, even greater policy uncertainty in the future.

HISTORICAL BACKGROUND

The West since its earliest times had looked to the East, and particularly to Washington, D.C., to shape its collective destiny. Unlike the East, the West is owned in large part by the federal government. While the East was made up of the original thirteen colonies and its relatively stable and traditionalistic political units, the West was carved out of the military conquest of the Mexican-American War and reflected the desire to build a great nation under the rubric of manifest destiny. The East had traditionally looked to its local government to mediate the competing groups vying for political recognition at the local level. With no absentee landlord and a highly differentiated economy based on a diverse set of manufacturing industries, the East has not needed Washington for the same reasons as the West.

As a region, the West has been shaped and developed by a variety of public and private land use laws throughout its history. Moreover, its political representatives have had a strong hand in shaping those laws. The Homestead Act (1862), the

Desert Lands Act (1891), the Newlands Reclamation Act (1902), the Mining Act of 1872, and the Taylor Grazing Act (1934) are just a few of the laws which have had a significant impact on the development of the Western states and their economies. These acts are aimed at disposal, management, and/or development of the lands and resources of the West. However, despite the strong regional identification of the people and state officials in the West, there are increasingly stark differences among them. While federal statutes that affect public lands have generally had a "one size fits all" cast to them, they have had varying effects on the economic and political development of the several Western states. Consequently, Nevada stands as an extreme example of the adverse effects that federal land policy may produce.

Looking back over the history of the land now known as the State of Nevada, one is struck by what hasn't changed as much as by what has. The physical changes to this arid, sparse land have been nothing less than spectacular. Technological advances in water delivery systems and dams have wrought a thriving tourist destination out of a desert that no one wanted to claim 150 years ago. Nevada and its principal cities of Las Vegas and Reno boast of having some of the highest growth rates in the country; in the early 1990s approximately 5,000 people a month were pouring over its borders into Clark County alone. Judging by the influx of people and the booming economy, there is seemingly nothing to keep Nevada from realizing a strong and prominent place in this nation as the dawn of a new century arrives. What has not changed, however, has been the convoluted relationship that the people in the state have with not only the actual workaday apparatus of government, but with the very idea of government itself.

Nevada is unique in that it is, and historically has been, largely owned and controlled by various absentee landlords, California railroad magnates and Eastern financiers were among the more notorious absentee landlords to hold sway in Nevada. The most prominent landlord, however, is the federal government. Nevada is also unique in that the results of uncoordinated and contradictory governmental policies, seemingly aimed at achieving conflicting goals, have been more extreme in their outcomes in Nevada than in other Western states, thereby inciting extreme reaction, from the myriad interests in the state. The picture painted of Nevada's relationship to the federal government is a complex one involving a wide range of institutions and people hampered in their relationship with the administrative state by the conflicting means by which they seek to address problems. Often the picture reveals that good intentions are not even a good starting point (Nelson, 1995). The consequences of various land use and disposal policies on the part of the federal government have not spoken with one clear voice, so it is not surprising that the voices raised in anger against those policies are lacking in harmony or agreement. Over the last century and a half, federal policy regarding Western lands has moved (or rather lurched) from disposal of perceived wasteland to resource management to environmental protection. The court rulings executive orders, and congressional legislation that have both sparked and defined these movements play up the lack of clear motivation from one transition to another. The result is a patchwork of traditional and contemporary constituents all laying claim to some standing regulation, law, or ruling, all conflicting and denying one another simultaneously. Still, in the midst of this there are many uninformed residents of the state, many who are innocently ground up in the process; others, of course, are clearly responsible for manipulating that process to serve their own needs.

The myth of the old West is a powerful one, and it often obscures the issues and alternatives for the very real West of today. Western land disposal policies of the nineteenth century were not in accord with the realistic development potential of the state considering its geologic and meteorological characteristics. The newly acquired territories were quickly opened up and used to solve a number of social problems, from inexpensive payments to veterans to sources of revenue for the national government (Nelson, 1995: 7, 14). Policies such as the Homestead Act were based on the objective of populating the Western territories with self-sufficient farmers. Instead, this and other policies perversely produced land owners and resource users in Nevada, as well as throughout the West, who were heavily dependent on the deep pockets of the federal government to make up for the shortfall between what the land could support and what the land was forced to support. This is a fact to which we shall return in concluding this analysis.

Originally, the land we know as Nevada was part of the vast and vacant Utah territory. The whole region was arid and stippled with mountain ranges and basins, earning the name of the Great Basin. Those persons in charge of the territorial government were Mormon settlers out-running the latest wave of confrontation, moving forever Westward in search of land where they would be left to their own devices. They chose forbidding areas as a point of religious conviction and as a way of securing some measure of distance from misunderstanding gentiles. For Mormons, doing the work of God meant changing wastelands into paradise. They had little appreciation for the value of untouched land and little tolerance for the cut-and-run exploits that had attracted many others to the dry Western expanses. In addition, prospectors and cattlemen drifted onto future Nevada land in search of a big strike or free range. These explorers and exploiters were a ragtag bunch. The kind of government they needed was not the orderly one guided by a higher purpose that the Mormons were offering from their outpost in Salt Lake; instead, they sought an ad hoc polity driven by economic and logistical necessities (Elliot, 1987: 55-68; Mosser and Soden, 1993). Government was only called for in order to settle disputes or assign rights to property; few other needs were to be considered as matters of public policy. As such, the miners and grazers petitioned to have the area designated as its own territory in order to get out from under the direction of the Mormon leaders in Salt Lake.

The nature of prospecting prevented those involved from developing a land ethic or communal spirit that is so closely associated with farming in the eastern and midwestern states. No one wanted to own any of the land within the state until a claim was struck, and even then ownership of the claim was sought rather than the titled ownership of the land. When a claim is played out, it's time to move on to the next prospect. Miners working the desolate areas in the Nevada territory developed legal arrangements that suited their needs for assuring that the wealth of a given claim would go to the rightful owner while eliminating many of the other responsibilities that accompany ownership should the claim prove to be worthless. Since towns that bustled with life one year could become ghost towns the next, flexible local charters were developed by mining interests to ensure that support services were provided with limited liability to the mining concerns and limited powers of governing. These arrangements were codified and protected by the newly formed territorial government. Thus, from the very start the State of Nevada began a pattern of requiring government to ratify or legitimate already existing practices (Elliot, 1987: 55, 68).

Although all Western states display a defiant expectancy when their projects and wants are at stake, possibly no other Western state has asked for so much with so little justification as has Nevada. The Nevada territory was rushed into statehood before it claimed the requisite number of settlers. Statehood allowed the Union to exploit Nevada's mineral riches to further the cause of the Civil War. When Nevada was brought into the Union, its territorial debt was cleared under the terms of its Enabling Act. Yet, in Nevada there was opposition to statehood based on the fear of federal taxation (taxation was negligible on the territory level), and the congressional delegations from Nevada challenged the propriety of federal oversight from the start (Elliot, 1987: 84, 89). In 1908, a barely populated and agriculturally deficient Nevada flexed enough local and national political muscle to have its demands (fantastic and arrogant at the time, prescient and cunning considering present day population growth) for water from the Colorado River written into the Republican National Convention platform (Jones and Cahlan, 1975: 52). On receipt of its school plot lands, Nevada, like her neighbor California, promptly sold its selections to private grazing interests at favorable prices (Ring, 1994: 10; Graf, 1990: 9). Nevada was always looking to the future and to the dollar it would bring.

Besides not having the correct number of settlers to have been granted statehood under any other circumstances but those of war and the discovery of silver, the settlers were not really correct in stature either. The Homestead Act was based on Lockean-Jeffersonian notions about good government being possible through good husbanding of the land. The Homestead Act did not work well (that is to say, as it was intended, inasmuch as it did not create scores of independent and self-sufficient political and economic agents) when applied to the sparsely watered lands of the West; in no state was that more apparent than in Nevada. Nevada is the most arid of the 50 states, with some parts receiving less than four inches of rain a year and where four one-hundredths of an inch is enough to cause flash floods because the soil is so poor. The grazers literally had the run of the land while Nevada was still a territory, and they quickly learned to exploit the weaknesses of the Homestead Act to monopolize water sources for their livestock by impersonating farmers (along with other ruses) (Cawley, 1993; Nelson, 1995: 31).

Grazers were not held, in those early days, in much esteem. They were thought to be a ruthless, opportunistic bunch quite unlike the ideal farmer of the Jeffersonian tradition who improves his land through the steady, humble application of his own labor. By contrast, rather than improving the land through honest labor, the grazer merely ran his herd over it, taking what he needed then moving on to the next place; a real world tragedy of the commons, many argue, continues to this day (Hardin, 1968). Despite the lack of traditional respect, in Nevada grazers won the day over the farmers and homesteaders, often through violent confrontation and intimidation (Nelson, 1995: 149).

Grazers, having the benefit of greater familiarity with the land, staked out the choice plots with water and outfoxed the homesteaders and their embodying act to corner the water supplies. Grazers also beat out the farmers by sheer force of nature-the soil and the rainfall were simply too poor to produce much more than hay for livestock fodder. Politically, the grazers out-gunned the beleaguered homesteaders as well. When land values were being categorized for tax assessments, the homesteaders ended up bearing the greatest proportionate share of tax valuation for assessment purposes. The railroads threatened blackmail against the state and local counties that tried to collect taxes coming even close to real use value (Elliot, 1987: 159). And the grazers? Early on they learned to own only small parcels-chiefly for growing winter feed-and to keep their herds on public lands maintained at public expense (Nelson, 1995: 149). The independence of the cowboy and ranch-owner, now mythologized in Western lore and literature, can appear to the cynical eye as merely an independence from responsibility rather than independence of spirit and intellect.

Nevadans and their congressional representatives were full of bluster against the restraints of federal ownership. But despite their free-market rhetoric, when they were given the chance to accept ownership of the land (but not the mineral resources), they respectfully declined. The 1931 recommendations of the committee on the Conservation and Administration of the Public Domain were such that lands not appropriated should be regulated. The federal government should retain the mineral rights to public lands, but those lands should be offered to the states. Whatever portions the states denied would subsequently be retained by the federal government. The Western states refused the recommendations and the land, thus ushering in the era of federal management (Cawley, 1993: 74, 5).

Although mining interests have had to contend with the changing policies of the federal government, it has been the grazers who have been most vocal, contentious, and politically active. Nevada, along with other Western states, has sent a number of powerful senators and representatives to Washington. These Western congressmen have had an impact on land use legislation far beyond the percentage of citizens they represent. The grazers and miners had their positions ratified by federal legislation. The Mining Act of 1872 held public lands open to mining at low cost. Francis Newlands of Nevada crafted the act that initiated the massive water projects that have "reclaimed" the desert, and Pat McCarran fought during the Depression to guarantee that existing grazing arrangements would be protected.

Nevadans consistently voted for conservative candidates who would fight for their projects, and soundly rejected conservatives who would not. Herbert Hoover had been a staunch proponent of returning federal lands to the states because he felt that the states were in a better position to manage those lands. Considering the free-market rhetoric of past and present-day Sagebrush Rebels, you would have thought that Hoover would have been given tremendous support. However, the states were not willing to take on the financial responsibilities of managing the lands, and the resource-based industries did not want to shoulder the burden of ownership either. When the Depression hit, ranching and mining interests called out for federal dollars; Hoover gave them free-market advice instead. Support for Franklin D. Roosevelt and his programs was overwhelming in the West, particularly in Nevada, which supported programs that primarily benefited state interests. Pat McCarran, one of the most powerful senators from Nevada, was one of the few Democratic senators to buck many of FDR's programs that would provide fiscal supports for national interests, yet worked tirelessly to assure the flow of federal dollars into Nevada (Elliot, 1987: 301-4). McCarran also used the power of the appropriations purse to accomplish what he could not do in open debate on the Senate floor (Cawley, 1993: 210).

When the Taylor Grazing Act was passed, advisory boards made up of stockmen associations set fees that the federal government was to collect and enforce. Nevada was the only state to challenge the act, despite the fact that the fees were considerably less than those charged by either private landholders or the state (Cawley, 1993: 76). Phillip Foss's interpretation of the Nevada challenge was that they did not want to throw out the federal government entirely because the federal government was useful in keeping out the competition and nomads. They did, however, want to secure the lowest possible access fees while enjoying some measure of federal protection (Cawley, 1993: 77) McCarran was successful in bringing the BLM, the federal agency charged with managing the range, into the tow of the stockmen (Cawley, 1993: 78). Despite their cries of being bullied by an uncaring federal government, Nevada grazers "demonstrated a consistent ability to use the political system to their best advantage" (Cawley, 1993: 80).

The Sagebrush Rebellion of the early 1980s was in many ways merely a continuation of past tactics and relationships. What had changed over time was the growth in influence and popular support of the environmental movement, coupled with an increasing number of urban recreationalists intent on using their share of the land resources pie. The economic and environmental abuses of years of accommodation to business and resource interests had come home to roost. The American people had taken a new look at their environment and had demanded change. Many simply wanted better management of public lands, while others asked for preservation and long-term protection. The Reagan years brought a calm to the Sagebrush fires as the president accommodated many of their demands without any wholesale changes to the policy process (Cawley, 1993: 222; Nelson, 1995: 177, 178). The Bush administration backed away from some of the more controversial policies of Reagan, rekindling the Sagebrush ire. It was, however, the Clinton administration with its endorsements from the Sierra Club, among other major environmental groups, that inspired a full-fledged rebirth of the Sagebrush Rebellion, now sometimes known as the Wise-Use Movement (WUM), coupled with a burgeoning Property Rights Movement that is fighting government regulation as a taking under the Fifth Amendment. These groups trade databases and mailing lists, but their missions are not exactly the same. The Sagebrush Rebels of the West realize that most of the lands presently owned by the government would be too expensive for state management, and they would be vulnerable to sale to the private sector, conceivably closing off access permanently. More than anything, they are pressing for more control over the policy process--a return to the political control they had held before the 1960s--rather than outright ownership. The Property Rights Movement has its largest base in the South and East, where regulations regarding sensitive lands and endangered species are running headlong into development interests.

What is disturbing about the tenor of these neo-Sagebrush Rebels and their Fifth Amendment friends is the violent rhetoric that is more and more followed by violent acts against environmentalists and federal employees. Although reports of violence come from all over the country, Nevada has seen more than its share. During 1994 and 1995, a BLM office in Reno and a Forest Service office in Carson City, Nevada were bombed. The summer of 1995 also saw the vehicle of a Forest Ranger blown up outside of the ranger's home in the early morning hours.

As mentioned earlier, it is amazing how much has not changed in the past 150 years. At the time of its statehood, Nevada was a state that had little besides its mineral wealth to offer, and a great pile of debt to be cleared; the debt which was incurred as a territory came about while trying to claim the mineral wealth with that the state is naturally endowed (Elliot, 1987: 73). Public domain was, from the very beginning, land that no one had claimed at the time of statehood (Elliot, 1987: 84). The range did not receive enough rainfall or inflows from rivers to support ranches with clearly demarcated property lines. Instead, the rugged terrain of Nevada could just barely support the cattle and sheep within its borders if they were constantly moved from one basin to another. The nature of the land precluded the kind of pastoral cattle farms of the East, and the grazers fought as much among themselves as with the government over access to prime grazing areas. The range wars of the 1800s were fought with guns, not by means of politics nor by the word of law. Eventually, the grazers themselves realized that federal management would be better than living by gun and by sabotage. The latest round of antifederalist movements has exposed how little our state institutions have changed during this long period. We are still fighting the same battles with the same crude weapons.

THE SAGEBRUSH REBELLION OF THE 1980s

Nevadans, for all their lack of legal ownership of the majority of their state, had for a long time wielded tremendous power in the halls of Congress and within the agencies sent to manage them (Nelson, 1995: 169; Graf, 1990; Cawley, 1993). In fact, activities in Nevada went virtually unnoticed except for its two cities of Reno and Las Vegas, world-renowned for quick divorces, quicker marriages, and gambling. As the policy landscape changed dramatically in the 1960s, more and more attention was paid to the workings of quiet dusty counties such as Nye just north of bustling Las Vegas (Cawley, 1993: 98). With this new-found attention came new battle lines and the developments that manifested themselves in the

Sagebrush Rebellion and its successors.

The 1960s witnessed a sea of change on the national political scene, which had ramifications throughout every level of government. Foremost among these changes was the area of environmental protection, which became a major issue to people of all walks of life. Despite analytical warnings to the contrary, the salience of environmental concerns has survived for a generation (Downs, 1972). Dying lakes, burning rivers, and smog thicker than molasses galvanized public opinion around taking greater care of the environment--and not just for health reasons. The growing urban middle class had discovered its national parks, and along the way discovered that areas they thought to be pristine, natural settings were, in fact, active sites of extractive and consumptive commercial use by the mining, timber, and grazing industries. This new political awareness and urgency brought forth the passage of another round of major legislation. The Wilderness Act (1964), the Endangered Species Act (1973), and the National Environmental Planning Act (NEPA, 1970)--with its mandate to study the impacts of human activities on the natural environment in the form of Environmental Impact Statements (EISs)-- ushered in a whole new set of federal acronyms and agencies, bringing with them a whole new set of operating and managerial demands. These laws had effects throughout the whole country, but they had a particular impact on the West.

Although many writers cite a different incident as the spark that ignited Nevada's Sagebrush Rebellion in the late 1970s and early 1980s, all seem to agree that Nevada was the center of resistance to the new policy changes on the federal and local levels. Nancie Marzulla cites the 1964 moratorium on claiming desert land for farming as "the turning point in the history of U.S. land policy" (Marzulla, 1995: 3). Marzulla asserts that the moratorium sparked the Sagebrush Rebellion in Nevada. As evidence, Marzulla cites pressure from then Nevada Attorney General Robert List as the reason then-Secretary of the Interior Cecil Andrus recalled the moratorium in 1978. William L. Graf writes, "As in previous incidents, Nevada was in a position of leadership. Throughout the early 1970s, the Nevada Legislature's Select Committee on Public Lands explored the possibilities of transferring federal lands into state ownership. This activity was the result of complaints by ranchers with grazing permits who claimed that their financial security was threatened by the changing administrative climate" (Graf, 1990: 225). An excerpt from the Press Release regarding the findings of Nevada's Select Committee commented on the state of federal to Western states relations as, "Both a general attitude and a specific set of actions. The general attitude reflects the feeling that federal policies affecting the West, are made in ignorance of conditions and concerns in the West, that those policies are made for a so-called national constituency without regard for Western problems, and that this 'colonial' treatment is going to get worse" (Quoted in Cawley, 1993: 96). The Sagebrush Rebels wrapped themselves in the clothes of the beleaguered patriot. They rallied around issues of "states rights" and demanded control over their own economic destinies. Such rhetoric carried weight because in part it was a manipulation of national sympathies for a local (and as far as profit was considered, private) cause, and partly because it reflected the genuine loss of power that the ranchers were experiencing.

Grazers had enjoyed such control over the BLM, the agency charged with overseeing the management of public rangelands, that many accused the agency of having been "captured" by the grazers. Under the provisions of the Taylor Grazing Act, crafted by Nevada's Pat McCarran, local grazing districts were created and members of advisory boards were chosen from those districts. As shrewd as this arrangement was, it was also born of some very practical considerations: the grazers were familiar with the rangelands, lands about which very little information was known. By the 1970s this arrangement was being challenged more and more by outsiders, and by newcomers to the state finding new homes in the urban areas of Nevada.

In 1972, the Federal Advisory Committee Act attempted to answer the growing criticisms of advisory boards to the federal agencies. By 1976, the regulatory structure that had been dominated by stockmen for stockmen until the 1960s had been completely overhauled and realigned with the passage of the Federal Land Policy and Management Act (FLPMA). As a result, livestock interest's percentage of representation on advisory boards diminished to 12 percent by 1980 as compared to the 100 percent membership in 1940 (Cawley, 1993).

In the period from 1960 to 1978, Nevada lost 17 percent of its grazing access to the public range due to combinations of laws and policies of various governmental agencies (Cawley, 1993: 136). Ranchers, especially in Nevada, rely almost entirely on BLM land and feel any reduction is a threat to their way of life. This reliance goes beyond range feed for their cattle; grazers have long been allowed to use their grazing permits as collateral. Since they owe debts against the lands that they graze, they feel entitled to all the same rights as a mortgage holder. Of course, this is the result of short-term planning on the part of the various financial and political institutions that allowed public land to be mortgaged by private individuals in the first place.

Environmental groups challenged grazers and their practices on public lands by focusing their attack on the various agencies with oversight on public lands in the courts. The environmentalists were able to put tremendous pressure on the BLM through the courts, suggesting that the BLM and other agencies were not following the mandates legislated under NEPA and demanded greater accountability and access to BLM policies and practices. Environmental groups relied extensively on agency reports regarding practices on public lands, such as the BLM's "Effects of Livestock Grazing on Wildlife, Watershed, Recreation and Other Resource Values in Nevada," a 1977 General Accounting Office report entitled, *The Public Rangelands Continue to Deteriorate* that pointed to the abuses of public lands under the care of the BLM with the central use of those lands being grazed, and a 1980 BLM study concluded that grazing allotments should be reduced substantially (Cawley, 1993).

To understand the depth of the change in federal land policy, it is necessary to take a closer look at FLPMA. FLPMA arose out of a challenge to BLM management of public rangelands mounted by the Natural Resources Defense Council (NRDC), an influential environmental group that relies heavily on the courts to seek redress for environmental damages or practices. In their landmark case, *NRDC v. Morton*, NRDC showed that the BLM was not following the EIS mandates in order to determine the impact of grazing on public lands and "alerted Congress to the deplorable condition of BLM lands and to the failure of the Taylor Act, leading directly to passage of the Federal Land Policy and Management Act of 1976" (Plater, 1992: 690). Besides shedding light on the activities of grazers, FLPMA sought to formally recognize the interests of other users of public lands by calling for a "multiple use, sustained yield" standard of management (Plater, 1992: 686). While the act "also protects grazing permittees to a limited extent on the whole, however, FLPMA represents a condemnation of past stewardship and requires that the BLM utilize a broader approach to public rangeland management" (Plater, 1992: 690).

Another aspect of FLPMA, the Wilderness Review, also stood to reduce grazing allotments. But most important to the grazers, the act mandated that federal managers "must try to accommodate all resource uses to the extent possible, giving priority to none-at least on the broad scale-and consideration to all" (Plater, 1992: 694). Equal treatment and management is difficult at best; and the act, while detrimental to the former position of grazers, still contained contradictions that hampered its overall policy goals. Sustainable yield mandates requiring managers to work toward maintaining *perpetual, high level* annual resource outputs of *all* renewable resources" are qualified by the "impairment" standard (Plater, 1992: 193, 194, emphasis in original). The impairment standard accounts for the health of the resource inputs such as soil, water, and ground cover. No permanent damage to these inputs is supposed to occur under federal management. However, maintaining high-level yields for grazers can and does conflict with high level yields for other resource uses and users. Here again is an example of policies and institutions that try to support conflicting goals and practices without any real success.

Environmentalists were not, however, the only outsiders challenging the grazers on public lands. Ranchers had been drawing fire from federal agencies before the environmental movement asserted itself. Fiscal problems with the arrangement of ranchers and the BLM up to the 1960s began to attract more and more attention. The Office of Management and Budget (OMB) pushed hardest for economic efficiency regarding the rangelands by demanding that higher grazing fees be charged that were more in keeping with market values. Accordingly, "a major study of Western livestock grazing was conducted in the mid-1960s" (Nelson, 1995: 95). A Forest Service study in 1972 also concluded that "livestock grazing was economically unwarranted in many areas in the Western United States" (Nelson, 1995: 96). The recommendations to concentrate efforts only in economically viable areas would have led to a 49 percent reduction in the total area grazed by the year 2000 (Nelson, 1995: 96). Naturally, attempts to dramatically raise fees or to drastically reduce the range allotments was met with indignation, suspicion, and protest.

Despite the dictates of laws such as FLPMA and the increasing oversight of the OMB, cattlemen remained a determined and wily political force. The arguments and the tactics the Sagebrush Rebels have employed display a certain political savvy despite their claims to average-citizen-standing as well as a certain cynical manipulation of an admittedly complex system. They have developed an intriguing argument around the Equal Footing doctrine, suggesting that "the federal government must 'return' the [public] lands to the various states, because when the states were admitted to the union all of the area within their borders should have been state-owned, as in the thirteen original colonies. This legal argument had as a flaw the fact that the federal government had obtained the Western lands through purchase or by international conflict. Western states carved from these federal lands had not been previously owned by the states" (Graf, 1990: 228). The Enabling Act that brought Nevada into the union required it to cede to the federal government all unappropriated lands. The Nevada Sagebrush Rebels have challenged that statehood act from its earliest days.

The Equal Footing argument relies on the appearance that because of the overwhelming federal ownership of land in Nevada, the state is severely limited in its economic activities as compared to Eastern states that contain no federal lands. Given that the federal government controls more than three-quarters of the state's land, this argument carries a certain superficial appeal. Nye County, however, one of the most rambunctious sites of Sagebrush Rebellion, is larger than Rhode Island and Vermont combined. Add to that the fact that the West is currently experiencing vibrant economic growth while the East is stumbling toward stability and is losing population after a lengthy economic depression. If we are to take the Equal Footing argument as posed by the Sagebrush Rebels seriously, then each state can claim some kind of inherent disadvantage to some other or others and seek redress through the courts in the form of undoing the terms of its statehood.

Some of the key politicians from Nevada on the local and national level who were fighting during the 1980s for state transfer or control of public lands were Representative James Santini, who sponsored the Western Lands Act in the House, coordinated with legislation in the Senate initiated by Utah's Orrin Hatch to transfer public lands into state hands; Dean Rhoads, the state senator from rural Nevada who sponsored the first Sagebrush Rebellion bill that was copied by other state legislatures in the West; and Paul Laxalt, who served as an influential member of the Reagan administration. Laxalt used his position to urge the president to openly support and recognize Sagebrush concerns. Although these efforts did not culminate in the actual transfer of public lands into the hands of the Western states, credence and prominence were accorded to their cause on a national level (Cawley, 1993: 222, 223).

This recognition and partial return of political power calmed the Sagebrush Rebels throughout much of the 1980s. Also, Cawley cites the nonfuel mineral "crisis" of the late 1970s and early 1980s as having a parallel impact on public land policy that was helpful to the Sagebrush cause. Although the issues involved in mineral policy did not directly correspond to those of the Sagebrush Rebels, Cawley points out that "the very fact that the mineral situation can be expressed as a crisis adds support to those who seek greater access to the public lands" (Cawley, 1993: 156). So whether the Rebels were successful or not, access to public lands remained a central part of public land policy. However, the Bush and Clinton administrations' policies, as well as the continually changing dynamics between urban and rural resource uses, caused the Sagebrush Rebels to circle the wagons once more in the 1990s in the face of a threat of a further reduction in their political position.

THE NEO-SAGEBRUSH REBELLION OF THE 1990s

If the Sagebrush Rebellion of the 1980s exposed the tensions and conflicts between the Western states and the federal government, the rebellion of the 1990s exposed the growing tensions between urban and rural resource development, between extractive and consumptive resource users, and between individuals and the larger community. In the 1990s the Neo-Sagebrush Rebels and the wise-use movement (WUM) charged into the battle over government regulation in general and environmental regulation in particular. While these groups are largely funded by resource-based industries that have a financial stake in weakening environmental regulations, they often point to their grassroots support.

It would, however, be naive to deny that these groups hold some value to the citizens of rural, resource-dependent communities. Cattlemen who once enjoyed a tremendous amount of political influence over the policy decisions that would directly affect their lives increasingly feel isolated and marginalized. The rural communities that had once depended on resource-based industries that paid livable wages are seeing those jobs disappear only to be replaced by menial and low-paying service sector jobs for the tourism sector and recreation industries (Ring, 1995: 8-12; Elliot, 1995: 24-28). In the Elliot *Newsweek* article, the Old and New West are described as at odds with one another over jobs and the uses of scarce resources. The Old West offers public land use and decent paying jobs; the New West offers vacationers, recreationists, and escaped Californians along with menial service jobs.

The new battlelines in the Sagebrush Rebellion of the 1990s are drawn along Fifth Amendment "takings" lawsuits and calls for county control that carry along with them an even more individualized conception of proper land management practices. The State of Nevada is no longer a sympathetic partner in the Rebel fights against federal regulation. The state increasingly realizes what the transfer of public lands would mean to its budget. While the state may be capable of managing public lands currently in the federal domain, the costs would be at least the same, and in some areas possibly higher (Gardner, 1995). In addition, Nevada must increasingly cater to its urban centers and provide them with scarce resources for further population growth and recreation areas.

In Nevada, it may be argued that federal state relations have come full circle. In the past, Nevada attorneys general had initiated some of the Sagebrush shots heard "round the country." But in 1991, when rancher Wayne Hage launched his suit against the Forest Service, claiming that restriction of his grazing allotment constituted a "taking" under the Fifth Amendment, Nevada Attorney General Frankie Sue Del Papa took the side of the federal government and environmental groups such as the National Wildlife Federation. For her efforts, Del Papa was soundly attacked by ranchers and by Sagebrush original, Dean Rhoads. Del Papa defended her position by stating that she was asked to take up the case by the Nevada Department of Wildlife. She countered charges that she was representing special interests by asserting, "It's my responsibility to represent the entire state of Nevada, not just special interests. The Nevada Department of Wildlife shares the Forest Service's concern that a ruling in favor of a permittee who has abused lands would pressure federal agencies to acquiesce to special interests on multiple-use land" (Christensen, 1992: 5).

This incident is not the end of conflict between the state's Attorney General's Office and local ranchers. Nye County is suing the federal government for control of public lands. Nye's officials are following in the path blazed by those in Catron County, New Mexico, which is considered the home of the County Supremacy movement. County Commissioner and rancher, Dick Carver, who walks around with a copy of the U.S. Constitution in his pocket, is claiming that the federal government has no legal title to the public lands it manages and regulates. The federal government responded by suing the county in 1995, after county officials passed resolutions claiming the right to manage 10 million acres of federal land within county borders (Bates, 1995a: B3). The state was asked by the federal government to join in the suit. Not long after the state was invited to join in the action, Nye County District Attorney Robert Beckett charged that "Nevada's inclusion would raise several new factual issues regarding claims on unappropriated lands and that the federal government was trying to moot Nye County's assertions" (Bates, 1995a: B12). The Sagebrush State becomes more fractious as time passes and conflicts over resources and land mount.

The legacy of the 1980s Rebellion still has congressmen touting the benefits of state control, if not outright ownership of public lands. Some Western governors are backing proposed legislation sponsored by James Hansen of Utah in the House of Representatives and Craig Thomas of Wyoming in the Senate that would turn over BLM land to the states (Knickerbocker, 1995: 8). "Elected officials at the state and local level can be held directly accountable for the effect of their decisions," says Arizona Governor Fife Symington (R), while "no such direct accountability exists for federal land managers" (Knickerbocker, 1995:8). By contrast, Nevada's governor, Bob Miller, is very critical of proposals to turn over management of public lands to the state. Miller's press secretary, Richard Urey, voiced concerns that transfer of lands would have fiscal impacts that are enormous and would take into account services such as reforestation, fire management, erosion and many more, commenting that "the federal government has borne those costs. To shift those responsibilities to the state casts a shadow of mounting costs on state taxpayers" (Associated Press, 1995). Urey cited figures from a recent BLM report noting that the agency had paid "$73.6 million in direct transfers and services compare[d] with $39.1 million in revenues from BLM-managed lands in Nevada in 1994" (Associated Press, 1995).

While Wayne Hage is lionized by the property rights movement in the East and the wise-use movement in the West because of his "takings" suit against the federal government and its burdensome regulations, ranchers are not above using those same regulations to protect their resources against the encroachment of urban areas. In 1989, the Las Vegas Valley Water District filed for permits on water rights in four northern counties. The outcry against the "water grab" was quick and fierce. Ranchers gathered to protest the district's action, blazing the slogan: Remember Owens Valley! Besides protest and high rhetoric, the ranchers joined forces with environmentalists in forcing the district to prepare Environmental Impact Statements before going any further with the permits (Pappa, 1990: E1, E5). While somewhat peripheral to this issue, the so-called water grabs point out the urban-rural distinction in Nevada and the nature of regional disputes, which, in part, direct our considerations, especially the degree to which preferences about public lands issues are reflected in the general public based on region of residence (Gerlak and Soden, forthcoming).

PUBLIC OPINION AND THE PUBLIC LANDS DEBATE IN NEVADA

Critical to understanding the issue of public lands in Nevada is the nature of the state's political dynamics and how they are a function of the geography of Nevada. Like other Western states, Nevada has a few urban cores, but geographically remains primarily rural in nature. Characterized as a state of fierce individualists in the literature on political culture (Elazar, 1984), the state has changed from the nation's most rural state at the end of World War II, to the most urban in the late 1990s. The public's views have taken on new dimensions as the state continues to grow at an unprecedented rate; newcomers are demanding higher levels of services from government and are expressing expectations for public goods and services that are new to Nevada politics. To understand these dynamics in relationship to the current debate about public lands and natural resources, public opinion data is used to assess the general public's positions. Using survey data collected in the fall of 1995, public opinions are considered across the three regions of Nevada that define the state's *de facto* political units.

Because of its size, Nevada is fragmented into three large regions, equal in size to many Eastern states. The urban north includes the Reno-Sparks and Carson City areas and serves as the core for the northern half of the state. The urban south is made up of Clark County, home to Las Vegas, and is the nation's fastest growing community. Outside of these areas are the rural counties of Nevada, that include the largest land areas but a population that pales in comparison to the urban areas. Politically, the northern and southern parts of Nevada have been at odds for decades, with Reno historically dictating to Las Vegas well into the second half of this century. The dramatic growth in the Las Vegas area has shifted the balance of power southward, but on most issues there remains a north-south split. Added to this are the rural areas that are politically weak and dependent on the natural resources in their areas for their economic and political livelihoods. Because of these well-documented differences (Soden and Herzik, forthcoming), a thorough analysis of the public's stance on public issues must likewise consider the tri-regional character of the state.

THE STUDY

The results reported here are based on a telephone survey of 1,213 Nevada residents conducted in the fall of 1995 by researchers at the University of Nevada campuses at Reno and Las Vegas. To assure representation of each of the three political regions and comparability across the regions, approximately equal numbers of surveys were completed in the urban north (389), the urban south (399), and the rural region (425).

FINDINGS

In the conflictual atmosphere attendant to the public lands debate in Nevada, it is first necessary to obtain an overview of the general public's contemporary preferences by recalling the previous discussion of how the current situation developed. Table 9.1 reports public attitudes on a statewide basis for four policy options for public lands management-options with their roots in the political discussions that have occurred over the past decade and before. When asked if Nevada should have ownership of all lands within the state now owned by the federal government, nearly one-half (49.6%) either strongly agreed or agreed with this policy option. About one-third (32.3%) either disagreed or strongly disagreed with this policy. In light of the momentum of the wise-use and property rights movement in the state and the expansive growth of the two major urban areas into previously federally controlled lands, these findings would seem to reflect the general mood of the state's politics. When queried about whether the state should have the right to veto uses of federal lands in the state, three quarters of Nevadans (75.2%) either agreed or strongly agreed with the policy option. In light of the great concern about the federal role in Nevada associated with defense-related activities both in southern and northern parts of the state, with grazing and mining practices, and the controversy attendant to the proposed high-level nuclear waste repository at Yucca Mountain, 100 miles north of Las Vegas, or the historical uses of the Nevada Weapons Test Site, Nevadans responded strongly to their concerns that they have little to say about how federal lands are utilized despite the impact these uses have on them.

Much of the current debate centers around whether federal control over natural resources and public lands best represents the broad range of public interests in the nation. When asked whether federal control over lands protects the environment, Nevadans shared mixed perspectives with one-third (33.8%) agreeing or strongly agreeing with federal stewardship. In comparison, less than 40 percent (39.3%) disagreed or strongly disagreed with the view that federal control provides protection of the environment. One-quarter of the respondents were neutral on this issue, suggesting a basis for the considerable controversy associated with federal lands. Such controversy may well lie within perspectives on environmental

Table 9.1
Public Attitudes Regarding Federal Lands Policy in Nevada: Statewide, 1995

Policy	Strongly Agree	Agree	Neutral	Disagree	Strongly Disagree
		Percent Responding			
State Ownership[a]	14.9	34.7	18.1	27.8	4.5
State Veto of Use[b]	20.9	54.3	12.6	10.6	1.5
Federal Stewardship[c]	3.8	30.0	26.9	34.6	4.7
No Change[d]	2.3	23.7	23.9	42.0	8.2

a. The question read: "Nevada should have ownership of all lands within the state now owned by the federal government. Please tell me whether you strongly agree, agree, neither agree nor disagree, disagree, or strongly disagree."
b. The question read: "Nevada should have a veto over the uses of federal lands within the state. Please tell me whether you strongly agree, agree, neither agree nor disagree, disagree, or strongly disagree."
c. The question read: "Federal control over lands protects environmental interests. Please tell me whether you strongly agree, agree, neither agree nor disagree, disagree, or strongly disagree."
d. The question read: "There is no need to change the ownership of land between state and federal government in Nevada. Please tell me whether you strongly agree, agree, neither agree nor disagree, disagree, or strongly disagree."

protection as much as state's rights and federal control. It also suggests that a considerable swing group exists among the general public that could--through its support or lack thereof--turn the tide of public opinion about public lands issues.

The status quo was also proposed as an option, although over one-half (50.2%) of respondents record disagreement with a policy of no change in the current ownership arrangements between the federal government and the state. Overall, these data suggest considerable room for political maneuvering by both proponents and opponents of federal land control. Further analysis is, however, required to see if the framework of political regions within the state helps explain in greater depth the current controversy, especially if the rural commitment to the Sagebrush and wise-use movements is as strong as suggested in the extant literature.

Moving beyond the views held on a statewide basis, Table 9.2 provides a perspective on the four policy options based on region of residence. When we look at the four policy options by the state's subregions, we see both concurrence and divergence. The respondents from the southern urban area of Clark County concur with rural residents that state ownership of federal lands is a preferred option (47.6% and 57.9% for southern urban and rural, respectively), while residents in northern urban Nevada are inclined to be less supportive of a change in ownership as evidenced by 10 percent less in agreement with this option from that region and disagreement over 40 percent (44.5%). The continuance of growth in southern Nevada requires transferring federal lands to private ownership, that-in conjunction with the broad-based support of the wise-use movement in rural Nevada, as documented in the earlier sections of this chapter-lends itself to an anti-federal point of view. When taken together, these findings are consistent. The findings in northern Nevada are, however, interesting. First, they may reflect trends more supportive of a government role that do not exist in the urban south or the rural areas of the state. This argument appears supported by the data on federal protection of the environment, where we see residents from northern urban areas showing stronger agreement with a federal protection role (42.7%) than their rural and southern urban counterparts (32% and 27.1%, respectively).

Rural residents seem most adverse to federal protection, perhaps because they are the ones who see it on a daily basis, or in light of current trends reflecting a cynicism about the federal government's ability to manage resources. While it appears that there is little day-to-day resentment in rural areas with federal control according to some elected officials, there is a general public discontent with Washington and management of rangelands and the like from afar.

Support for change in public lands policy is, not surprisingly, broadest in the rural areas as evidenced by nearly 60 percent (58.6%) reporting disagreement with a policy of no change in the current lands ownership structure. In addition, these rural opinions receive support from both urban regions where well over 40 percent likewise disagree with a status-quo/no change policy (47.6% and 43.6% for northern urban and southern urban, respectively).

Concern for public lands among the state's residents is multifaceted in origin. In both the northern and southern parts of the state, broad concerns have arisen over water needs, especially proposed transfers from rural areas to urban centers. At another level, military presence throughout the state, ranging from bombing ranges, the famous "Top Gun" school's relocation to Nevada, the Test Facility at Tonopah, and the famed and secretive Area 51, has served as an economic impetus from one perspective, but a restriction of access to the public lands of the state from another. Added to this, the congressional decision to only consider Nevada as a site for a proposed high-level nuclear waste repository has raised the ire of the state's citizenry, reflected in the renaming of the legislation as the "Screw Nevada" bill, while the end of the Cold War has left the state's residents in a quandary about what to do with the Nevada Weapons Test Site, that served as the nation's nuclear weaponry laboratory for 40 years (See for an overview, Soden and Herzik, forthcoming).

With a history recording low levels of input by citizens of the state into many federal land use decisions, it is not surprising that there is broad concurrence across all three regions for a state right to veto federal uses of lands. Over two thirds

(66.2%) find agreement with this policy in the southern urban area, nearly three-quarters in the northern urban area, and over 85 percent in the rural region.

Table 9.2
Public Attitudes Regarding Federal Lands Policy in Nevada: Region, 1995

Policy Region	Strongly Agree	Agree	Neutral	Disagree	Strongly Disagree
State Ownership*					
Northern Urban	8.7	33.9	12.9	38.3	6.2
Southern Urban	17.8	29.8	26.1	22.3	4.0
Rural	17.9	40.0	15.5	23.3	3.4
State Veto of Use*					
Northern Urban	11.8	60.7	8.2	16.2	3.1
Southern Urban	19.3	46.9	24.6	8.3	1.0
Rural	30.8	55.5	5.4	7.8	0.5
Federal Stewardship*					
Northern Urban	6.7	36.0	22.6	31.4	3.3
Southern Urban	2.8	24.3	36.8	32.1	4.0
Rural	2.1	29.9	21.4	40.0	6.6
No Change*					
Northern Urban	3.1	29.6	19.8	40.9	6.7
Southern Urban	2.3	23.3	30.8	37.6	6.0
Rural	1.6	18.6	21.2	47.1	11.5

* Chi-Square significant at p = .0000

IMPLICATIONS

In light of these results, it would appear that while there is general statewide consensus about public lands policies, there is stronger preferences for less federal control and a change in the status quo in rural areas. From one point of view, this would seem to be the inverse of the past, when rural areas more closely aligned with the federal government to escape state intervention into their affairs. From another, it suggests general discontent with the past and a trend of overall discontent with federal control that exists in a number of regulatory realms and has been reflected in the nation's ballot boxes throughout the 1990s.

In consideration of the range of conflicts that abound over public land issues it is tempting, but difficult, to find easy answers to policy issues. People on both sides of an issue wish to influence policy that has an affect on them. The idea of direct influence exposes the deeply held values of independence. But when faced with pragmatic situations people will reach out to any mechanism that will forward their cause, whether it means attacking federal regulation when it threatens your livelihood or whether it means espousing regulations when they protect you from private or competing public interests that also threaten to destroy your way of life. Thus, if you look on the West and government policy regarding public lands trying to find rational, self-interest at work, you will be disappointed.

Continued competition for scarce resources, chief among them being water, will further complicate any political, economic or ideological analysis of the citizens of Nevada and the West at large. While Dean Rhoads championed the interests of the West against the impositions of the federal government in the 1980s, even he now concedes that the conflicts traditional resource uses are complex and admits the need for oversight. Compare the sentiments in these two statements:

Not only do we have to contend with present management policies that restrict production, we must look ahead apprehensively to wilderness review, grazing environmental impact statements and more rules, regulations, and restrictions. It is these apprehensions and fears of what's coming next that has contributed to a mood and movement in the West that has been called the Sagebrush Rebellion. This movement not only embraces livestock grazing, but mineral and oil exploration and development, recreation, and urban growth as well. Dissatisfaction, anxiety and fears about future policies among all these interests have led to frustrations and resentments of a regional nature that combine into the so-called sagebrush rebellion. (quoted in Cawley, 1981: 250, 251)

That was said at the height of the movement in the early 1980s. Today, Rhoads sees resource use as an issue that can divide traditional resource users rather than solidify them into a vast regional force. This passage comes from a 1994 edition of *High Country News*:

Dean Rhoads, a state senator and rancher from Elko County, says that ranchers and farmers stand to lose big if dewatering [a practice used by large-scale mining operations to remove enough water so that the land can be mined] is not carefully regulated. Rhoads says he is alarmed by the rate at that gold mines are buying up agricultural land so that they can dewater the aquifers and "dry up the fields for 40 years." Rhoads worries that water rights bought from ranchers as compensation for dewatering will eventually be sold to metropolitan areas like Reno when the pumps are shut off. (Thompson, 1994: 6)

One thing that should be pointed out is the centrality of water to the economies of the Western states, whether on the local or state level. The West is so arid that water must be brought to cities and towns, and even to cows and mining operations. Water that is consumed by one purpose cannot serve another. Land policy really becomes subservient to the distribution and politics of water. The competition for this resource brings the tensions within the development and use industries into sharp relief. Even without environmental concerns, battles for water would have become increasingly more common.

Rural discontent aside, the majority of the state's political clout is found in the urban areas. From this perspective, the lack of political clout places rural residents in a position of relative political and economic weakness vis-à-vis their urban counterparts. This view suggests that despite a preferred future of a change in the public lands structure, rural areas are at a loss, because: (1) their participation is ineffective because of a lack of political skills, coherent strategy or broad-based support in urban areas; (2) they become excluded from channels of policy and decision making because of preferences for urban issues and the geography of the state; and, (3) the preponderance of federal activity in the state may simply overwhelm proponents of a change in the lands ownership structure, or other issues on the political and social agenda will be determined to be more important. In this case, the opportunity costs associated with health care, education and crime-- consistently the most salient political issues--when compared to the opportunity costs of the public lands debate, will yield a calculus that pushes the lands issue to one side.

It is noteworthy that when faced with the prospect of condos over cows, many ranchers are forming alliances with environmental groups to keep their land. The Nature Conservancy is the chief group promoting such alliances. In Nevada, the Nature Conservancy has helped to keep small family ranches from foreclosure and improved the stewardship of the land in the process (DeVereaux, 1995: 6; Nature Conservancy Newsletter, 1994: 4). These kinds of alliances are a far cry from the environmentalist versus rancher bumper sticker battle of: "Cattle-free in 93!" versus "Cows Galore in 94!," or the T-shirt slogan, W.R.A.N.G.L.E.R.S., Western Ranchers Against No Good Liberal Environmental Radical Shitheads. While cattle may not belong home on the range in a perfect world, such a world does not exist. These and other small projects between environmental groups and those people dependent on resource-based livelihoods may prove to find reasonable solutions to the conflicting interests and goals attached to public lands.

CONCLUSIONS

Like many Western states dealing with change brought about by an influx of population and a change in the political structure, Nevada is facing a crisis in its public lands management. On the most severe side of the equation, it may well be that violence will escalate about the uses of, rights associated with, and management practices employed on public lands. At the other extreme, there may be little change as the current stampede against federal control lessens in time and the opportunity costs of the range of public policy issues is determined. Change is, however, occurring. The traditional forces that set the agenda for public lands management for the twentieth century are in a state of flux. The iron triangle of federal land management agencies, powerful Western congressmen, and a powerful natural resource user group of ranchers, agriculture interests, and mining, is facing a challenge to their control. States rights is a powerful issue that cannot be dismissed when ownership of lands is overwhelmingly in the hands of federal landlords. And massive urban growth in population places a new set of users in proximity to federal lands they feel they have the right of access to for recreation and other purposes often at odds with ranching and mining. Western members of Congress are also discovering that the monopoly they once enjoyed in making decisions about Western federal lands issues is gone as a new generation on the hill looks at Western lands management with fiscal austerity in mind and/or a concern for the integrity of the natural resources. Added to this, a new clientele has emerged in the last three decades as environmental interest groups have increased their stature with the public (Soden, 1995b) which increasingly demands and receives input into the decision-making process.

This study finds that the public lands issue in Nevada is both similar to and distinct from that found in other states. Issues of population growth are overwhelmingly changing the political parameters of Nevada. Regional differences exist that are quite distinct and suggestive of a high potential for conflict. Yet the set of issues facing a state under dramatic growth may, in the end, lead to a reduction in the drama attendant to the public lands debate. While the political geometry of the state is indeed changing, a rational process at both state and federal levels, including new forces from all spectrums of environmental interests, will most likely see incremental change with only a few new actors. James Hulse (forthcoming), one of the state's most noted historians, sets forth some basic facts that suggest less radical change than many expect. First, despite the push for state control, Nevada would remain the state with the smallest percentage of its lands in private control, still lop-sided on the gaming and tourist sector for tax revenue, and unlikely able to afford managing the vast lands currently in the federal domain. Second, Nevada has relatively scant natural assets to support public lands. Mining is limited to a few areas, grazing restricted by the aridity of the state, and agriculture very restricted. Third, Nevada's history is as a petitioner for federal patronage, ranging from the Newlands project in the early part of the century, Hoover Dam, to later federal military largess. Despite special interests predominant in some rural areas of the state that have repeatedly tried to mount a Sagebrush Rebellion, logic and law pronounce them improbable in the long run.

What then, we might ask, can lead to a change? Population growth will continue to cast a shadow over the public lands debate as urban areas such as Las Vegas must trade for federal land or cease expansion. Coupled with this are urban recreationists who see the adjacent lands of the Great Basin as their playground rather than the domain of ranchers and miners. Accordingly, by their sheer numbers they will force changes and seek policies consistent with a more informed environmental protection perspective. Lastly, political change will follow in the wake of this growth, as new residents demand *more, not less* from government and take political matters out of the reigns of the traditional individualistic oriented Nevada and place it into a political milieu that will reflect traditions of other Western states that have already experienced their booms, such as Arizona, California and the states of the Pacific Northwest.

Part III: Case Studies

Chapter 10

The Siouxon Valley in the Gifford Pinchot National Forest

Richard Hansis

As the human population has grown and urbanized, values have changed over time; one consequence of value changes has been that the competition for influence over the disposition of public forest lands has heated up. Controversies over general forest issues as well as arguments as to the best uses for specific places have been fueled by people with diverse timber, special forest product, amenity, and land ethic interests. People with these often conflicting interests are increasingly involved in challenging forest managers because of increased uses for forests and because of laws mandating public participation in natural resource policy processes (Stankey and Clark, 1991). Although multiple use has been the longstanding mandate for National Forest management, in practice timber production was the chief objective of governmental management. Now, as other than utilitarian values come to the fore, managers need to be able to know whether they have included the full range of values expressed regarding forests when they make public policy decisions. Values, that is, "conceptions of the desirable" (Kluckhohn and Strodtbeck, 1961), as a key part of culture, are "contested, temporal, and emergent" (Clifford, 1988: 19). Societal meaning toward places, then, will unfold as the different interests try to make their views known and gain acceptance as the legitimate way of managing resources. One such place is the Siouxon (pronounced soo-son) Valley in the southwestern portion of the Gifford Pinchot National Forest.

The forest, located in southwest Washington, has been one of the top two timber-producing national forests in the country. In 1988, under the impetus of a timber production driven USDA Forest Service, the harvest reached 514 million board feet (mbf) (Hirt, 1994); however, production dropped rapidly to where its harvest level under the current Northwest Forest Plan is projected to be 71 mbf in 1997. In addition to being a top timber producer, the Gifford Pinchot has been designated an urban national forest: that is, a federal forest located within 50 miles of a metropolitan area of one million or more residents. This designation reflects the presumption that the Gifford Pinchot is likely to have a heavy impact from visitors who want to engage in outdoor recreation and that more demands for access will be made than resources would be available to accomodate. Different from most other urban natural forests, especially those of southern California, the Gifford Pinchot is *both* a major producer of timber and a heavily used recreation area.

The Siouxon, one of the few remaining nearly pristine lowland valleys located near the greater Portland, Oregon metropolitan region, has become a site for conflict between people with commodity and noncommodity values, as well as a site for differences among recreationists. Hiking, mountain biking, and horseback riding in the valley's roadless area of 12,000 acres is accessed by a paved road to a trailhead a quarter of a mile from the stream. Clear, cold water dropping over several waterfalls in an area that had not been logged since large fires burned in the early part of the century serves as a powerful lure to recreationists. A paved road from which large clearcuts can be seen going almost all the way to the banks of another creek serves as a gateway.

By 1990, the Forest Service began to proclaim the "New Perspectives" program within which the "New Forestry" would be practiced on public lands. Jerry Franklin, closely associated with the development of the ideas of the New Forestry, received a grant to study the valley and recommend forest management practices. At approximately the same time, Region 6 (comprising Washington, Oregon, and Idaho) of the USDA Forest Service suggested that an "Integrated Resource Analysis" be done before planning any specific projects in a given area. In spite of these initiatives, the sense of Forest Service personnel involved in the project was that timber production was still the goal of the agency and the heart of the Forest Plan for the Gifford Pinchot National Forest. In 1989, before dramatic reductions in harvests occurred, three timber sales were planned for the Siouxon Valley. These mixed messages led to a drawn-out process of decisions being made and then rescinded. It was decided to carry out an integrated Environmental Impact Statement, not specific to any project but rather to the whole valley. An integrated EIS, though, is not the same thing as an Integrated Resource Analysis, which is an assessment of existing conditions rather than a presentation of a set of alternatives and their associated impacts. Five scoping meetings with the public were held in various sites between November 1990 and February 1991. In May of 1991, the possibility of studying Siouxon Creek as a potential Wild and Scenic River was raised as an issue once more; this time an analysis of "seen areas" for visual impacts indicated that timber harvests would be curtailed. The issue of doing an Integrated Resource Analysis also was raised again several months later. To carry this out, the Interdisciplinary Team of Forest Service employees assigned to the Siouxon needed its efforts supplemented by outside expertise in the assessment of social values toward the Siouxon Valley in order to do a complete Integrated Resource Analysis. The following case study reports the results from that research and provides an interpretation of them. Soon after the study was completed, the Northwest Forest Plan was issued. The Siouxon Valley was included in the Late-Successional Reserve area, meaning that only limited silvicultural practices that enhance late successional (old growth) characteristics can be practiced.

METHODS

Interviews: Before survey research was carried out, interviews using a draft questionnaire were conducted with participants in the Siouxon valley planning process. These interviews were used both to gain a more in-depth reflection of the views of interested parties and to test the meaningfulness of the questionnaire. Even in this group, some people had thought deeply about many of the issues that the questionnaire raised while others had not given them much thought. The latter part of this statement holds even more strongly for the general public. The strength of the in-depth interview is that it allows for more nuances in understanding to be communicated; in addition, it facilitates more careful thinking about issues. Care was taken to avoid the problem of strategic bias, a manner of answering that the respondent or interviewee would use to influence policy outcomes, which usually is done by the purposeful overstating of views. The depth allowed by interviewing is gained at the expense of high cost or loss of breadth; consequently, survey research was also carried out as part of the study.

Survey Research: Survey questionnaires were sent to random samples of the public in the Greater Portland area, the Greater Vancouver area, and the rural counties contiguous to the Gifford Pinchot National Forest. In addition, visitors to the Siouxon Valley and participants in the Siouxon Valley planning process were surveyed. All surveys were conducted during September and October 1992. Survey design and implementation followed Dillman (1978). For each sample a mail questionnaire was sent to prospective respondents with subsequent reminders (up to three) for those who did not return the survey. Response rates for all samples reached over 67 percent.

Respondents were first asked some general questions concerning federal forest lands, defined as lands owned by the public and managed by the federal government (Bureau of Land Management and the USDA Forest Service) for multiple uses. Their responses paralleled those reported by Steel, List, and Shindler (1993) in their national survey of forestry issues.

ORIENTATIONS TOWARD ROADLESS AREAS

The future disposition of roadless areas on national forests remains a focus of conflict among natural resource interest groups, even in places such as the Gifford Pinchot where the wilderness designation issue has been largely resolved. Among the nonwilderness roadless areas on the Gifford Pinchot National Forest is the Siouxon Creek watershed, which remains unroaded except along the upper ridges.

Respondents were asked to agree or disagree with eight statements about the disposition of roadless areas. They were given the following definition ROADLESS AREAS are areas of Federal Forest which contain at least 5,000 acres without any roads. They are similar to wilderness areas, except that wilderness areas are set aside by Congress as places where road-building, timber harvest, and other developments cannot take place. Roadless areas may be opened up to a much wider range of forest activities."

The rural sample was most likely to support development of roadless areas, while forest plan participants and recreation visitors were least likely to do so. However, there was widespread support even among the rural sample for relatively low levels of development in roadless areas. A majority of all four groups agreed that some roadless areas should be preserved as reservoirs of future old growth. Participants also supported preserving them as future wilderness--a view that was supported by slightly more than half of the overall sample, but was rejected by the rural subsample. Some of the visitors and participants felt that wilderness designation would be the only way that the Siouxon could be protected from the whims or pressures to which Forest Service decision makers are subject. Only an act of Congress could then open the area for timber production.

Others of this group felt that designation as a research natural area is the most appropriate manner for this area to be protected. Some people who do not generally support turning all roadless areas into wilderness areas want the Siouxon to be so designated because of the uniqueness of the area. For them, the context of the Siouxon, one of the few relatively undisturbed, accessible lowland forests left in the southern portion of the Gifford Pinchot, makes it unique. This not-in-my-backyard (NIMBY) response is common to many places where people have memories of attractive landscapes and family/friend outings. Not only did people express opposition to changing a place they have become attached to over the years, but they also projected their feelings to their children and grandchildren; they want to know that this specific place will still be here for them to enjoy.

There was little evidence of support for high levels of timber cutting in the survey results. A large majority of all four samples disagreed with a statement that roadless areas should be managed primarily for timber, and a smaller majority of all four samples agreed that timber harvesting would adversely affect the character of such areas. Some visitors and planning participants felt that by managing primarily for timber, the Forest Service would be perpetuating its past practices of turning the public domain into quasi-private land not being managed for uses other than tree harvesting. None of the groups agreed with the idea that timber harvesting is acceptable if it is done without being visible or without building roads. Each sample agreed that helicopter logging would be preferable to conventional ground-based logging. Some visitors and planning participants felt that invisible logging, whether in the Siouxon or along roads (but hidden by a strip of trees), is deceitful. If logging is to take place, they do not want it hidden. Others, although generally against logging in roadless areas, are reacting to their past experience with large clearcuts: they would likely find selective thinning and harvesting acceptable (Hansis, 1995).

It seems clear that forest resource development other than timber harvest may be more acceptable to citizens; respondents tended to disagree with a statement that campground development adjacent to a roadless area would adversely affect its character. Most visitors and planning participants interviewed, though, were very concerned about the size and type of development of areas in the Siouxon.

ORIENTATIONS TOWARD WILD AND SCENIC RIVERS

While Congress passed "omnibus" (statewide) wilderness legislation for Washington State in 1984, no omnibus wild river preservation bill has yet been enacted. Consequently, the fate of eligible rivers on the Gifford Pinchot has yet to be decided. It is possible that several Gifford Pinchot streams (including Siouxon Creek) will be proposed for protection under the Wild and Scenic Rivers Act. Because of this, managers need to know a good deal more about the preferences of forest users and the public regarding the preservation and management of wild rivers.

As in the previous section, opinions were measured by asking survey respondents to agree or disagree with eight specific statements. Respondents were told that "Congress passed the National Wild and Scenic Rivers Act to balance river development with river protection," and were asked to respond based on the following definitions:

WILD rivers are entirely free-flowing and essentially unpolluted. Shorelines are primitive and access is generally limited to trails.

SCENIC rivers are entirely free-flowing and essentially unpolluted. Shorelines are largely primitive and undeveloped, but are accessible in places by roads.

In general, less difference in responses across sample groups occurred than in the previous set of questions. The greatest differences pertained to issues of logging, off-road vehicle use, and visitor use limitations. Although wanting to see the positions they espouse enacted, some visitors and participants saw the necessity of compromising to accommodate the interests of other people. Willingness to recognize the different claims of other people seems a common response among people who are not polarized on public land issues.

There was overwhelming support from all sample groups for a statement that all rivers currently eligible for Wild or Scenic River status should be kept in that condition by law. A majority of all groups agreed that trails for hikers only are desirable within wild and scenic river corridors, while a majority disagreed that trails should also be set aside for use by horse riders or mountain bikers. Some participants and visitors felt that if an area were large enough, separate trails could be established if the numbers of different users were great enough and if illegal use and abuse could be avoided by doing so. Most opposed multiple trails even though they did not personally desire the interaction with other types of trail users. Hikers were especially less desirous of sharing trails with mountain bikers. There was overwhelming disagreement with a statement supporting off-road vehicle use within Wild/Scenic corridors, although there was twice as much agreement among rural respondents as others (18% for rural residents, less than 10% for all other groups).

A slight majority of all groups except rural Washington residents supported the concept of limits on visitor numbers for Wild/Scenic rivers, even though visitors/participants saw that possibility as a last resort because they would hate to see the Siouxon become so popular that limits would be needed. A majority of all groups disagreed with statements that it is OK to hear, or to see at a distance, logging activity from within a Wild/Scenic corridor. Washington residents (rural and urban/suburban) were more willing than activists or urban Oregonians to accept evidence of logging within wild/scenic corridors. Some visitors/participants who were interviewed suggested that it would depend upon the distance away, the type, and the days of the week.

SIOUXON VALLEY MANAGEMENT PREFERENCES

This section outlines public sentiment concerning the future management of the Siouxon Valley Drainage in the Gifford Pinchot National Forest. For those respondents who had heard of the area, 27.1 percent of the Portland area sample, 49.5 percent of the Vancouver area sample, and 46.2 percent of the rural Washington sample had visited Siouxon Valley. This information is important in that it provides baseline information on public exposure to the site and thus knowledge of its features.

Survey respondents were provided with five different management options, ranging from road construction and timber harvesting to keeping the area roadless and managing primarily for primitive outdoor recreation (see Table 10.1). Opinion regarding future management of Siouxon Valley is diverse and differs considerably across the area's geography. Over 60 percent of Portland area respondents and 57.8 percent of visitors and planning participants would like to see Siouxon Valley "kept unroaded and managed primarily for primitive forms of outdoor recreation." For the Vancouver area and the rural Washington samples, there appears to be little consensus for any of the management options provided. However, 42.4 percent of the rural Washington sample favor management for multiple use, including both timber harvest and road construction.

One management option that appears to have wide support among the Portland area, Vancouver area, and visitors/planning participants is managing the Siouxon Valley primarily for outdoor recreation. When combining the first three management options, all but the rural Washington sample have strong majorities of people wanting management for recreation.

The supplemental management preferences for the Siouxon Valley were obtained from the visitors/participants sample described previously. Opinions on management preferences were solicited by asking respondents not only to agree or disagree with management options, but also to respond to the desirability of contingencies associated with agreement, or in some cases, disagreement. Four management alternatives and relevant contingencies were addressed.

Table 10.1
Management Preferences for the Siouxon Valley Drainage

Question: Which statement BEST matches your opinion about the appropriate future management of Siouxon Valley?

Percentage Selecting

Siouxon Valley should be kept unroaded and only minimally managed to maintain its current condition.	Portland	10.9
	Vancouver	15.8
	Rural Wash.	4.0
	Visit-Participant	18.3
Siouxon Valley should be kept unroaded and managed primarily for primitive forms of outdoor recreation.	Portland	60.9
	Vancouver	26.3
	Rural Wash.	15.2
	Visit-Participant	57.8
Siouxon Valley should be managed primarily for outdoor recreation, including development of facilities and roads where needed.	Portland	10.9
	Vancouver	13.6
	Rural Wash.	21.2
	Visit-Participant	6.7
Siouxon Valley should be managed for multiple uses including timber harvest, but logging should occur only if it can be done without roads.	Portland	2.2
	Vancouver	16.7
	Rural Wash.	17.2
	Visit-Participant	8.9
Siouxon Valley should be managed for multiple uses including timber harvest, and roads may be built if necessary to meet management goals.	Portland	15.2
	Vancouver	27.6
	Rural Wash.	42.4
	Visit-Participant	8.3

SUPPLEMENTAL MANAGEMENT PREFERENCES FOR SIOUXON VALLEY VISITORS AND PARTICIPANTS

The data presented in Table 10.2 provide information about the desirability of developed campsites with water and toilet facilities adjacent to the parking lot at the end of the paved access road. It also includes a contingency for the "yes" response: the number of campsites preferred. A slight majority of the visitors would not support the development of campsites, while a majority of the participants would support this management option. The contingency question on the number of developed campsites preferred also suggests that the greatest plurality of visitors prefer the most restrictive alternative (1, 5 campsites) while the greatest plurality of participants prefer the somewhat less restrictive alternative (6, 10 campsites).

Table 10.2
Orientation Toward Additional Campsites in Siouxon Valley

Question: Currently, there are no developed campsites with water and toilet facilities adjacent to the parking lot at the end of the paved access road. Would you be willing to support the development of campsites?

	Visitors	Participants
YES	43.8%	64.5%
NO	56.3%	35.5%

If "yes" above, what is the number of campsites you prefer to see developed?

	Visitors	Participants
1, 5 Campsites	41.7%	29.4%
6, 10 Campsites	34.5%	35.3%
11, 20 Campsites	22.6%	24.7%
21, 50 Campsites	1.2%	10.6%

The data presented in Table 10.3 provide information about the desirability of Scenic River designation of Siouxon Creek, with the current access road and trails left in place and with timber harvest restrictions within a corridor one-quarter mile on either side of Siouxon Creek. A strong majority of both visitors and participants supported this option.

A contingency question was designed to provide information about the effects of visitor density on decisions to visit the area. Planning participants and visitors were asked to choose the number of encounters with groups of one or more people that would cause them to avoid visitation. The largest plurality of both visitors and participants indicated they would be disinclined to visit the area if the number of encounters was in the 11, 25 groups range.

Some interviewed participants and visitors did not feel that restrictions on visitation would be appropriate, except in extreme circumstances. Even though the number of encounters might exceed what would be desirable, they would only accept restrictions as a last resort. "I would hate to see it come to that" was a common observation. The accessibility of this area and the consequent possibility of "spur of the moment" visits led people to disfavor restrictions even though their own enjoyment might be diminished.

Table 10.3
Support for Scenic River Designation of Siouxon Creek

Question: One of the alternatives for the Siouxon Creek area is for designation of the Creek as a Scenic River. The 5701 access road and existing trails would be allowed. However, timber harvesting within a corridor one-quarter (1/4) mile on either side of Siouxon Creek would be precluded. Would you support the designation of Siouxon Creek as a "Scenic River?"

	Visitors	Participants
YES	78.9%	75.0%
NO	21.1%	25.0%

This designation would not place limits on the number of people utilizing the area. What is the number of encounters with groups of one or more people on a visit that would cause you not to visit?

	Visitors	Participants
1, 5 Groups	3.8%	8.8%
6, 10 Groups	23.1%	27.2%
11, 25 Groups	37.1%	39.7%
26, 50 Groups	30.1%	15.4%
51, 100 Groups	5.9%	8.8%

Table 10.4 contains contingency responses to a Wild River designation of Siouxon Creek. The description of this alternative in the survey was the same as the description of the Scenic River, with the modification that this designation may require the closure of the paved access road of approximately three miles into the area. Therefore, the question for respondents was their willingness to employ nonmotorized means of access to the trails adjacent to Siouxon Creek. A large majority of visitors, and an even larger majority of planning participants, indicated a willingness to employ nonmotorized means of access. A contingency question for the "yes" respondents was to inquire about the number of round-trip miles they would be willing to walk/hike to gain access. The response to this question is best interpreted as a wish by "yes" respondents for the most desirable walk/hike distance. The largest plurality of visitors preferred a two-mile round-trip access. A simple majority of the respondents preferred the one and one half-mile, two-mile, or three-mile options. The results obtained from the participants were somewhat bimodal, with the greatest plurality choosing seven miles. However, an even greater plurality chose the one half-mile, two-mile, or three-mile options. Those who chose the one and one half and two mile distances seem to be engaging in wishful thinking inasmuch as the road that would have to be closed is three miles long.

Also contained in Table 10.4 are results from a contingency-like question addressed to the "no" respondents. For the visitor sample the most frequent response was to agree that they were not willing to spend the time required to gain access. The second most frequent reason for giving a "no" response by visitors was to agree that this option was not restrictive enough of timber harvesting. For the planning participants' sample, the most frequent response was to agree that this option was not restrictive enough for timber harvesting, while another group of respondents rejected the option because it was too restrictive of timber harvesting.

Closure of the access road accompanying Wild River designation elicited mixed reactions by visitors and planning participants alike. Some who support Wild River designation would not support closure of the road because of their desire to make Siouxon Creek accessible to people who do not have the physical capabilities of hiking to the creek. Others suggested that the access road would allow a larger constituency to see the area, and by so doing, support strict protection of the forest. Strategic thinking of this type reveals a sophisticated trading off of a desire to see roads closed to protect the area versus the need to mobilize people to influence the direction of Forest Service policy.

To provide information about the visitors and planning participants' preferences for a Wilderness Area designation of Siouxon Creek, they were asked to agree or disagree with two alternative management plans requiring congressional approval and the elimination of timber harvesting in an area which may or may not coincide with the roadless area of approximately 12,600 acres of Siouxon Valley. The first alternative asked for approval or disapproval if current access is maintained. Large majorities of both visitors and participants endorsed this alternative. The second alternative asked for approval or disapproval of Wilderness Area designation if this also required the closure of the access road that gets people three miles closer to the most attractive areas of Siouxon Creek. A diminished majority of visitors and

Table 10.4
Support for Wild River Designation of Siouxon Creek

Question: Another alternative for the Siouxon Creek area is to designate it as a Wild River. This designation would preserve trails, but may require the closure of the 5701 paved access road of approximately three (3) miles into the area of Siouxon Creek. Timber harvesting within a corridor one-quarter (1/4) mile on either side of Siouxon Creek would be precluded. Would you be willing to employ non-motorized means of access to the trails adjacent to Siouxon Creek?

	Visitors	Participants
YES	68.4%	83.8%
NO	31.6%	16.2%

If "yes" above, what is the number of round-trip miles you would be willing to walk/hike to gain access to Siouxon Creek?

	Visitors	Participants
½ Mile	7.6%	3.6%
1 Mile	9.2%	7.1%
1 and ½ Miles	10.7%	8.0%
2 Miles	23.7%	11.6%
3 Miles	16.0%	17.0%
4 Miles	7.6%	14.3%
5 Miles	7.6%	8.0%
6 Miles	4.6%	5.4%
7 Miles	13.0%	25.0%

If "no" above, why not? (Circle all that apply)

	Visitors	Participants
Not willing to spend time to gain access.	50.9%	3.6%
Not physically able to gain access.	7.3%	14.3%
Not restrictive enough of timber harvesting.	30.9%	53.6%
Too restrictive of timber harvesting.	1.8%	21.4%
Multiple reasons suggested.	9.1%	7.1%

participants endorsed this more restrictive alternative. A mistrust of what some visitors and participants feel is the arbitrary and changeable nature of U.S. Forest Service decisions was evident in interviews on this issue. Thus, congressional designation of the area as wilderness was seen, even by a former Forest Service manager, as a way to make sure that their special place was protected.

CONCLUSION

This chapter, a revised version of a study originally undertaken to apprise forest managers of values toward a specific place, demonstrates the complexity of natural resource values. It is not enough to know place of residence (rural/urban) to determine the positions that people will take on general natural resource issues. It is also not enough to know whether or not people have a direct relationship to forest-based employment. We can, however, see some trends from socioeconomic information collected in the survey. But, answering general questions to resource-based issues cannot always predict how people will react to a specific place that they know well and to which they have strong attachments. Any hope of using Rokeach's (1973) method to establish peoples' value priorities in order to determine how they may react to specific proposals in known places must be strongly tempered by an understanding of the context in which these value priorities operate. It is important to know that the Siouxon Valley is one of the last little-logged lowland valleys in the Portland-Vancouver metropolitan area, and that many people from diverse backgrounds have had a long love affair with it.

The "culture wars" over natural resources based on differences in whether a person believes that resources are to be used for the material good (utilitarians) or that nature has intrinsic value sometimes seem to be portrayed as a rural-urban split. Although some truth resides in these portrayals, partial truths may conceal more than they reveal because diversity is found in both rural and urban populations (Brandenburg and Carroll, 1993). Complexity, value contradictions, and change characterize individuals as well as people grouped by interests, class, and place of residence. Although portions of rural and urban populations could be expected to react similarly whatever and wherever natural resource issues occur, large numbers of people will make their decisions based on values and context.

Chapter 11

Citizen Values and Participation in the Tongass National Forest Debate

Bruce Shindler

As natural resource agencies attempt to implement ecosystem-based management on federal forests, gaining public acceptance of forest practices has become a central issue. In response, agencies have developed specific processes to obtain public feedback on proposed management activities. These efforts, however, are most frequently used to gain public acceptance of a single action or project plan. Although outcomes may allow the agency to proceed with its proposed activity, they usually do little in the way of helping managers understand the public's motivations or preferences for managing the larger forest ecosystem.

A recent planning process on Alaska's Tongass National Forest-to reduce clearcutting practices in favor of alternative (partial) harvesting techniques-provided an opportunity to go beyond simple assessments of public preferences for one treatment over another. Initially, the Forest Service was interested in the social acceptability of various silvicultural treatments in terms of their visual quality. Researchers from Oregon State University approached the visual acceptability issue on the Tongass as one element in the broad range of forest values that may have a contextual relationship to other elements. Findings from qualitative research provided a rich body of information that went well beyond visual quality preferences.

MANAGEMENT ISSUES

Increasing public concern over management of national forest lands has resulted in confusion, conflict, and great pressure for change. Consequently, resource professionals face increasing pressure to implement management strategies that deviate from traditional forestry practices (Brunson, 1993). It is not clear which specific changes will be found acceptable, but shifting public attitudes strongly suggest management that adopts a more holistic, ecosystem-based approach is preferred over standard commodity-based policies (e.g., Shindler, List, and Steel, 1993; Dunlap, 1992). Recognition that change is necessary has led the Forest Service to undertake a new management directive.

Introduced as "new perspectives" and later changed to "ecosystem management," this new direction is meant to shift the focus from timber production to the sustainability of forest ecosystems; in doing so, management policies will address concerns about biodiversity, long-term site productivity, and social consequences (Stankey and Clark, 1992). Thus, ecosystem management encompasses a collection of planning strategies and silvicultural methods. When applied systematically at varying spatial and temporal scales, the techniques can imitate patterns of natural disturbance more closely than traditional high-yield forestry (Brunson and Shelby, 1992). Salwasser (1990) described the methods as an attempt to develop a scientifically sound and socially acceptable forestry of the future.

Until recently, however, little attention had been given to the acceptability variables involving alternative harvest practices. If opposition to clear-cuts is based on visual aesthetics, then alternative practices that reduce the visual impact should be more accepted by the public. But as Brunson (1993) has pointed out, since we do not know exactly what opposition (or support) is based on, a new practice may be no better in the mind-and eyes-of the public than the practice of clearcutting. Most likely, it is overly simplistic to suggest that controversies in forest management can be adequately addressed by adjusting silvicultural techniques to improve visual quality. Social acceptability concept is pervasive nature and questions will need to do more than ask people which landscape scene they like best. Public acceptance of management activities most probably will be influenced by beliefs about ecological processes, aesthetic values, agency motives, and perceived feasibility of achieving some desired future condition (Forest Ecosystem Management Assessment Team, 1993).

APPROACHING THE ACCEPTABILITY ISSUE

Southeast Alaska provides an interesting mix of publics. The area is well entrenched in timber extraction activities, but is also a prime commercial fishery and more recently has experienced a boom in nature-based tourism. Native American tribes have a substantial presence, and a number of environmental groups have also gained a foothold in the last decade. Largely a region comprised of islands, self-reliance and a sense of community permeate social conditions in the region. Many residents depend on natural resources, in one form or another, for their livelihood. As might be expected, a certain distrust exists for values brought in by interlopers from the "lower 48."

Implementing ecosystem management on the Tongass National Forest meant translating public values and incorporating these views into supportable policies. In addition to examining alternative harvest practices, which served as the guiding premise, the study evolved to allow more in-depth assessment of public attitudes. We sought to (1) understand how people feel about alternative harvesting within the range of forest management options, including factors that influence their judgments, and (2) identify underlying concerns that may be related to the acceptability of ecosystem management practices.

To tap the local perspective, focus group and individual interviews were conducted with a cross-section of interest groups and the general public during the summer of 1994. Sessions included use of questioning techniques and photographs of alternative harvest units (½ acre patch cuts, early commercial thins, two-story stands, and single tree retention sites). No ranking of photos was done, instead they were used generally as a means to facilitate and stimulate discussion. Questions included citizens' expectations for management, judgments of practices including clearcutting and alternative harvesting, and related concerns over a move to ecosystem management. Travel distance, time, and resources limited research to the greater Stikine area (Petersburg, Kake, Kupreanof, and Ketchikan), but the nature of the findings suggests some generalizability to a larger region may be reasonable.

PUBLIC PERSPECTIVES SUMMARY

As with other recent research (Wondolleck and Yaffee, 1994; Brunson, 1993), findings from the Tongass indicate that the social acceptability of alternative harvest practices (or any ecosystem management practice) is related more to a group of factors than to any single reason. For example, people are more likely to find a practice acceptable if they:

* Can visualize how it will look

* Understand its effects on sustaining the natural characteristics of the surrounding forest

* Feel the practice will benefit the local community

* Believe in the information they have received from agency sources

* Are given an opportunity to have a meaningful role in the planning process.

As anticipated, some difference of opinion existed among groups on the polar ends, but a good deal of general agreement was also apparent. Perceptions and concerns are summarized in the following six categories.

VISUAL QUALITY IS IMPORTANT

Scenic quality was a significant factor in almost everyone's judgment, and within this context alternative harvest practices are preferable to the present practice of clear-cutting. Generally, preferences were for practices that leave more trees, no slash on the ground, and do not depend on logging camps or storage facilities. Similarly, more road building for increased access to harvest sites will be problematic; according to the public, sufficient roads already exist on federal lands. Small disturbances like patch cuts or individual tree selection that maintain scenic quality are likely to be more acceptable.

It is not likely that alternative treatments will be acceptable everywhere, however. "Special views" from homesites or other important scenic areas were a primary concern, and any proposed harvest will require the active involvement of affected stakeholders. These NIMBY responses reflect an important first reaction in public judgments about the acceptability of any resource practice (Paehlke and Torgensen, 1990). Attempts to change the characteristics of special places will have to account for these initial, and often emotional, responses among the affected parties. Although the public may be receptive to partial harvests instead of clear-cutting, a prudent management approach may be to tread slowly and softly.

DO NOT SHORTCHANGE AMENITY USES

For much of the public, nontimber uses of the forest are as important as, or more important than, harvesting activities. Local citizens identified four such uses that were basic to their daily lives. First, subsistence uses are essential to many people in southeast Alaska as a primary or secondary source of goods. Although hunting and gathering activities are normally associated with the Native American way of life--and still are a major component of tribal livelihoods in this region--other local residents also depend on the forest for food or fuelwood. As a long-term practice, none of the public wanted subsistence use relegated to a lesser status to accommodate more harvesting of any kind.

Second, all participants generally expected that their recreation opportunities-access to trails, jeep roads, recreational cabins, and natural areas-would be maintained as alternative harvests were planned. Typically, harvests that occur near recreation sites are "bad" (Martinson and Baas, 1992), and it will be important to consider how well these traditional uses are protected (or enhanced) by partial harvesting.

Third was a concern closely associated with recreational use. Tourism is becoming an important activity and residents had strong expectations that their essential natural resources would be maintained. Most acknowledged that the main travel corridors seem to be well protected, but were worried about other lesser known hunting, fishing, and kayaking sites being subject to alteration. Certainly, the ability to engage in tourism activities is important to visitors from other parts of the country, but local sentiment is also based on concerns for economic opportunities as timber interests decline.

The importance of protecting native wildlife was the final common theme. Most everyone shared the view that the presence of animals like bald eagles, moose, bear, and salmon were important to enjoying life in Alaska. As elsewhere, opinions about the harvest levels necessary to sustain sufficient wildlife habitat broke down across commodity/preservation lines. However, the majority would oppose any planned harvests until questions of protecting species habitat had been addressed.

UNCERTAINTY ABOUT ECOSYSTEM MANAGEMENT

The uncertainties of ecosystem management, particularly spatial and temporal issues, seem central to public acceptance of new practices. People were often reticent to express their feelings about alternative harvesting (and other Ecosystem Management [EM] practices) simply because they did not have a great deal of experience on which to judge it. Others were concerned with how this particular brand of new management would be implemented. Numerous questions remain about the effects of partial harvests on forest composition, wildlife, healthy watersheds, and traditional public uses. The acceptability of new management practices will be closely associated with how the public perceives the risks involved.

Perceptions of risk often involve the extent to which consequences of an action are localized (Fischoff, Lichtenstein, Slovic, Derby, and Keeney, 1981). When communities consist largely of forest users, local outcomes merely up the ante for controlling risk factors. Forest managers will need to demonstrate sound stand selection processes and dispel perceptions of highgrading that seem to accompany partial harvest techniques. The size of harvest units needed for alternative treatments is likely to be another contentious issue. Loggers wanted no reduction in timber volume overall, while most others wanted no increase in the land base required for harvesting. The general perception seems to be that small will be better, as long as it is cost effective.

Findings suggest that experimentation with alternative methods might be supported, particularly if the local public understands the rationale, research questions, and potential outcomes of the proposed practice. As knowledge of conditions and consequences increases, we have seen that public evaluations can change (Stankey, 1993). For example, studies of forest users have shown that increased awareness about the role of fire in forest ecosystems is associated with support for policies that introduce fire into forest landscapes (McCool and Stankey, 1986). Questions about the effects of partial harvests on wildlife, fish habitat, and healthy watersheds are important-even among those with no apparent ties to forestry issues-and will need to be addressed.

SUSTAINABLE HARVESTS THAT ARE COST EFFECTIVE

Naturally extreme opinions exist on either end of the spectrum, but timber production on the Tongass has generally been viewed as a traditional and legitimate use of forest land. More recent reactions have added concerns over long-term sustainability of ecosystems, about wholesale shipments of logs out of the region (particularly to Japan), and for revenues that contribute more to the local economy. Fears exist about irreversible depletion of forest resources, and that it will be done with little benefit to local communities.

As elsewhere in the Pacific Northwest (Shindler et al., 1993), it is apparent that the public's preferred option for the Tongass is the middle ground of managing for multiple objectives. The perception persists, however, that the Forest Service is still managing for timber first and foremost, frequently at the expense of other resources. For example, many citizens were concerned that agency budgets for nontimber programs (e.g. recreation and wildlife management) may be sacrificed to pay the costs associated with alternative harvesting.

The public will have to be shown that the multiple objectives philosophy of ecosystem management has actually been adopted by the Forest Service. Although few were able to define sustainability themselves, citizens felt it was important for the agency to demonstrate that sustainability can be achieved. The public's willingness to accept the compromises inherent in ecosystem management may depend on their perception of whether these practices can be fairly implemented and can work on behalf of local citizens. In other words, using alternative practices to continue harvesting in southeast Alaska may be endorsed only to the extent they do not come at the expense of other forest values or the local economy.

COMMUNITY-ORIENTED MANAGEMENT

How local communities view the sincerity of agency actions is likely to be a determining factor in ecosystem management's overall success. The Tongass staff was regularly commended for its educational outreach like school programs and interpretive activities as positive links with the community. Even individual staff members, acting as ordinary citizens in volunteer roles, generated dividends for the agency. These informal contacts, particularly in small communities, are an important source of information and influence. People are more likely to regard their friends, relatives, or neighbors as credible sources of information (as opposed to government employees assuming official roles). On the Tongass, citizens recognized that these informal contacts could provide a basis for improved cooperation on broader, more substantive issues.

In many cases, however, southeast Alaskans were the most critical of the Forest Service's formal communication efforts and public involvement activities. Reflecting a now common concern shared by publics in other locations, low marks were generally given for meetings where the public was invited to speak up on planning issues. Typical complaints included a failure to present options appealing to a range of views, lack of concern for citizens' points of view, and nonattendance by high level administrative staff. In addition, the agency was often seen as preoccupied with technical analyses. Citizens cited a reliance on extensive and complex computer data, the production of numerous maps and GIS overlays that are difficult for the public to assimilate, and the seemingly impersonal and calculated manner in which the agency collects citizen input. Instead, the public expects a community-oriented approach that respects the opinions of local residents.

Legitimization of the public participation process appears essential. Tongass residents have coined the phrase "the illusion of public input" to describe the extent of their involvement. The most emotional responses came from those who felt they were given little opportunity to be heard or that their comments were not taken seriously. From an agency standpoint, most national forests are wrestling with the public involvement issue. In the rush to "do public involvement," many have neglected to address the important question about defining the agency's relationship with the public and just what role it is willing to let the public play. Recognizing this omission, an interest group member from the Pacific Northwest recently stated his frustration in a letter to the BLM:

The agencies must define the reasons for involving the public in a much more precise manner. I am not interested in attending a never ending series of meetings if they are just supposed to make me feel better because I was involved. . . . I have spent too much of my life attending public meetings in which a diverse public voiced their views only top have the agencies make the final decision that no one liked. (Mickey, 1993)

Often the public is asked to participate in planning sessions without clarification of the decision points or how those decisions are to be made (Priscoli and Homenuck, 1990). Clarification of roles and agency commitments is particularly important to the front line personnel who are being asked to engage the public. They cannot make these important decisions on their own and the public will not believe them anyway. The definition of roles and responsibilities is a forest-wide (if not agency-wide) action that can empower first-line public contact staff to carry out community-based management.

CREDIBILITY ISSUES

It is reasonable to say that on the Tongass (as in many other locations), the public is disgusted with the politics surrounding the natural resource debate. Many citizens view the current political climate as constraining the Forest Service from taking the leadership role they think the agency should play. Some cited micromanaging of forest lands by far-off federal bureaucrats, others saw large interest groups applying inordinate pressure that bogged down the system. Dunlap (1992) observed that these conditions erode public confidence. Even when the agency is *unable* to provide answers to resource questions--as is often the case in the ambiguous, complex task of managing large ecosystems--it can lead to the perception of an *unwillingness* to do so. As a consequence of such views, we see a distrusting public who is suspicious of institutions and politically driven processes.

Part of the credibility fallout on the Tongass is public perception over the agency's ability to manage. Concerns emerged about Forest Service personnel who were not in touch with the land they were responsible for managing. Reasons cited include (1) agency staff is too busy attending workshops or seminars, (2) the perception of a revolving door at the ranger district level through which employees move on to other jobs, and (3) recent cutbacks that mean staff cannot spend enough time in the field or are placed in jobs for which they have not been adequately trained. Many locals know the forest lands well; they are disturbed when land managers do not share the same knowledge. Additional concerns were reflected in opinions about front-line personnel who seem to simply echo agency-wide policy directives instead of being sensitive to local issues. Even when people had trust in an individual staff member, they did not necessarily trust the agency to allow the individual to do the right thing.

It is no wonder that agency staff feel they are frequently dealing with a contentious public. One reason people or groups are so combative is that they think it is often the only choice they are given (Wondolleck and Yaffee, 1994). It simply is the only way they can engage a confusing and sometimes unfriendly system. If given another avenue, the public would probably welcome a more collaborative, community-based approach.

MANAGEMENT CHALLENGE

There are very few traditional either/or decisions remaining in natural resource management. Asking people to make such simplistic judgments as choosing one scenic view over another involves much more than a visual preference. Socially acceptable ecosystem management of the future will not be single-issue management. From this case study, it is apparent that local citizens view practices like alternative harvesting as involving a range of issues and a complexity of choices.

It seems essential that management decisions be seen as social choices reflecting both scientific dimensions and the values and beliefs of the community (Stankey, 1993). We will need to devise methods to include people in real-life decisions, with the consequences of choices out on the table. Inherently, the outcomes become more durable because of their social acceptability. If we expect ecologically and economically informed judgments about alternative harvest (or any other) practices, we will need to learn how to more properly frame the questions.

Chapter 12

An Oregon Case Study: Families, Gender Roles, and Timber Communities in Transformation

Jennifer Gilden

Timber communities in the Pacific Northwest are experiencing economic fluctuations and dramatic cultural, technological, and ecological changes. The last decade has proven particularly difficult for forest-products workers and their families. Government regulations, increased mechanization, fluctuating market forces, and negative public opinion have created an atmosphere in which many residents of timber towns feel apprehensive and uncertain about the future of their communities, their families, and themselves.

The nature of timber harvesting and production makes it a predominantly male enterprise in which the roles of men and women have been clearly defined and embodied in a system of symbols and stereotypes. Interviews and ethnohistorical data suggest that women's roles have undergone subtle changes throughout the development of the industry. In the logging camps of the late 1800s and early 1900s, women were helpmates who labored alongside their husbands, performing domestic work for the benefit of the community--cooking, cleaning, organizing, and providing a "civilizing" influence (Churchill, 1965; Fleetwood, 1988). With technological developments in the industry and the home, logging camps gave way to towns that were removed from the immediate supply of timber. Men were able to commute to logging sites and women remained in town, where they were responsible for the domestic sphere. Now, as timber supplies become increasingly scarce, men dedicated to the industry find themselves required to commute long distances and they are sometimes separated from their families for days or weeks. Those without steady forest jobs, in contrast, are often homebound, caring for children while their wives are at work.

Interviews suggest that the traditional sexual division of labor was accepted and encouraged by both men and women, and both have made attempts to maintain it despite economic and cultural change. In the early 1990s, stress resulting from a cutback in harvestable timber challenged the gender roles that had been associated with a more stable industry, and although the economy proved more resilient than residents had feared, important cultural changes have taken place. Women have attempted to diversify within their traditional caretaker roles, taking on a wide variety of wage labor, including political activism, in addition to their domestic work; while those men who are unable or unwilling to leave the timber industry have sought to remain within its cultural parameters.

BACKGROUND

This ethnographic study took place in a valley of Oregon's North Santiam River, known to residents as "the Canyon." It is a strongly timber-oriented community, in the process of adapting to an economic and social crisis that reached its peak in the early 1990s after the *Dwyer* decision, a timber sale injunction aimed at protecting the northern spotted owl. Although opinions and emotions regarding the decision are still strong, they have mellowed with the years and many of residents' worst fears regarding the future have not materialized. In retrospect, some residents consider the period to have been a difficult yet valuable maturing process for Canyon communities.

The research effort included a series of interviews with 28 women, men, and children, combined with fieldwork in Mill City, where I conducted an evaluation of the Mill City/Gates 4-H Youth Development Program in 1994. The study concentrated on families who remain at least partially involved in the industry, either as loggers (including choker setters, buckers, fellers, climbers, and others associated with the removal of trees from the forest) or millworkers. Participant-observation, survey results, casual conversations, documentary research, and reviews of popular and academic literature were also used in the development of these findings. Because research on the timber industry has focused almost exclusively on the masculine perspective (the works of Marchak [1983] and Warren [1992] are exceptions), interviews for this study were conducted primarily with women and girls.

The population of the Canyon is approximately 4,000, and most of the research was conducted in Mill City/Gates, the largest Canyon community, which has a combined population of 2,000. The Canyon runs east to west from the mountains adjacent to the Mt. Jefferson wilderness area to the rolling hills and farmland at the edge of the Willamette Valley. The hills surrounding the Canyon are covered with Douglas fir in all stages of maturity, from old-growth forest to third-growth tree farm; many residents can point to forests that they or their forebears logged. Cougar, bear, elk, deer, and coyotes, as well as smaller wildlife including the northern spotted owl, can be found in the area. Camping, hiking, fishing, and hunting for both food and sport are popular activities for Canyon residents and tourists.

The exploitation of the Canyon's environment--including timber, water, gold, copper, and aesthetic beauty--has been the foundation of its economy since the early years of settlement in the late 1800s. Lumber mills were the primary employers in most Canyon towns, and many mills and towns have been constructed and abandoned through the years. Currently, several locally owned mills are operating, although two have recently "downsized." A recent influx of nontimber families--including retirees, Californians, and "welfare families" attracted by the Canyon's affordable housing--has drawn criticism from long-time residents; however, with the possible exception of Idanha, where timber workers are becoming increasingly scarce, Canyon residents still consider their communities "timber towns." As one logger said, "Everyone in the Canyon has something to do with wood."

Residents have traditionally possessed a strong sense of community, although they feel that this is eroding due to recent economic declines. They celebrate and reinforce their communities' timber orientation by decorating their homes and restaurants with painted saw blades and sepia photographs of loggers standing on the giant stumps of ancient trees that are no longer available to the Canyon's mills. The color yellow is a symbol of support for the timber industry, and the pickups and utility vehicles popular in the Canyon often sport yellow balls decorated with fir trees on their radio antennae. Yellow flags emblazoned with Mill City's logo, which depicts the Santiam River flowing from a round saw blade, hang from telephone poles along the streets, and yellow signs declaring support for the timber industry, or reliance on timber dollars, commonly appear on the walls of businesses and homes. Stewart's grocery store, a Mill City institution, still sells clothing for timber workers--including heavy boots spiked with caulks ("corks"), striped "hickory" shirts, helmets, jeans and flannels--and local businesses are frequented by workers covered with mud and debris collected during a day working in the woods.

In recent years, the community's sense of confidence has been shaken as the timber industry has come under increasing criticism by the general public. From high school girls to retired loggers, residents repeatedly express their belief that they are filling a necessary niche in American society by providing vital forest products. They stress their deep concern about the future of the environment and their conviction that the timber industry can exist along with healthy forests, and they believe they are being unfairly villainized by urbanites and preservationists who understand neither their close feeling of connection to their environment, nor the economics, operations, or values of the timber industry.

Perhaps because of its name, Mill City drew considerable media coverage during the spotted owl debate, and residents frequently complain of negative and inaccurate press and television reporting. They express frustration that their once-valued vocation is now derided by the media and by the very people who use the forest products they provide:

It does something to a male's image if they can't support the family. But I mean, this happens to other people in other industries . . . but the one other thing in the timber industry, is that you're a bad person now too. Cause you have destroyed the environment. Or whatever. So not only do you have to work hard, but you have all these people spittin' on you, hollerin' at you, belittling you. (Female retail worker, 7/11/95)

Despite residents' common commitment to the industry, timber harvesting has rarely provided a stable economic base, either in the Canyon or elsewhere. The seasonal nature of the work and its dependence on favorable weather conditions contribute to instability at the individual and family level. Particularly in the early years of the industry, both logging and millwork were extremely dangerous occupations with little job security, low pay, no insurance, and a predominance of single, transient, male workers. Despite the professed efforts of government and industry to ensure stability through a steady supply of timber, timber towns continue to suffer from widespread technological, economic, and cultural changes. The industry is affected by such diverse factors as worldwide demand for timber, price fluctuations, the weather, political decisions, social values, foreign and domestic competition, mechanization of logging and milling, and the varying efficiency of mills. Between 1970 and 1990 the number of sawmills in the Pacific Northwest decreased by 30 percent (Brunelle, 1990); however, lumber production increased as mills became more efficient and less labor-intensive. Although many Canyon residents recognize these causes of economic distress, "preservationists," the Forest Service, and the Clinton administration are popular objects of blame. In the early 1990s the crisis was symbolized by the spotted owl and by Opal Creek, a nearby stand of old-growth forest continues to be the focus of heated debate.

COMMUNITY STRESS

Canyon communities are fortunate in having locally owned and operated mills that possess large tracts of timberland and that have weathered economic declines more successfully than mills in other areas. Nevertheless, residents have experienced extreme stress, particularly with the 1989 *Dwyer* decision aimed at the protection of the northern spotted owl. Residents regarded this decision as a direct threat to the future of the timber industry in the Canyon, as well as evidence that they had been forsaken by the government. Partly because of a lack of harvestable timber, many workers were temporarily or permanently laid off. Some families moved away in search of timber work elsewhere, while others chose to leave the industry altogether:

There are more students enrolling, transferring and re-enrolling. There are a lot of split families, single parents . . . this has increased over the years. Since the timber crisis, families haven't stayed as long as they used to . . . plans are always changing. One family . . . moved to . . . where there was more timber work. Now their daughter . . . wants to graduate at Santiam with her friends. Before, people were able to stay here until their kids graduated. (Male high school teacher, 8/31/95)

Opinions regarding environmental issues also caused friction among residents. Not surprisingly, prevailing public opinion was highly antipreservationist, and many residents felt obligated to align themselves behind an extreme and vocal minority. Several informants indicated that public discourse about the timber industry has been dominated by extremists on both sides; as one woman said, "The two radical sides are screaming so loud that you can't hear the people in the middle. And yet we're the ones that are gonna end up being crushed by it."

During this period of uncertainty, many residents questioned the future existence of their communities. In conversations recorded by Seideman (1993) and myself, concerned citizens compared their situation to that of Valsetz, a logging town that was razed by Boise Cascade in 1984 after timber in the area was depleted. Although circumstances in Valsetz were quite different from those in the Canyon, the community's distressing fate serves as a potent symbol of Canyon residents' fears for the future. As one logger's wife said,

My daughter was in tears more than once, afraid that dad was going to lose his job . . . that the school would have to close and we would have to move. . . . It was hard to reassure her that those things weren't going to happen, because we didn't know if they would happen. . . . It was upsetting. I remember feeling depressed and angry; it was pretty hard. (Logger's wife/retail worker, 9/6/95)

In reality, the problems faced by the community are more chronic than the dramatic Valsetz example, and include unemployment, underemployment, increased levels of domestic violence, and broken families. Youth are particularly at risk. A combined lack of activities, jobs, and parental guidance has led to severe problems among many of the Canyon's youth. As a middle-school teacher noted, "Basically, with kids in this town, it's early partying, early sexual experiences, and early motherhood." Other problems include alcohol and drug abuse, child abuse, and gang-related activities. The community's ability to address these problems will depend heavily on both the timber economy and residents' attitudes toward change.

THE STEREOTYPED LOGGER

The culture of the timber industry is colorful and complex, and like many natural-resource occupations, including the milling, mining, and hydropower upon which the economy of the Canyon is partially based, it has a strong male orientation. The popular literature of the logging industry, from folklore about the legendary logger-giant, Paul Bunyan, to Ken Kesey's *Sometimes a Great Notion*, is filled with symbols and images that celebrate the masculinity of the logger. Popular logging literature, particularly before the 1980s, describes the stereotypical logger as being tough, daring, honest, generous, superstitious, and romantic (Andrews, 1968)--"a breed apart" from other men, immune to pain, independent, obsessed with his work, close to nature, honest, and chivalrous toward women and small animals. The timber worker's close connection to his calling is a common theme: "The logger is the victim of a certain obsession, like a fever, and he will never willingly turn his back on his way of life," writes Pierre (1979: 7). Margaret

Elley Felt, the wife of a gyppo logger, writes on the same subject (1963: 17):

Once I did manage to lure him away from the woods, but not for long. Finally yielding to my constant "Why must you work at logging? Why can't you come home every night, like other husbands?" he gave in and went to work in the shipyards .... He worked there for exactly three weeks--and they were the longest three weeks of my life. He was miserable.

This stereotype reflects the American ideal of a laborer who is independent and capable of providing for his family through his own hard work, without the necessity of formal education. Carroll and Lee (1990: 148), in their study of occupational community among timber workers, write that loggers view themselves as "extreme, rugged individualists . . . whose survival and prosperity are based almost exclusively on individual initiative, skill, and hard work." This stereotype is echoed and maintained by timber companies and workers, including those I spoke to in Mill City. It is an ideal toward which modern loggers continue to strive.

The danger inherent in logging is both romanticized and deplored. The mortality rate for logging is over 20 times the national average for all occupations (Fortmann, Kusel, and Fairfax, 1989), and most timber workers can tell vivid stories of crushed and broken bones. Because it is difficult for loggers to get health insurance, these dangers are not taken lightly by timber workers or their families. Nevertheless, economic necessity pressures loggers to continue working despite physical injuries: "They get injuries, but they just tough it out . . . My dad's broken his ankle before and worked with it broken, just cause he didn't have the benefits . . . they just put a special boot on and go to work" (Female high school student, 8/1/95).

The risk associated with logging puts special pressure on the women who remain at home. Women in logging families cope with worry about the safety of their loved ones on a daily basis. "My most major fear is that he'll get hurt," said a logger's wife. "If we fight, I make sure in the morning that I tell him I love him .... I get very scared." An older wife took a different approach: "You can't think about that. You *can't* think about that. Unless you want to torture yourself."

Despite improvements in forest technology, danger continues to be part of the romantic mythology of the timber culture and is celebrated in stories about the "logging life." As one former logger in Mill City said,

Until you've gotten up at 3:30 in the morning, climb out of that crummy just as the sun's bustin' over the top of Mount Jefferson, get your first lungful of really clean air, have a cup of coffee while the gear's warmin' up, go to work, and bust your ass all day long in a job that could kill you anywhere within the next 30 minutes to three hours, and end that day--you don't know what the experience is. It gets in your psyche, it gets in your soul. It's a part of you.

WOMEN'S ROLES

In general, the wives and mothers of timber workers do not share in either the glory or the danger of timber work. Women have traditionally played a supporting role in timber families, and feminine stereotypes are not as clearly defined as those for men. Literature about the timber industry has focused on the danger, humor, and adventure of the logging profession rather than the more mundane work performed by women in logging camps and towns. Women's roles, and their connection to the industry itself, have been defined through their relationships with the men in their families and communities.

Popular literature provides little testimony regarding the actual status of women in lumbering. Nelligan (1929) and Lucia's (1975) stories about early logging camps suggest that women fell into two categories: those the loggers respected and those they did not. Wives, sweethearts, and camp cooks were worthy of respect, while the prostitutes and "floozies" who congregated in cities like Portland were not. In most popular, nostalgic literature about logging these are the only options open to women, although there is evidence that their occupations were quite a bit more diverse. Although they performed different functions, women in early logging camps took part in daily activities, often maintaining the creature comforts that were lacking in the woods. One woman's work in a turn-of-the-century logging camp (Churchill, 1965) included housework, cooking, bearing and raising children, "civilizing" the working men, cleaning and dressing wounds, and setting broken bones, all in primitive conditions. Another woman, working in a camp in the 1940s, performed the traditional "women's work" of cooking, cleaning, and laundry as well as driving and repairing trucks, bookkeeping, payroll, purchasing, and operating heavy equipment (Felt, 1963). One informant noted that although most women in the Canyon's past were housewives and mothers, many were widowed early as a result of logging accidents, and turned to business or farming to earn a livelihood. Boarding house operators, farmers, schoolteachers, elk-skin glove manufacturers, restaurant owners, pharmacists, dry-goods store owners, and even a 1920s photo shop owner are included among the women of the Canyon's past.

Since the 1950s, women's labor in the Canyon has been centered in the home, and much of it has been devoted to ensuring domestic tranquility. Timber culture is strongly patriarchal and although women exercise a certain amount of control over the home, their husbands often have the final authority. Traditionally, men's work has received more attention and respect than women's work, and uncertainty connected to the future of the timber industry has magnified its role in sustaining the family. Primary importance is placed on the husband's ability to function effectively. Early rising is a prominent characteristic of timber work, and when asked what qualities made a good logger's wife, one informant said it was the ability to get up at 4:00 a.m. to make your husband lunch. Wives, and sometimes girlfriends, often rise early to help their partners prepare for the day. In the summer, when the forest fire danger increases, they rise earlier--sometimes at 2:00 a.m. Given timber workers' long hours, this early-morning rising also provides an opportunity for husbands and wives to communicate.

At the end of the day, care must be taken to ease the husband's transition from the woods to the home. Loggers' wives note that because their husbands work long hours in stressful jobs such as choker setting, bucking, or climbing, they come home exhausted and prefer not to be involved in daily domestic details.

[My father and brother were loggers.] I've heard . . . them go, "You know, I can't handle this tonight; don't stress me out; I don't want to get in a fight; all my concentration has to be on my job tomorrow. I can't be tired, I can't be thinking about this problem." Because the job is so dangerous. Either cutting trees or choker setting, driving the truck, you know, your concentration has to be on what you're doing in those mountains. (Female professional worker, 8/10/94)

Male workers' concentration on their occupations, and their subsequent lack of participation in domestic work, does afford women the freedom to make daily household decisions without interference from their husbands. Informants note that in a traditional timber family, a husband turned his paycheck over to his wife, who made the decisions and purchases necessary to keep the household operating smoothly; the husband's authority was invoked only when a serious problem or expensive purchase presented itself. Many traditional families still retain this structure, while in others the wife is given a monthly allowance. As one logger's wife said, "He pays me. I take care of the kids . . . the home part."

The domestic work of timber women is characterized by its diversity. In the early camps, as now, women were "jacks of all trades" who contended with limited economic resources, physical isolation, frequent work accidents, the prolonged absences of their husbands, and constant worries about their husbands' and families' safety. Although the culture emphasizes the stress inherent in logging, informants note that women experience stress as well:

[My mom] does more than my dad does. . . . She does a lot of mentally stressful things, you know, like organizing and planning and calling and going to the store and running here and there and doing everything and cooking dinner and [making] sure Kid One and Kid Two are organized to go here and there at this certain time. . . . She's the one who always gets dumped on. She's the one who doesn't ever get new clothes. (Female 18-year-old, 8/1/95)

Along with traditional "women's work," women also perform duties that are not typically feminine, such as chopping wood, repairing cars and trucks, and using power tools. One informant noted that while women did both "men's" and "women's" work, men only did "men's" work. Women described this performance of men's work with a sense of pride, both in their abilities and the belief that women outside timber communities would not be willing or able to perform this kind of manual labor. As a 16-year-old girl said, "I know how to cook; I can clean; I can sew; I can build things; I can fish; I can hunt . . . you learn everything!"

Women with jobs outside the home often speak of their domestic functions with a touch of nostalgia, noting that economic stress now forces them to work away from their families. Although some high-school-aged women express irritation with mens' expectations regarding these gender roles and are now pursuing college and future careers, many other Canyon women retain their allegiance to tradition. As one woman said, "That's one thing we're really lucky with, is that I don't have to work."

Despite the economic necessity for many women to work outside the home, paid employment opportunities for women in the Canyon are scarce and career-track opportunities are extremely rare. The primarily employers of women in the Canyon include restaurants, motels, grocery stores, gift shops, mill and timber company offices, schools, and the farms and canneries at the west end of the Canyon. As Irland and Gamson ([1974], cited in Humphrey 1990) and Marchak (1983) found in their studies of timber communities, women in the Canyon are confined primarily to the service and low-paid administrative sectors, where they work to supplement household incomes when necessary. This "floating reserve" of labor, as Marchak calls it, functions as a buffer for families experiencing economic stress.

Despite the community's timber orientation, logging and mill work is almost exclusively reserved for men. Although women are often hired for office work at local mills, they are rarely hired to do manual labor, and the mill that is almost universally regarded as the "best" in Mill City--the highest-paying and the most stable--will not hire female laborers ("you don't even ask"). Informants note that women do occasionally work at less physically demanding veneer mills, and lumber mills in other areas of Oregon are also known to hire female laborers. Logging work is non-existent for Canyon women; even if it were available, most of the women I spoke to showed no interest in working in the woods. Their attitudes regarding women's roles are implied in their comments:

[It's] disgusting, dirty, manual labor. Given the hours, and given the work conditions, it's a rare woman who's going to want to do it. It's pretty hard to think of being a young mother, you get on the crummy [van to the worksite] at three o'clock in the morning; and when you come in fourteen hours later, you're awfully tired to be taking care of children. (Female mill office worker, 5/17/95)

I think the physical labor of it is really hard on a woman, plus . . . having to be in the woods all day--it's a little easier for a man to pee in the woods . . . I think it would be really hard for a woman to work in the woods with a bunch of men. (Female high school teacher, 8/31/94)

Just by nature . . . women are more emotional, I think, and more fragile than men. Not always true, but . . . generally. (Female high school student, 8/1/95)

Women's wage labor in the Canyon is closely associated with their family status. At the time of my research, there were no formal childcare facilities available in the Canyon. Jobs at the local schools were particularly desirable for this reason, as they allow women to be near their children and also provide insurance and other benefits. These jobs, along with jobs driving school buses and providing childcare, also fall within the accepted gender roles. For women without immediate childcare needs, the most lucrative jobs exist 30 miles away in Salem's state offices and shopping malls.

One unexpected effect of the timber crisis, given the traditional emphasis on women as domestic workers, has been the movement of women into the public arena (Warren, 1992; interviews). Increasingly, positions in city councils, planning commissions, and community development organizations are being filled by women. At the time of my research, two mayors in the Canyon were women; women comprised the majority of the members on Idanha's sewer committee and planning commission; and women were active in Mill City's economic development committee. Female informants suggest the lack of involvement by men in these areas is due to the fact that they are either too tired, too busy, too demoralized, or simply uninterested in these primarily volunteer positions. In the early 1990s, while men struggled to find or retain their work in the industry, women also became responsible for much of the pro-timber organizing taking place in the Canyon. In response to Earth First! timber sale protests, women and children went into the forest--"out on the line"--to show support for the loggers. These grassroots protests developed into rallies at the state capital, at the timber summit in Portland, and eventually in Washington, D.C. Although men were also active at these rallies, it seems that much of the organizing was accomplished by women, taking advantage of their extensive social networks and teaching themselves the skills to be effective grassroots organizers. Some activists insist that their involvement is due more to family commitment to the industry than a desire to become politically visible; as one woman said, "I either helped [my husband] out for our fight for survival, or we probably would have got a divorce." Even as they discuss their marches in Washington and meetings with senators, however, these women express a desire for the industry, and for families, to return to their traditional states.

Prospects for young people have been dramatically affected by the changing economy of the Canyon. For young, unmarried women who wish to be independent of their families, the lack of opportunities in the timber industry, combined with the distance and the expense of transportation to Salem, leads to a frustratingly limited occupational outlook:

If guys drop out [of high school], they're in the mill; if girls drop out, they're having kids . . . . If you stay in Mill City from the time you graduate, then there's not a lot of hope. I mean, yeah, you can get by and stuff, but generally what's going to happen is you're going to work in the mill. (Female college student, 8/8/94)

This lack of opportunity is encouraging many young women to enter college. As one student said, "I couldn't ever find a job anywhere around here that would support me without an education." Although junior-high and high-school students share many of their parents' values regarding the timber industry, the environment, and gender roles, they do not expect, and are not expected, to follow in the footsteps of their mothers and fathers. Both parents and children express the view that the timber industry is an unreliable source of employment, and there is new impetus for children to complete high school, perform well academically, and go on to college. In the timber families I contacted, parents did not hope for their children to continue in the industry, despite the fact that some of the families had been logging or millworking for several generations.

ADAPTING TO CHANGE

Challenges to the timber economy have upset the traditional division of labor along gender lines. In some cases, women have taken jobs outside the home and unemployed husbands have stayed home to care for the children, a complete role reversal that places stress on all parties. More often, male workers are required to leave home for longer periods of time as they work farther and farther away. They may spend weekdays or even weeks away, living in a mobile home while they work at a site. As one logger's wife described it,

They come home late Friday night, they sleep all day Saturday, because they're so tired, and of course they've gotta go to bed early on Sunday night because they have to wake up-- they've gotta get down there and drive four hours to work. . . . Really, I think you just exist to pay your bills. And the little things like fun in life--you don't have time for it. You don't have the money for it, either. . . . You just kinda communicate through letters, little notes on the counter. No bonding. If you haven't bonded before this, you're outta luck.

The increasingly frequent absence of men leads women to assume new responsibilities in the household, making decisions that previously would have fallen to their husbands. At times this leads to a growing sense of independence among women, causing friction when returning husbands expect to resume the role of primary decision maker in the home. Challenges to the patriarchal orientation of the community are discouraged. One informant noted that men felt threatened by wives who proved themselves capable during their absences, and in the early 1990s an effort to form a women's support group was vetoed by husbands who objected to it.

Some of the ways in which families have adapted to economic and social stress are described above. Some couples have divorced; many have left for logging work in Washington, Alaska, or other states; and others have quit the timber industry altogether, sometimes taking advantage of retraining programs to attend college. For most families in the Canyon, reliance on the social networks and kin relationships that extend throughout the Canyon and into other timber communities has been an important resource. Job seekers and working mothers in need of child care frequently take advantage of the complex web of in-laws, step-families and cousins that make up the community. "We're related to almost everybody in town," said one housewife. Recent in-migrants to the community who lack family ties face a distinct disadvantage, although after a period of time most are accepted into the social web. Those without relations can still benefit from the community's strong emphasis on neighborliness: "One of the nice things about Mill City is everyone knows everyone--they'll do things for each other."

Although the stress and exhaustion caused by underemployment in the early 1990s resulted in increased family violence, alcoholism, and suicide attempts, surviving this difficult period brought many families closer together. Women say that adapting to the crisis has led some husbands to see their wives as more equal and more worthy of respect, and that their marriages have benefited as a result.

Among the timber workers and their wives who remain in the Canyon, there is a sense of having survived a "trial by fire," a "shakedown" that has weeded out all but the most dedicated of timber families.

Among those who remain, women's work inside and outside the home has been an essential adaptive mechanism. Because of the wide range of domestic duties they perform, women in the Canyon are generalists who are capable of working in a wide variety of fields. Many have held several jobs at once while continuing to fulfill their domestic duties. Because women in these communities lack the commitment to the timber industry that restricts their husbands, and because few career-track jobs are available to them, women are more able to take stop-gap temporary jobs, which they add and drop as necessary. In contrast, their husbands often continue to look for work in the timber industry or in other fields that require manual labor.

There is an assumption, voiced by both women and men--and echoed in the stereotype of the "obsessed" logger--that true timber workers are both incapable and unwilling to work in other fields. As one logger said, "I'm a basic guy. Not everybody can sit behind a desk. . . . People keep telling me I have choices, but I don't. I can go back in construction, but at this point I've given up. . . . I'm just doing what I gotta do." The fact that manual labor is readily available and requires little training, and that other high-paying jobs are extremely rare, reaffirms this belief. As one woman said, "The guys I graduated with in 1988 said they wouldn't work in the mills or the woods, but now they are. Most are like, 'What else can we do?' Some tried other things, and ended up coming back."

Combined with economic realities and a lack of formal education, the strong sense of commitment that timber workers feel for the industry, as described by Carroll and Lee (1990) in their studies of occupational community among loggers, functions as a handicap in their adaptation to a changing industry. Although many wives of timber workers share their husbands' strong commitment to the industry, timber work is not an option for them and they do not share the vocational restrictions of their husbands. As a result, husbands find themselves relying more on their wives' occupational abilities--a situation many find hard to accept.

The changes in the timber economy have caused both men and women to reassess their roles in the family and the community. Ironically, aspects of the timber culture including men's strong commitment to the industry, women's required occupational flexibility, and the consuming nature of timber work, combined with current economic distress, are having a destabilizing effect on gender roles. Women are attempting to retain their roles as supporters of their husbands even as they are pushed by necessity into wage labor, and by interest or commitment into community activism. At the same time, men are experiencing the weakening of their culturally dictated role as authority figure and provider. Together, they must try to balance the expectations embodied in the stereotypes and ideals of their culture with the realities of an economy in transformation.

References

Aaron, H., T.E. Mann, and T. Taylor, eds. (1994). *Values and Public Policy*. Washington, D.C.: The Brookings Institution.

Abramson, P., and R. Inglehart. (1995). *Value Change in Global Perspective*. Ann Arbor: University of Michigan Press.

Ajzen, I., and M. Fishbein. (1980). *Understanding Attitudes and Predicting Social Behavior*. Englewood Cliffs, N.J.: Prentice-Hall.

Aldrich, H.E. (1979). *Organizations and Environments*. Englewood Cliffs, N.J.: Prentice-Hall.

Alm, L.R. and S.L. Witt. (1995). "Environmental Policy in the Intermountain West: The Rural-Urban Linkage." *State and Local Government Review* 27 (Spring): 127–136.

American Forests. (1994). "Results of Nationwide Survey on Forest Management." Washington, D.C.: Unpublished Report.

Andrews, R.W. (1968). *Timber: Toil and Trouble in the Big Woods*. New York: Bonanza Books.

Arnold, J. (1994). "Counties Take Lead as Sagebrush Rebellion Rides Again." *County News*, April 4. Washington, D.C.: National Association of Counties.

Arrondale, T. (1994). "The Sagebrush Gang Rides Again." *Governing* 7 (March): 38–42.

Associated Press. (1995). "Miller Against State Handling Federal Land," *Las Vegas Review Journal*. Sunday, August 8.

Balmer, D.G. (1991). *State Elections Services in Oregon*. Princeton, N.J.: Citizens' Research Foundation.

Barnes, D.A. (1987). "Strategy Outcome and the Growth of Protest Organizations: A Case Study of the Southern Farmers' Alliance." *Rural Sociology* 52 (2): 164–186.

Barnett, J.D. (1915). *The Operation of the Initiative, Referendum, and Recall in Oregon*. New York: MacMillan Co.

Barton, W. (1992). "Telling Our Story," *Journal of Forestry* 90 (1): 3.

Bates, W. (1995a). "State Considers Nye Lawsuit" *Las Vegas Review Journal*. Sunday, August 25.

_____. (1995b). "Nye County Opposes State Role in Suit," *Las Vegas Review Journal*. Sunday, September 1.

Batt, T. (1995). "Bryan: Residents in Rural Nevada Not at War with Government," *Las Vegas Review-Journal*. Sunday, September 16, 1995: 7b.

Beale, C., and G.V. Fuguitt. (1990). "Decade of Pessimistic Nonmetro Population Trends Ends on Optimistic Note." *Rural Development Perspectives* 6: 14–18.

Beard, C.A., and B.E. Shultz. (1912). *Documents on the State-Wide Initiative, Referendum and Recall*. New York: MacMillan Co.

Bell, D. (1973). *The Coming of Postindustrial Society*. New York: Basic Books.

Benson, J. K. (1975). "The Interorganizational Network as Political Economy." *Administrative Science Quarterly* 20: 229–249.

Berman, D.R. (1993). *County Governments in an Era of Change*. Westport, Conn.: Greenwood Press.

Berry, J.M. (1989). *The Interest Group Society*. Glenview, Ill.: Scott, Foresman.

Blahna, D. (1990). "Social Bases for Resource Conflicts in Areas of Reverse Migration." In *Community and Forestry: Continuities in the Sociology of Natural Resources*, ed. R. Lee, D. Field, and W. Burch. Boulder, Colo.: Westview Press.

Borrelli, P. (1988). "The Ecophilosophers." In *Crossroads: Environmental Priorities for the Future*, ed. P. Borrelli. Washington, D.C.: Island Press.

Boundary Backpackers v. Boundary County. (1994). No. CV93–9955 (Idaho 1st Jud. Dist. Ct. Jan. 27).

Brandenburg, A.M., and Carroll, M.S. (1993). "The Stakeholder Groups of the Siouxon Creek Drainage: Constituencies in Rural Community Clusters Surrounding the Gifford Pinchot National Forest." Report to the Wind River Ranger District.

Brechin, S., and W. Kempton. (1994). "Global Environmentalism: A Challenge to the Postmaterialism Thesis." *Social Science Quarterly* 75: 245–69.

Brown, G., and C. Harris. (1992). "The USDA Forest Service: Toward the New Resource Management Paradigm?" *Society and Natural Resource.* 5: 231–45.

Brown, R.B., H.R. Geersten, and R.S. Krannich. (1989). "Community Satisfaction and Social Integration in a Boomtown: A Longitudinal Analysis." *Rural Sociology* 54 (4): 568–86.

Brunelle, A. (1990). "The Changing Structure of the Forest Industry in the Pacific Northwest." In *Community and Forestry: Continuities in the Sociology of Natural Resources,* ed. R.G. Lee, D.R. Field, and W.R. Burch Jr. Boulder, Colo.: Westview Press.

Brunson, M.W. (1993). "Socially Acceptable Forestry: What Does it Imply for Ecosystem Management?" *Western Journal of Applied Forestry* 8 (4): 1–4.

Brunson, M.W., and J. Kennedy. (1994). "Redefining Multiple Use: Agency Responses to Changing Social Values." In *A New Century for Natural Resources Management*, ed. R.L. Knight and Sarah Bates. Washington, D.C.: Island Press.

Brunson, M.W., and B. Shelby. (1992). "Assessing Recreational and Scenic Quality: How Does New Forestry Rate?" *Journal of Forestry* 90 (7): 37–41.

Brunson, M.W., and B.S. Steel. (1994). "National Public Attitudes Toward Federal Rangeland Management," *Rangelands* 16: 77–81.

Bullard, R. (1994). *Dumping in Dixie: Race, Class, and Environmental Quality*, 2nd ed. Boulder, Colo.: Westview Press.

Buttel, F.H. (1992). "Environmentalization: Origins, Processes, and Implications for Rural Social Change." *Rural Sociology* 57 (1): 1–27.

_____. (1987). "New Directions in Environmental Sociology." *Annual Review of Sociology* 13: 465–488.

Buttel, F.H., and W.L. Flinn. (1977). "Conceptions of Rural Life and Environmental Concern." *Rural Sociology* 42 (4): 544–55.

Caldwell, L. (1992). "Globalizing Environmentalism: Threshold of a New Phase in International Relations." In *American Environmentalism*, ed. R. Dunlap and A. Mertig. Philadelphia: Taylor and Francis, Publishers.

Calvert, J. (1987). "Partisanship and Ideology in State Legislative Action on Environmental Issues." Paper presented at the Annual Meetings of the Western Political Science Association, Anaheim, Calif., March.

Carroll, M. (1995). *Community and the Northwestern Logger: Continuities and Changes in the Era of the Spotted Owl.* Boulder, Colo.: Westview Press.

Carroll, M., and R. Lee. (1990). "Occupational Community and Identity Among Pacific Northwestern Loggers: Implications for Adapting to Economic Changes." In *Community and Forestry: Continuities in the Sociology of Natural Resources*, ed. R. Lee, D.R. Field, and W.R. Burch Jr. Boulder, Colo.: Westview Press.

Catton, W., and R. Dunlap. (1980). "A New Ecological Paradigm for Post-Exuberant Sociology." *American Behavioral Scientist* 24: 15–47.

Cawley, R. McGreggor. (1996). *Federal Land, Western Anger: The Sagebrush Rebellion and Environmental Politics.* Lawrence: University of Kansas Press.

_____. (1981). *The Sagebrush Rebellion and Environmental Politics.* Unpublished manuscript.

Christensen, J. (1992). "Nevada Sides with Environmentalists Against Rancher." *High Country News*, July 25, p. 13.

Christianson, E.H., and T.A. Arcury. (1992). "Regional Diversity in Environmental Attitudes, Knowledge, and Policy: The Kentucky River Authority." *Human Organization* 51: 99–108.

Churchill, S. (1965). *Big Sam.* Garden City, New York: Doubleday.

Cigler, B.A. (1993). "The Special Problems of Rural County Governments." In *County Governments in an Era of Change* ed. David R. Berman. Westport, Conn.: Greenwood Press.

_____. (1994). "The County–State Connection: A National Study of Associations of Counties." *Public Administration Review* 54 (Jan/Feb): 3–11.

Clary, D.A. (1986). *Timber and the Forest Service.* Lawrence: University of Kansas Press.

Clifford, F. (1993). "Cow County Tells U.S. to Back Off." *Los Angeles Times.* April 4, pp. A3, A20.

Clifford, J. (1988). *The Predicament of Culture.* Cambridge, Mass.: Harvard University Press.

Cobb, R.W., and C.D. Elder. (1983). *Participation in American Politics: The Dynamics of Agenda Building*, 2d ed. Boston: Allyn and Bacon.

Cohen, C. (1971). *Democracy.* Athens, Ga.: University of Georgia Press.

Conary, J.S., and D.L. Soden. (1996). *Public Attitudes, Risk Perceptions and the Future of the Nevada Test Site.* Harry Reid Center for Environmental Studies and Southwestern Social Science Research Center, University of

Nevada, Las Vegas.

Coufal, J.E. (1989). "The Land Ethic Question." *Journal of Forestry* 87 (6): 22–24.

Cramer, L.A., J.J. Kennedy, R.S. Krannich, and T.M. Quigley. (1993). "Changing Forest Service Values and Their Implications for Land Management Decisions Affecting Resource-Dependent Commuties." *Rural Sociology* 58 (3): 475–491.

Cronin, T.E. (1989). *Direct Democracy: The Politics of Initiative, Referendum, and Recall.* Cambridge, Mass: Harvard University Press.

Crowfoot, J.E., and J. Wondolleck. (1990). *Environmental Disputes: Community Involvement in Conflict Resolution.* Washington, D.C.: Island Press.

Culhane, P.J. (1981). *Public Lands Politics: Interest Group Influence on the Forest Service and the Bureau of Land Management.* Baltimore, Md.: Johns Hopkins University Press.

Dahlgren, P., and C. Sparks. (1991). *Communication and Citizenship: Journalism and the Public Sphere in the New Media Age.* New York: Routledge.

Dake, K., and A. Wildavsky. (1991). "Individual Differences in Risk Perception and Risk-Taking Preferences." In *The Analysis, Communication, and Perception of Risk,* ed. B.J. Garrick and W.C. Gekler. New York: Plenum Press.

——————. (1990). "Theories of Risk Perception: Who Fears What and Why?" *Daedalus* 119 (4): 41–60.

Dalton, R. (1988). *Citizen Politics in Western Democracies: Public Opinion and Political Parties in the United States, Great Britain, West Germany and France.* Chatham, N.J.: Chatham House.

Dalton, R., and M. Kuechler. (1990). *Challenging the Political Order: New Social and Political Movements in Western Democracies.* New York: Oxford University Press.

Daly, H., and J.B. Cobb. (1990). *For the Common Good: Redirecting the Economy Toward Community, the Environment, and a Sustainable Future.* Boston: Beacon Press.

Dearborn, P.M. (1993). "Local Property Taxes: Emerging Trends." *Intergovernmental Perspective* 19 (3): 10–13.

Deavers, K. (1989). "Rural Development in the 1990s: Data and Research." Paper presented at the Rural Social Science Symposium, American Agricultural Economics Association, Baton Rouge.

DeBonis, J. (1989). "A Letter to the Chief of the U.S. Forest Service," *Inner Voice* 1 (1): 4–5.

Dennis, S., and E.R. Zube. (1988). "Voluntary Association Membership of Outdoor Recreationists: An Exploratory Study." *Leisure Sciences* 10: 229–245.

DeSantis, V.S., and T. Renner. (1994). "The Impact of Political Structures on Public Policies in American Counties." *Public Administration Review* 54 (May/June): 291–295.

Devall, B., and G. Sessions. (1985). *Deep Ecology, Living as if Nature Mattered.* Salt Lake City: Peregrine Smith Books.

DeVereaux, C. (1995). "Supporting an Island in the Sky," *The Weekly,* August 9.

Dietrich, W. (1992). *The Final Forest: The Battle for the Last Great Trees of the Pacific Northwest.* New York: Simon and Schuster.

Dillman, D. (1978). *Mail and Telephone Surveys: The Total Design Method.* New York: John Wiley.

Dillon, W.R., and M. Goldstein. (1984). *Multivariate Analysis: Methods and Applications.* New York: John Wiley.

Doherty, S. (1993). "Oregon's Not-so-Sweet Home," *Newsweek* 114 (Dec. 11): 55.

Douglas, M., and A. Wildavsky. (1982). *Risk and Culture: An Essay on the Selection of Technical and Environmental Dangers.* Berkeley: University of California Press.

Dowdle, B. (1984). "Perspective on the Sagebrush Rebellion." *Policy Studies Journal* 12 (3): 473–482.

Dowie, M. (1994). *Losing Ground: American Environmentalism at the Close of the Twentieth Century.* Cambridge, Mass.: MIT Press.

_____. (1992). "American Environmentalism: A Movement Courting Irrelevance." *World Policy Journal* 9 (1): 67–92.

Downs, A. (1972). "Up and Down with Ecology." *Public Interest* 28 (Summer): 38–50.

Draffan, G.L. (1987). *Information and Environmental Activism.* Masters thesis. University of Washington, Seattle.

Dunlap, R.E. (1992). "Trends in Public Opinion Toward the Environment: 1965–1990." In *American Environmentalism: The U.S. Environmental Movement 1970-1990,* ed. R.E. Dunlap and A. Mertig. Philadelphia: Taylor and Francis.

Dunlap, R.E., J. D. Grieneeks, and M. Rokeach. (1983). "Human Values and Pro-environmental Behavior." In *Energy and Material Resources: Attitudes, Values, and Public Policy, ed.* W.A. Cann. Boulder: Westview Press.

Dunlap, R.E., and A. Mertig. (1992). "The Evolution of the U.S. Environmental Movement from 1970 to 1990: An Overview." In *American Environmentalism: The U.S. Environmental Movement 1970-1990,* ed. R.E. Dunlap and A. Mertig. Philadelphia: Taylor and Francis.

Dunlap, R.E., and K.D. Van Liere. (1978). "The New Environmental Paradigm: A Proposed Measuring Instrument and Preliminary Results." *Journal of Environmental Education* 9 (Summer): 10–19.

Eaton, A.H. (1912). *The Oregon System: The Story of Direct Legislation in Oregon: A Presentation of the Methods and Results of the Initiative and Referendum, and Recall, in Oregon, with Studies of the Measures Accepted or Rejected, and Special Chapters on the Direct Primary, Popular Election of Senators, Advantages, Defects and Dangers of the System.* Chicago: A.C. McClurg.

Eckersley, R. (1992). *Environmentalism and Political Theory: Toward an Ecocentric Approach.* Albany: State University of New York Press.

Egan, T. (1991). "Fighting for Control of America's Hinterlands." *Journal of Forestry* 89 (4): 26–29.

Elazar, D.J. (1984). *American Federalism: A View From the States,* 3d ed. New York: Harper and Row, 1984.

Elliot, R.R. (1987). *History of Nevada,* 2d. ed., Lincoln: University of Nebraska Press.

Elliott, M. (1995). "The West at War." *Newsweek* 126, August 17, 1995, p. 3.

Erm, R. III. (1993–94). "The 'Wise Use' Movement: The Constitutionality of Local Action on Federal Lands Under the Preemption Doctrine." *Idaho Law Review* 30: 631–70.

Etlinger, C. (1994). "Urbanization Puts Squeeze on Wildlife." *Idaho Statesman,*

Sept. 20, p. 1B.

Fairfax, S.K., and R.M. Cawley. (1991). "Land and Natural Resource Policy II: Key Contemporary Issues." In *Politics and Public Policy in the Contemporary American West*, ed. C.S. Thomas. Albuquerque: University of New Mexico Press.

Falen, F.J., and K. Budd-Falen. (1993–94). "The Right to Graze Livestock on the Federal Lands: The Historical Development of Western Grazing Rights." *Idaho Law Review* 30: 506–524.

Felt, M.E. (1963). *Gyppo Logger.* Caldwell, Idaho: Caxton Printers.

Fischoff, B., S. Lichtenstein, P. Slovic, S.L. Derby, and R. Keeney. (1981). *Acceptable Risk.* Cambridge: Cambridge University Press.

Fiske, E. (1991). "Controversial Issues as Opportunities: Extension's Effectiveness in Resolving Environmental Disputes." *Journal of Extension* 29: 26–28.

Flanagan, S. (1982). "Changing Values in Advanced Industrial Society." *Comparative Political Studies* 14: 99–128.

Fleetwood, E. (1988). *Just a Few of Our Memories, 1888–1988.* Mill City, Oregon: Self-Published.

Force, J. and K. Williams. (1989). "A Profile of National Forest Planning Participants." *Journal of Forestry* 87 (1): 33–93.

Forest Ecosystem Management Assessment Team. (1993). *Forest Ecosystem Management: An Ecological, Economic, and Social Assessment.* Washington, D.C.: U.S. Government Printing Office.

Fortmann, L. (1988). "Predicting Natural Resource Micro-Protest," *Rural Sociology* 53 (3): 357–67.

Fortmann, L., and J. Kusel. (1990). "New Voices, Old Beliefs: Forest Environmentalism Among New and Long-standing Rural Residents." *Rural Sociology* 55: 214–32.

Fortmann, L., J. Kusel, and S.K. Fairfax. (1989). "Community Stability: The Forester's Fig Leaf." In *Community Stability in Forest-Based Communities* ed. L. Fortmann. Portland, OR: Timber Press.

Fortmann, L., and P. Starrs. (1990). "Power Plants and Resource Rights." In *Community and Forestry: Continuities in the Sociology of Natural Resources*, ed. R. Lee, D. Field, and W. Burch. Boulder, Colo.: Westview Press.

Fouhy, E. (1994). "The Dawn of Public Journalism." *National Civic Review* 83: 261.

Freemouth, J. (1993). "Federal Land Management in the West." In *Environmental Politics and Policy in the West*, ed. Zachary Smith. Dubuque, Iowa: Kendall/Hunt Publishers.

Freudenberg, N., and C. Skinsapir. (1992). "Not in Our Backyards: The Grassroots Environmental Movement." In *American Environmentalism: The U.S. Environmental Movement,* ed. R. Dunlap and A. Mertig. Bristol: Taylor and Francis.

Freudenburg, W., and B. McGinn. (1987). "Rural-Urban Difference in Environmental Attitudes: A Closer Look." Paper presented to the Rural Sociological Society, Madison, Wis., August.

Gallup International. (1992). "The Health of the Planet Survey." Preliminary report prepared by Riley Dunlap, George Gallup, Jr., and Alec Gallup. Princeton, N.J.: George Gallup International Institute.

Gallup Poll Monthly. (1991). "Americans Report High Levels of Environmental

Concern, Activity." (April): 6–12.

Gallup Report. (1989). "Environment Regaining a Foothold on the National Agenda." (June): 2–12.

Galston, W. (1992). "Rural America in the 1990s: Trends and Choices." *Policy Studies Journal* 20: 202–11.

Gardener, T. (1995). "Panel Told Nevada Could Manage Lands Better Than Feds, But at a Price." *Las Vegas Review Journal,* September 30: B7.

Gaventa, J. (1980). *Power and Powerlessness: Quiescence and Rebellion in an Appalachian Valley.* Urbana: University of Illinois Press.

Gerlak, A., and D.L. Soden. (Forthcoming). "Rural vs. Urban Preferences: Water Transfers and Intra-State Politics in Nevada." In *Towards 2000: Public Policy in Nevada,* ed. D.L. Soden and E. Herzik. Reno: University of Nevada Press.

Gilles, J.L., and M. Dalecki. (1988). "Rural Well-Being and Agricultural Change in Two Farming Regions." *Rural Sociology* 53 (1): 40–55

Gilligan, C. (1982). *In a Different Voice: Psychological Theory and Women's Development.* Cambridge, Mass.: Harvard University Press.

Goodpaster, K.E. (1978). "On Being Morally Considerable." *Journal of Philosophy* 25 (6): 308–325.

Gore, Albert. (1992). *Earth in the Balance: Healing the Global Environment.* New York: Dutton.

Gorham, L., and B. Harrison. (1990). *Working Below the Poverty Line: The Growing Problem of Low Earnings in Rural and Urban Regions Across the United States.* Washington, D.C.: Aspen Institute.

Gottlieb, R. (1993). *Forcing the Spring: The Transformation of the American Environmental Movement.* Washington, D.C.: Island Press.

Gottlieb, R., and H. Ingram. (1989). "The New Environmentalists." *The Progressive* (August): 14–15.

Graf, W.L. (1990). *Wilderness Preservation and the Sagebrush Rebellions.* Lanham, Md: Rowman and Littlefield Publishers, Inc.

Graham, H. (1991). "Americans Report High Levels of Environmental Concern, Activity." *Gallup Poll Monthly* (April): 6–12.

Gramling R., and W.R. Freudenburg. (1990). "A Closer Look and 'Local Control': Communities, Commodities, and the Collapse of the Coast." *Rural Sociology* 55 (4): 541–558.

Greber, B., and N. Johnson. (1991). "What's All This Debate About Overcutting?" *Journal of Forestry* 89 (11): 25–30.

Greenpeace Guide to Anti-Environmental Organizations. (1993). Berkeley, Calif.: Odonian Press.

Gregoire, C.O. (1994). AGO1994 No. 10. Office of the Washington State Attorney General, Olympia, Wash.

Greider, T., and L. Garkovich. (1994). "Landscapes: The Social Construction of Nature and Environment." *Rural Sociology* 59 (1): 1–24.

Gundersen, A. (1995). *The Environmental Promise of Democratic Deliberation.* Madison: University of Wisconsin Press.

Habermas, J. (1981). "New Social Movements." *Telos* 49: 33–37.

Hansis, R. (1995). "The Social Acceptability of Clearcutting in the Pacific Northwest." *Human Organization* 54: 95–101.

Hardin, G. (1968). "The Tragedy of the Commons." *Science* (December 13): 1243–48.

Hart, J.W. (1995). "National Forest Planning: An Opportunity for Local Governments to Influence Federal Land Use." *Public Land Law Review* 16 (Spring): 137–61.

Hays, S. (1991). "The New Environmental West." *Journal of Policy History* 3 (3): 223–48.

Hays, S.P. (1959). *Conservation and the Gospel of Efficiency, The Progressive Conservation Movement, 1890–1920.* Cambridge, Mass.: Harvard University Press.

Heberlein, T.A. (1981). "Environmental Attitudes." *Zeitschrift für Umweltpolitik* 4: 241–70.

Heisler, M., ed. (1974). *Politics in Europe: Structures and Processes in Some Postindustrial Democracies.* New York: McKay.

Helvarg, D. (1994). *The War Against the Greens.* San Francisco: Sierra Club Books.

Hendee, J., R. Gale, and J. Harry. (1969). "Conservation, Politics and Democracy." *Journal of Soil and Water Conservation* 24: 212–215.

Herzik, E., and J. Dobra. (1994). "What's Science Got to Do With It? The Use of Public Opinion in Developing Nuclear Waste Policy." In *Proceedings of the Fifth Annual International Conference of High-Level Radioactive Waste Management,* La Grange, Ill.: American Nuclear Society.

Hibbard, M., and J. Elias. (1993). "The Failure of Sustained-Yield Forestry and the Decline of the Flannel-Shirt Frontier." In *Forgotten Places: Uneven Development in Rural America,* ed. T.A. Lyson and W.W. Falk. Lawrence: University of Kansas Press.

Hirt, P. (1994). *A Conspiracy of Optimism: Management of the National Forests Since World War Two.* Lincoln: University of Nebraska Press.

Holechek, J.L., R.D. Pieper, and C.H. Herbel. (1989). *Range Management: Principles and Practices.* Englewood Cliffs, N.J.: Prentice Hall.

Howell, S., and S. Laska (1992). "The Changing Face of the Environmental Coalition: A Research Note." *Environment and Behavior* 24: 134–44.

Hulse, J.W. (1991). *The Silver State: Nevada's Heritage Reinterpreted.* Reno: University of Nevada Press.

————. (Forthcoming). "Nevada and the Twenty-First Century." In *Towards 2000: Public Policy in Nevada,* ed. Dennis L Soden and Eric Herzik. Reno: University of Nevada Press.

Humphrey, C.R. (1990). "Timber-Dependent Communities." In *American Rural Communities,* ed. A. Luloff and L. Swanson. Boulder, Colo.: Westview Press.

Hungerford, A. (1995). "Custom and Culture Ordinances: Not a Wise Move for the Wise Use Movement." *Tulane Environmental Law Journal* 8 (Summer): 457–504.

Huntington, S. (1974). "Postindustrial Politics: How Benign Will it Be?" *Comparative Politics* 6: 147–77.

Idaho Association of Counties. (1993). *Idaho Public Lands Facts and Figures 1993 Edition.* Boise: Idaho Association of Counties.

Idaho Department of Commerce. (1994). *County Profiles of Idaho.* Boise: Economic Development Division, Idaho Department of Commerce.

Inglehart, R. (1995). "Public Support for Environmental Protection: Objective Problems and Subjective Values in 43 Societies." *PS: Political Science and Politics* (March): 57–72.

_____. (1990). *Culture Shift in Advanced Industrial Society*. Princeton, N.J.: Princeton University Press.

_____. (1977). *The Silent Revolution: Changing Values and Political Styles Among Western Publics*. Princeton, N.J.: Princeton University Press.

Inglehart, R., and S. Flanagan. (1987). "Values in Industrial Societies." *American Political Science Review* 81: 1289–1319.

Ingram, H., and D. Mann. (1989). "Interest Groups and Environmental Policy." In *Environmental Politics and Policy: Theories and Evidence*, ed. J. Lester. Durham, N.C.: Duke University Press.

Iyenger, S., and D. E. Kinder. (1987). *News that Matters: Television and American Opinion*. Chicago: University of Chicago Press.

Jenkins-Smith, H., and P. Sabatier. (1993). "The Dynamics of Policy-Oriented Learning." In *Policy Change and Learning: An Advocacy Coalition Approach*, ed. Paul Sabatier and Hank Jenkins-Smith. Boulder, Colo.: Westview Press.

Jones, F.L., and Cahlan, J.F. (1975). *Water: A History of Las Vegas*, vol. 1. Las Vegas Valley Water District.

Jones, R.E., and R. Dunlap. (1992). "The Social Bases of Environmental Concern: Have They Changed Over Time?" *Rural Sociology* 57 (1): 28–47.

Kanamime, L. (1995). "U.S. vs. Them: West's Ranchers Raising Cain with New Land Revolt." *Salt Lake City Tribune*, April 2, p. 2.

Keisling, P. (1992). *Oregon Blue Book*. Salem: State of Oregon.

Kellner, D. (1990). *Television and the Crisis of Democracy*. Boulder, Colo.: Westview Press.

Kelman, S. (1992). "Adversarial and Cooperationist Institutions for Conflict Resolution in Public Policymaking." *Journal of Policy Analysis and Management* 11: 178–206.

Kim, Jae-On, and C.W. Mueller. (1978). *Factor Analysis: Statistical Methods and Practical Issues*. Beverly Hills, Calif.: Sage Publications.

King, J. (1989). "Yogurt Eaters for Wilderness." *Sierra* (January/February): 22–23.

Kittredge, W. (1996). *Who Owns the West?* San Francisco: Mercury House Publishers.

Kleinbaum, D., and L. Kupper. (1978). *Applied Regression Analysis and Other Multivariate Methods*. Boston: Duxbury Press.

Kluckhohn, F. R. and Strodtbeck, F. L. (1961). *Variations in Value Orientations*. Westport, Conn.: Greenwood Press.

Knickerbocker, B. (1995). "Fight Over Changing How the West Is Run." *Christian Science Monitor*, August 10.

Kolar, A. (1993). Testimony of Arlene Kolar, Boise County Clerk, Before the Idaho House Resources and Conservation Committee. Feb. 11, 1993. Transcript provided by the Idaho Association of Counties.

Krakauer, J. (1991). "Brown-Fellas." *Outside* 16 (Dec): 69–72.

LaPalombara, J.G. (1950). *The Initiative and Referendum in Oregon: 1938–1948*. Corvallis: Oregon State College Press.

Laumann, E.O., and D. Knoke. (1987). *The Organizational State: Social Choice in National Policy Domains*. Madison: University of Wisconsin Press.

Laumann, E.O., and F.U. Pappi. (1976). *Networks of Collective Action: A Perspective on Community Influence Systems*. New York: Academic Press.

Lawrence S. (1992). *Linking Citizens to Government: Interest Group Politics at*

Common Cause. Cambridge: Cambridge University Press.

Lawson, M. (1986). "The Impact of the Farm Recession on Local Governments." *Intergovernmental Perspective* 12 (3): 17–23.

Leopold, A. (1966). *A Sand County Almanac, with Essays on Conservation from Round River.* New York: Sierra Club/Ballantine Books.

————. (1949). *A Sand County Almanac.* New York: Oxford University Press.

Leuthold, D., and A. Scheele. (1971). "Patterns of Bias in Samples Based on Telephone Directories." *Public Opinion Quarterly* 35: 249–257.

Lewis, T. (1995). "Cloaked in a Wise Disguise." In *Let the People Judge,* ed. John Echeverria and R.B. Eby. Washington, D.C. and Covelo, Calif.: Island Press.

Lindbloom, C.E. (1977). *Politics and Markets.* New York: Basic Books.

List, P., ed. (1993). *Radical Environmentalism, Philosophy and Tactics.* Belmont, Calif.: Wadsworth Publishing Co.

Lovrich, N., and J. Pierce. (1986). "The Good Guys and Bad Guys in Natural Resource Politics: Content and Structure of Perceptions of Interests Among General and Attentive Publics." *Social Science Journal* 23: 309–326.

Lowe, G.D., and T.K. Pinhey. (1982). "Rural-Urban Differences in Support for Environmental Protection." *Rural Sociology* 47 (1): 114–128.

Lucia, E. (1975). *The Big Woods: Logging and Lumbering, from Bull Teams to Helicopters, in the Pacific Northwest.* Garden City, N.Y.: Doubleday.

Lunch, W.B. (1994). Luncheon Presentation: Annual Meeting of the Pacific Northwest Political Science Association.

Machlis, G.E., and J.E. Force. (1988). "Community Stability and Timber-Dependent Communities." *Rural Sociology* 53 (2): 220–34.

Madison, J., A. Hamilton, and J. Jay. (1982). *The Federalist Papers.* New York: Bantam Books.

Mansbridge, J. (1983). *Beyond Advocacy Democracy.* Chicago: University of Chicago Press.

Marando, V.L., and R.D. Thomas. (1977). *The Forgotten Governments: County Commissioners as Policy Makers.* Gainesville: University of Florida Press.

Marchak, P. (1983). *Green Gold: The Forest Industry in British Columbia.* Vancouver, B.C.: University of British Columbia Press.

Martin, K.E., and K.P. Wilkenson. (1984). "Local Participation in the Federal Grant System: Effects of Community Action." *Rural Sociology* 49 (3): 374–388.

Martinson, K., and J. Baas. (1992). *Understanding Effects of Harvesting Timber on Forest Recreationists.* Paper presented at Fourth North American Symposium on Society and Resource Management. Madison, Wis.

Marzulla, N.G. (1995). "The Property Rights Movement: How It Began and Where It Is Headed." In *Land Rights: The 1990s Property Rights Rebellion,* ed. B. Yandle. Lanham, MD: Rowman and Littlefield Publishers, Inc.

Mather, A. (1990). *Global Forest Resources.* Portland, Oreg.: Timber Press.

Mazurek, J.P. (1993). "Letter of Advice to Mike McGrath, Lewis and Clark County Attorney and Keith D. Haker, Custer County Attorney." Office of the Attorney General of the State of Montana, June 11, Helena, Mont.

McBeth, M., and R. Foster. (1994). "Rural Environmental Attitudes." *Environmental Management* 18: 401–411.

McCool, D. (1988). *Command of the Waters.* Berkeley: University of California Press.

McCool, S., and G. Stankey.   (1986). *Visitor Attitudes Toward Wilderness Fire Management Policy, 1971–1984.* USDA Forest Service Research Paper INT-357. Ogden, Utah.

McCoy, C. (1996). "Ruling Quashes Nevada County's Claim on U.S. Land." *Wall Street Journal,* March 18, 1996: B1.

McCurdy, H.E. (1984). "Public Ownership of Land and the Sagebrush Rebellion." *Policy Studies Journal* 12 (3): 483–490.

McDonnell, L.J., and S.F. Bates, eds. (1993). *Natural Resources Policy and Law: Trends and Directions.* Washington, D.C.: Island Press.

McQuillan, A.G. (1990).   "Is National Forest Planning Incompatible with a Land Ethic?" *Journal of Forestry* 88 (5): 21–37.

Meacham, T.E. (1994). "Public Roads over Public Lands: The Unresolved Legacy of R.S. 2477." *Rocky Mountain Mineral Law Institute Proceedings* 40 (Annual) 2, 60.

Menzel, D.C., V.L. Marando, R.B. Parks, W.L. Waugh Jr., B.A. Cigler, J.H. Svara, M. Reeves, J.E. Benton, R.D. Thomas, G. Streib, M. Schneider. (1992). "Setting a Research Agenda for the Study of the American County." *Public Administration Review* 52 (March/April): 173–182.

Merriam, C.E. (1903). *A History of American Political Theories.* New York: A.M. Kelley, Publishers.

Mickey, R. (1993). *Northwest Forestry Association Letter to the Bureau of Land Management,* November 16. Eugene, Oreg.

Milbrath, L. (1984). *Environmentalists: Vanguard for a New Society.* Albany: State University of New York Press.

Mitchell, R.C. (1979). "National Environmental Lobbies and the Apparent Illogic of Collective Action." In *Collective Decision Making: Applications from Public Choice Theory,* ed. C.S. Russell. Baltimore, Md.: The John Hopkins University Press.

Moehring, E.P. (1989). *Resort City in the Sunbelt: Las Vegas, 1930–1970.* Reno: University of Nevada Press.

Mohai, P. (1992). "Men, Women, and the Environment: An Examination of the Gender Gap in Environmental Concern and Activism." *Society and Natural Resources* 5 (1): 1–19.

Mosser, D. and D.L. Soden. (1993). "Rural Migration in Southern Nevada." *National Social Science Journal* 7 (2): 71-90.

Naess, A.   (1989).   *Ecology, Community and Life-Style.*   Cambridge: Cambridge University Press.

————.   (1973).   "The Shallow and the Deep, Long-Range Ecology Movement: A Summary." *Inquiry* 16: 95–100.

Nash, R. (1992). *Rights of Nature: A History of Environmental Ethics.* Madison: University of Wisconsin Press.

————. (1989) *The Rights of Nature, A History of Environmental Ethics.* Madison: University of Wisconsin Press.

————. (1973) *Wilderness and the American Mind.* New Haven, Conn.: Yale University Press.

National Federal Lands Conference. (1995). Personal Communication with Author.

Feb. 7, National Federal Lands Conference, Bountiful, Utah.

Nature Conservancy Newsletter. (1994). "Perseverance Pays off in Ruby Valley." Salt Lake City, Utah: Nature Conservancy.

Nelkin, D., ed. (1979). *Technological Decisions and Democracy: European Experiments in Public Participation.* Beverly Hills, Calif.: Sage Publications.

Nelligan, J. (1929). "The Life of a Lumberman." *Wisconsin Magazine of History* 13: 4–65.

Nelson, R.H. (1995). *Public Lands and Private Rights: The Failure of Scientific Management.* Lanham, MD: Rowman and Littlefield Publishers.

Nicholson, M. (1987). *The New Environmental Age.* New York: Cambridge University Press.

Noe, F.P., and W.E. Hammitt. (1992). "Environmental Attitudes and the Personal Relevance of Management Actions in a Park Setting." *Journal of Environmental Management* 35: 205–16.

Offe, C. (1985). "New Social Movements: Challenging the Boundaries of Institutional Politics." *Social Research* 52: 817–68.

O'Hara, E. (1995). "Property Rights and the Police Powers of the State." In *Land Rights: The 1990s Property Rights Rebellion,* ed., B. Yandle. Lanham, MD: Rowman and Littlefield Publishers.

Onuf, P.S. (1988). "New State Equality: The Ambiguous History of a Constitutional Principle." *Publius: The Journal of Federalism* 18 (Fall): 53–69.

Ostrow, R.J. (1995). "U.S. Sues County to Halt Seizure of Federal Land." *Los Angeles Times,* March 9, p. A3.

Owyhee County, Idaho. (1993). *Owyhee County Interim Comprehensive Land Use and Management Plan for the Federally and State Managed Lands in Owyhee County.*

Paehlke, R., and D. Torgenson. (1990). "Toxic Waste and the Administrative State: NIMBY Syndrome or Participatory Management?" In *Managing Leviathan,* ed. R. Paehlke and D. Torgerson. Lewiston, N.Y.: Broadview Press.

Pappa, E. (1990). "Rurals Battling a Dry Clark County: Water Importation Plan Faces Fight on All Sides," *Las Vegas Review Journal,* December 23.

Pell, E. (1995). "Stop the Greens." In *Let the People Judge,* ed. J. Echeverria and R.B. Eby. Washington, D.C. and Covelo, Calif.: Island Press.

Petracca, M.P. (1992). *The Politics of Interest: Interest Groups Transformed.* Boulder, Colo.: Westview Press.

Pierce, J.C., N.P. Lovrich, M.A. Steger, and B.S. Steel. (1993). "Public Policy, Political Culture and Generational Change in British Columbia." *International Journal of Canadian Studies* (Winter): 23–38.

Pierce, J.C., N.P. Lovrich, T. Tsurutani and T. Abe. (1989). *Public Knowledge and Environmental Politics in Japan and in the United States.* Boulder, Colo.: Westview Press.

––––––––. (1986). "Culture, Politics and Mass Publics: Traditional and Modern Supporters of the New Environmental Paradigm in Japan and the United States." *Journal of Politics* 48: 43–63.

Pierce, J.C., M.A. Steger, B.S. Steel, and N.P. Lovrich. (1992). *Citizens, Political Communication and Interest Groups: A Study of Environmental Organizations in Canada and the United States.* New York: Praeger Publishers.

Pierre, J. (1979). *When Timber Stood Tall*. Seattle: Superior Publishing.

Pinchot, G. (1910). *The Fight for Conservation*. New York: Doubleday, Page and Co.

_____. (1907). *The Use Book*. Washington, D.C.: U.S. Department of Agriculture.

Plater, Z. (1992). *Environmental Law and Policy: Nature, Law, and Society*. St. Paul, Minn.: West Publishing Company.

Plotkin, S. (1987). *Keep Out: The Struggle for Land Use Control*. Berkeley: University of California Press.

Priscoli, J., and P. Homenuck. (1990). "Consulting the Publics." In *Integrated Approaches to Resource Planning and Management*, ed. R. Lang. Alberta, Canada: Banff Centre School for Management.

Pross, A.P. (1992). *Group Politics and Public Policy*, 2d. Toronto: Oxford University Press.

Rabe, B. (1994). *Beyond NIMBY: Hazardous Waste Siting in Canada and the United States*. Washington, D.C.: The Brookings Institution.

Rasker, R. (1993). "Rural Development, Conservation, and Public Policy in the Greater Yellowstone Ecosystem." *Society and Natural Resources* 6: 109–26.

Reed, S.W. (1993–94). "The County Supremacy Movement: Mendacious Myth Marketing." *Idaho Law Review* 30: 525–53.

Reisner, M. (1986). *Cadillac Desert: The American West and Its Disappearing Water*. London: Penguin Press.

Richardson, V. (1993). "Clinton Warned to Soften Up on Riled West." *Washington Times*, November 28, A1.

Ring, R. (1995). "The New West's Servant Economy," *High Country News*, May 17.

_____. (1994). "State Lands: How Public Should They Be?" *High Country News*, August 25.

Rokeach, M. (1979). *Understanding Human Values: Individual and Societal*. New York: Free Press.

_____. (1973). *The Nature of Human Values*. New York: Free Press.

Rolston III, H., and J. Coufal. (1991). "A Forest Ethic and Multivalue Forest Management" *Journal of Forestry* 89 (4): 35–40.

Rosenau, P. (1992). *Post-Modernism and the Social Sciences: Insights, Inroads and Intrusions*. Princeton, N.J.: Princeton University Press.

Rosenthal, D.B., and J.M. Hoefler. (1989). "Competing Approaches to the Study of American Federalism and Intergovernmental Relations." *Publius: The Journal of Federalism* 19 (Winter): 1–23.

Rothenberg, L.S. (1992). *Linking Citizens to Government: Interest Group Politics at Common Cause*. Cambridge: Cambridge University Press.

Rothman, S. (1979). "The Mass Media in Postindustrial Societies." In *The Third Century*, ed. Seymour Martin Lipset. Chicago: University of Chicago Press.

Rudzitis, G., and H.E. Johansen. (1991). "How Important Is Wilderness? Results from a United States Survey." *Environmental Management* 15: 227–33.

Sabatier, P., J. Loomis, and C. McCarthy. (1990). *Your Views on Forest Planning, Questionnaire Results*. Davis, Calif.: Division of Environmental Studies, University of California, Davis.

Salazar, D. J. (1989). "Regulatory Politics and Environment: State Regulation of Logging Practices." *Research in Law and Economics* 12: 95–117.

Salazar, D., P. Garcia-Gonzalez, and D. Steinberg. (1990). "Political Resources of Environmental Groups in Washington State." Paper prepared for delivery at the 1990 Annual Meeting of the American Political Science Association, San Francisco.

Salisbury, R.H. (1975). "Interest Groups." In *Handbook of Political Science,* ed. F. Greenstein and N. Polsby. Reading, Mass.: Addison-Wesley.

Salwasser, H. (1990). *New Perspectives for Managing the National Forest System: What Is New Perspectives and Why Are We Doing It?* Washington, D.C.: USDA Forest Service unpublished manuscript.

Scammon, R.M., and A.V. McGillivray. (1985). *America Votes: Handbook of Contemporary Election Statistics*, 26. Washington, D.C.: Elections Research Center.

————. (1981). *America Votes: Handbook of Contemporary Election Statistics,* 24. Washington, D.C.: Elections Research Center.

Schattschneider, E.E. (1960). *The Semisovereign People.* Hinsdale, Ill.: Dryden Press.

Scherer, D., and T. Attig, eds. (1983). *Ethics and the Environment.* Englewood Cliffs, N.J.: Prentice-Hall.

Schlozman, K. L., and J. Tierney (1986). *Organized Interests and American Democracy.* New York: Harper and Row.

Schmidt, D.D. (1989) *Citizen Lawmakers: The Ballot Initiative Revolution.* Philadelphia: Temple University Press.

Schuman, D. (1994) "The Origin of State Constitutional Direct Democracy: William Simon U'Ren and The Oregon System." *Temple Law Review.* 67 (3): 947–963.

Seideman, D. (1993) *Showdown at Opal Creek.* New York: Carroll and Graf Publishers.

Shapiro, I., and R. Greenstein. (1990). *Fulfilling Work's Promises: Policies to Increase Incomes of the Rural Working Poor.* Washington, D.C.: Center on Budget and Priorities.

Shindler, B., P. List, and B.S. Steel. (1993). "Managing Federal Forests: Public Attitudes in Oregon and Nationwide." *Journal of Forestry* 91 (July): 36–42.

Siegelman, L., and E. Yanarella. (1986). "Public Information and Public Issues: A Multivariate Analysis." *Social Science Quarterly* 67: 402–10.

Simmons, C.J., B.A. Bickart, and J.G. Lynch Jr. (1993). "Capturing and Creating Public Opinion in Survey Research." *Journal of Consumer Research* 20: 316–29.

Simmons, D.D. (1982). *Personal Valuing, An Introduction.* Chicago: Nelson Hall.

Soden, D.L. (1995a) "Community Perceptions of National Parks as Economic Partners." *Journal of Park and Recreation Administration* 13 (Summer): 93–99.

————. (1995b). "Trust in Sources of Technical Information: Issue Specific or Consistency Over Time?" *Journal of Environmental Education* 26(2): 16–21.

————. (1989). "Community-Oriented Analysis: Viewing Policy Alternatives for the Gulf Coast Region." In *Marine Resource Utilization: Social Science Issues,* ed. E.P. Durrenberger. Mobile: University of South Alabama Press.

Soden, D.L., and E. Herzik, eds. (Forthcoming). *Towards 2000: Public Policy in*

Nevada. Reno: University of Nevada Press.

Stankey, G. (1993). *Defining the Social Acceptability of Forest Management Practices and Conditions.* Paper in Workshop Proceedings: Defining Social Acceptability in a Forest Management Context. Portland, Oreg: USDA Forest Service PNW Research Station.

Stankey, G., and R. Clark. (1992). *Social Aspects of New Perspectives in Forestry.* Milford, Pa.: Grey Towers Press.

―――――. (1991). *Social Aspects of New Perspectives in Forestry: A Problem Analysis.* Seattle, Wash.: Consortium for the Social Values of Natural Resources.

Steel, B., and M. Brunson. (1993). *Western Rangelands Survey: Comparing the Responses of the 1993 National and Oregon Public Surveys.* Vancouver: Washington State University, Vancouver.

Steel, B., P. List, and B. Shindler. (1993). "Conflicting Values About Federal Forests: A Comparison of National and Oregon Publics." *Society and Natural Resources* 7: 137–53.

―――――. (1992). *Oregon State University Survey of Natural Resource and Forestry Issues: Comparing the Responses of the 1991 National and Oregon Public Surveys.* Corvallis: Oregon State University.

Steel, B., D. Soden, and R. Warner. (1990). "The Impact of Knowledge and Values on Perceptions of Environmental Risk to the Great Lakes." *Society and Natural Resources* 3: 331–48.

Steel, B., M.A. Steger, N.P. Lovrich and J.C. Pierce. (1990). "Consensus and Dissension Among Contemporary Environmental Activists: Preservationists and Conservationists in the U.S. and Canadian Context." *Environment and Planning* 8: 379–93.

Steger, M.A., J. Pierce, B. Steel and N. Lovrich. (1989). "Political Culture, Postmaterial Values, and the New Environmental Paradigm." *Political Behavior* 11: 233–54.

Steger, M.A., and S. Witt. (1989). "Gender Differences in Environmental Orientations: A Comparison of Publics and Activists in Canada and the U.S." *Western Political Quarterly* 42: 627–50.

Stern, P., O. Young, and D. Druckman, eds. (1992). *Global Environmental Change: Understanding the Human Dimensions.* Washington, D.C.: National Academy Press.

Stone, C.D. (1987). *Earth and Other Ethics, The Case for Moral Pluralism.* New York: Harper and Row.

Sussman, G., and B. Steel (1991). "Support for Protest Methods and Political Strategies Among Peace Movement Activists: Comparing the United States, Great Britain and the Federal Republic of Germany." *Western Political Quarterly* 44: 519–40.

Tetlock, P.E. (1986). "A Value Pluralism Model of Ideological Reasoning." *Journal of Personality and Social Psychology* 50: 819–27.

Thomas, C.S. (1991). *Politics and Public Policy in the Contemporary American West.* Albuquerque: University of New Mexico Press.

Thompson, E. (1994). "Gold Mines Are Sucking Aquifers Dry." *High Country News,* June 13.

Tichenor, P.J., G.A. Donohue, C.N. Olien and J.K. Bowers. (1971). "Environment and Public Opinion." *Journal of Environmental Education* 2: 38–42.

Touraine, A. (1971). *The Post-Industrial Society: Tomorrow's Social History.* New York: Random House.

Tourangeau, R., and K.A. Rasinski. (1988). "Cognitive Processes Underlying Context Effects in Attitude Measurement." *Psychological Bulletin* 103: 299–314.

Tremblay, K.R., and R.E. Dunlap. (1978). "Rural-Urban Residence and Concern with Environmental Quality: A Replication and Extension." *Rural Sociology* 43 (3): 474–91.

Tribe, L., and Dorf, M.C. (1991). *On Reading the Constitution.* Cambridge, Mass.: Harvard University Press.

Tsurutani, T. (1977). *Political Change in Japan.* New York: McKay Publishers.

U.S. Bureau of the Census. (1994). *County and City Databook.* Washington, D.C.: U.S. Department of Commerce.

_____. (1992). *County Business Patterns, Oregon.* Washington, D.C.: U.S. Department of Commerce.

_____. (1991). *County Business Patterns, Oregon.* Washington, D.C.: U.S. Department of Commerce.

_____. (1990). *County Business Patterns, Oregon.* Washington, D.C.: U.S. Department of Commerce.

_____. (1988). *County and City Databook.* Washington, D.C.: U.S. Department of Commerce.

_____. (1986). *County Business Patterns, Oregon.* Washington, D.C.: U.S. Department of Commerce.

_____. (1985). *County Business Patterns, Oregon.* Washington, D.C.: U.S. Department of Commerce.

_____. (1984). *County Business Patterns, Oregon.* Washington, D.C.: U.S. Department of Commerce.

U.S. Department of Agriculture, Forest Service. (1984). *Land Areas of the National Forest System.* Washington, D.C.: U.S. Department of Agriculture.

U.S. Department of Interior, Bureau of Land Management Idaho State Office. (1995). *Instruction Memorandum ID-95-035*, March 10.

Van Liere, K., and R. Dunlap. (1980). "The Social Bases of Environmental Concern: A Review of Hypotheses, Explanations and Empirical Evidence." *Public Opinion Quarterly* 44: 181–97.

_____. (1981). "Environmental Concern: Does it Make a Difference How it's Measured?" *Environment and Behavior* 13: 651–84.

Vasu, M., D. Stewart, and G.D. Garson. (1990). *Organizational Behavior and Public Management*, 2d ed. New York: Marcel Dekker.

Walker, J.L. (1991). *Mobilizing Interest Groups in America: Patrons, Professions, and Social Movements.* Ann Arbor: University of Michigan Press.

Warren, K. (1992). *Role-Making and Coping Strategies Among Women in Timber-Dependent Communities.* Master's thesis, Seattle: University of Washington, College of Forest Resources.

Washington Association of Counties Meeting. (1993). Special Meeting on County Supremacy Initiatives in the West. Pasco, Wash., May.

Waugh, W.L., Jr. (1988). "States, Counties, and the Questions of Trust and Capacity." *Publius* 18 (Winter): 189–98.

Waugh, W.L., Jr., and G. Streib. (1993). "County Capacity and Intergovernmental

Relations." In *County Governments in an Era of Change*, ed. D.R. Berman. Westport, Conn.: Greenwood Press.

White, L., Jr. (1967). "The Historical Roots of Our Ecological Crisis." *Science* 155: 1203–07.

Wilderness Society. (1992). "Coming Soon to a County Near You." *New Voices* 1, (Sept.): 1–2, 7.

Wilkinson, C.F. (1992). *Crossing the Next Meridian: Land, Water, and the Future of the American West*. Washington, D.C.: Island Press.

Wilkinson, K.P. (1986). "In Search of the Community in the Changing Countryside." *Rural Sociology* 51 (1): 1–17.

Witt, S.L., and L.R. Alm. (1996). "A Typology of County Supremacy Ordinances: Results from a Four State Study." Paper presented at the Annual Meeting of the Western Political Science Association, San Francisco, March 14–16.

Wondolleck, J. (1988). *Public Lands Conflict and Resolution: Managing National Forest Disputes*. New York: Plenum Press.

Wondolleck, J., and Yaffee, S. (1994). *Building Bridges Across Agency Boundaries: In Search of Excellence in the U.S. Forest Service*. USDA Forest Service Research Report. Seattle, Wash.: PNW Research Station.

Worster, D. (1977). *Nature's Economy, The Roots of Ecology*. San Francisco: Sierra Club Books.

Wuerthner, G. (1991). "Paradigms and Paradoxes, Resource Managers Versus Ecocentrists." *Forest Watch*. 11 (6): 8–11.

Yankelovich, D. (1994). "How Changes in the Economy Are Reshaping American Values." In *Values and Public Policy*, ed. Henry Aaron, Thomas Mann, and Timothy Taylor. Washington, D.C.: The Brookings Institution.

————. (1991). *Coming to Public Judgment: Making Democracy Work in a Complex World*. Syracuse, N.Y.: Syracuse University Press.

————. (1981). *New Rules: Searching for Self-Fulfillment in a World Turned Upside Down*. New York: Bantam Books.

Zimmerman, J.F. (1987). "Initiative, Referendum and Recall: Government By Plebiscite?" *Intergovernmental Perspective* 13 (1): 32–5.

Index

Contributors

LESLIE R. ALM is an Assistant Professor in the Department of Political Science at Boise State University. He has published numerous articles and chapters on environmental policy and administration and has continuing interest in U.S.–Canada acid rain policy.

MARK BRUNSON is an Assistant Professor in the Department of Forest Resources at Utah State University. He has a continuing research interest and many publications in the social acceptability of forest and rangeland management practices.

KELLY DeVINE is a graduate student at the University of Nevada Las Vegas and specializes in environmental policy in the southwestern United States.

JENNIFER GILDEN is a graduate student in anthropology at Oregon State University. She has conducted much research on families in natural resource dependent–communities.

RICHARD HANSIS is an Assistant Professor in the Department of Anthropology at Washington State University Vancouver. He has conducted research in the areas of special forest products and the social acceptability of forest management practices.

PETER LIST is a Professor in the Department of Philosophy at Oregon State University. He has written several books and articles in the area of environmental ethics.

NICHOLAS P. LOVRICH is Director of the Division of Governmental Studies and Services and Professor of Political Science at Washington State University. He has written many articles and several books in the area of comparative environmental policy.

JOHN C. PIERCE is Dean of the College of Liberal Arts and Professor of Political Science at Washington State University. He has authored many articles and books in the area of comparative environmental policy.

DEBRA SALAZAR is an Assistant Professor in the Department of Political Science at Western Washington University. She has published various articles on environmental groups and policy.

BRUCE SHINDLER is an Assistant Professor in the Department of Forest Resources at Oregon State University. He has published many articles and monographs on natural resource management issues and ecosystem management.

CHRISTOPHER A. SIMON is a Ph.D. candidate in the Department of Political Science at Washington State University. He has worked and studied in the area of environmental conflict resolution.

DENNIS L. SODEN is Director of the Master of Public Administration Program and Associate Professor of Political Science at the University of Texas-El Paso. He has edited various books and published many articles on natural resource and environmental policy.

BRENT S. STEEL is Director of the Master of Public Affairs Program and Associate Professor of Political Science at Washington State University Vancouver. He has published many articles and a book on natural resource and environmental policy.

STEPHANIE L. WITT is Chair and Associate Professor in the Department of Political Science at Boise State University. She has published books and many articles on public policy.

ISBN 0-275-95695-4

90000>

9 780275 956950

HARDCOVER BAR CODE

DATE DUE

GAYLORD			PRINTED IN U.S.A.